MILESTONES

A HISTORY OF

MOUNTAIN VIEW, CALIFORNIA

BY MARY JO IGNOFFO

Managing Editor, Tom Izu
Editor, N. Grey Osterud

Published by the California History Center & Foundation,
De Anza College, 21250 Stevens Creek Blvd., Cupertino, CA. 95014.

Library of Congress Cataloging-in-Publication Data

Ignoffo, Mary Jo, 1955-
          Milestones: a history of Mountain View, California / by Mary Jo Ignoffo.
              p. cm. -- (Local history studies; v. 39)
          Includes bibliographical references and index.
          ISBN 0-935089-27-6 -- ISBN 0-935089-28-4 (pbk.)
            Mountain View (Calif.)-- History. I. Title. II. Series

              F869.M787 I36 2002
              979.4'73--dc21

                                  2002023894

Funded by John Arrillaga and Richard Peery to the Mountain View Historical Association.

Design by: Metro Design Center, Inc., Saratoga, California
Printing by: Pacific Press Publishing Association, Nampa, Idaho

Soft: ISBN 0-935089-28-4
Cloth: ISBN 0-935089-27-6

Photographs, except where otherwise credited, are from the Mountain View
History Center at the Mountain View Public Library.

Cover photo: Mountain View Train Depot, circa 1890's

TABLE OF CONTENTS

FOREWORD

Each city has its own unique history. Events, people and yes, even topography, shape its development. The story of Mountain View's beginning and the changes throughout the years has at last been written just as the city celebrates one hundred years of incorporation. *Milestones: A History of Mountain View, California* traces the evolution of the north Santa Clara County area from Indian villages to today's technological campuses.

Mary Jo Ignoffo, thorough researcher and skillful writer, brings the past alive with words and pictures. Newcomers will learn the significance of the Castro name, what attracted our varied nationality groups and how San Francisco's garbage helped build Shoreline Park. Old-timers will be reminded of the acres of flowering fruit trees each spring and of the *Macon* floating overhead.

All of these things are familiar to me having been born and raised near Castro Street in downtown Mountain View. A grandfather settled here in 1884, while other assorted relatives have lived in Santa Clara County since the early 1850s. I've seen the change from a small town with a busy main street where shopkeepers and professionals were all known by name, to the post WW II period of phenomenal growth. Orchards were replaced by subdivisions and businesses moved to shopping centers. *Milestones*, with its transportation theme, will make these times real for you.

Mary Jo Ignoffo and the Mountain View Historical Association are to be congratulated for giving us this interesting and authoritative history of Mountain View. Read and enjoy.

Barbara McPheeters Kinchen
City Historian
Mountain View, California

ACKNOWLEDGMENTS

This publication was funded by the generous contribution of John Arrillaga and Richard Peery to the Mountain View Historical Association. Their gift allows the entire Mountain View community to enjoy and ponder its history.

The Mountain View Historical Association, while Ralph Faravelli was president, approved the publication of a book on the history of Mountain View to be available for the centennial year, 2002. A book committee was formed, consisting of Wallace Erichsen, Barbara McPheeters Kinchen, Trudi Herrero Odbert, and Margaret Vidovich, to select the author and publisher. Fortunately, the nearby California History Center at De Anza College in Cupertino, California provided an excellent resource for this endeavor. This resulted in a contract with the center to publish the book as part of its Local History Series.

Former California History Center Director Kathi Peregrin gave this project serious direction, and when she retired, Tom Izu took over, keeping open channels of communication.

I am also grateful to Stocklmeir Library and Archives Librarian Lisa Christiansen for previewing the manuscript and offering insightful comments. Joni Motoshige, also on staff at the California History Center, skillfully managed many administrative details.

Each Historical Association committee member previewed the manuscript and offered suggestions. This process was more labor-intensive and took more time than any of these dedicated volunteers expected. I appreciate their patience and persistence.

The Mountain View History Center at the Mountain View Public Library is my favorite research facility in Santa Clara County. The center has an extremely well-catalogued photograph collection, and an extensive card catalogue—compiled by hand over a period of decades—with references to Mountain View newspapers, biographical articles, and local history books. In addition to its wonderful collection, the facility itself makes doing research a joy because of its easy computer hook-up, Internet access, and lighted research tables. The management of the center is owed my sincerest appreciation, especially Librarian Carol Fischer.

For about two years, I set aside Tuesdays to be at Mountain View's history center. I enjoyed the other friendly faces there including Edna Thompson, the late Anne Craik, Louise Fallon, Kathleen Lowe Owen, Dirk van Erp and Barbara Kinchen.

Several people agreed to be interviewed for this history, in person or by telephone including Victor Calvo, Joseph De La Fuente, City Manager Kevin Duggan, Ruth Job Erichsen, Wallace Erichsen, Ralph Faravelli, Barbara Kinchen, Richard Meyer, Judith Moss, Carol Olson, Martin Spangler, Jr., M. James Spangler, Edna Thompson, and Mary Lou Zoglin.

Diane Keenan has been the caretaker of a wonderful scrapbook dating from the establishment of the Mountain View Woman's Club in 1904, which belonged to her mother, Bea Grass. Keenan allowed me to include photos from it in this book and offered the scrapbook to the Mountain View History Center for safekeeping.

The late Mildred Gentry Winters had a passion for Mountain View history and her copious newspaper notes were useful for this project. The scholarship of two other publications was important to early chapters of this book and I would like to offer them special acknowledgment. They are *Inigo of Rancho Posolmi: The Life and Times of a Mission Indian* (Ballena Press, 1998) by Laurence H. Shoup and Randall T. Milliken. It is a comprehensive biography of a local Indian compiled from both anthropological as well as historical documents. The authors gave permission to reproduce two maps that were drawn for their study. Along the same lines, is Becky McReynolds' Master's Thesis for Stanford University entitled "Chinese Lives in Early Mountain View" (Center for Asian Studies, Winter 1996-97). Both were important sources for Mountain View's history and have been footnoted in the text.

I appreciate the work of Metro Design of Saratoga, California who designed this book and the book cover, especially Karl Schirrmacher and Carolyn Johnson.

Mountain View photographer Robert Weaver graciously loaned his photos. Photographs or illustrations were also borrowed from Trudi Odbert, Alice Oku, Stocklmeir Library and Archives, Santa Clara University Archives, and History San José.

This manuscript was edited by N. Grey Osterud of Acton, Massachusetts. She has become a friend over the past years since she was a professor of history at San Jose State University. Her style of editing is strong, clear, and prompt—all of which I really appreciate. I am also grateful to her for offering insight into some of the pitfalls of writing local history.

Working on this project has not been an entirely positive experience. The late Wallace Stegner once said "local history is the best history" because it is part of ourselves. I would also add that it can be the most emotionally-charged. Pressure is brought to bear on an author to include particular individuals, or families, or businesses, or neighborhoods. I have succumbed in some cases, and my refusal to include others has caused resentments. Both giving in to pressures and holding fast has a down side.

I do not live in Mountain View, but I was asked to write this history because I am a published, professional historian. Some believe, and have told me, that I am at a disadvantage for not living in the city. I have used the example that one does not need to have fought in the Revolutionary War to be a Revolutionary War historian. Living outside the community allows for an objective telling of the facts. Sometimes that objectivity ruffles feathers.

The very best part of writing this history has been getting to know some Mountain View people.

The city is blessed to have a City Historian like Barbara McPheeters Kinchen—a first-class historian and a professional of the highest integrity. I greatly admire her. I also appreciate Carol Fischer's friendly professionalism and her willingness to help locate sometimes obscure details.

Finally I would like to say thank you to my husband, Pat, for his quiet, but unwavering support, and for his good sense of humor. And to my children, Joey and Lisa, who have gotten into the habit of asking, "Is this a Mountain View day?"

There is a day
when the road neither
comes nor goes, and the way
is not a way but a place

Wendell Barry

PROLOGUE

As the twenty-first century dawns and time seems to propel us ever faster into the future, it is easy to ignore or overlook the past. Just two hundred and fifty years ago, a generation before the American Revolutionary War, the land on which Mountain View has developed was occupied by Indians who relied on the natural water and food sources of an abundant landscape. Today it is recognized the world over as part of the Silicon Valley.

Mountain View's history between the Indian occupation and the Silicon Valley phenomenon is marked by a series of milestones—moments in time when history is made or commemorated, moments when we can look back and see from where or how far we have come. For a town whose very genesis is on a highway, *El Camino Real* (the royal highway), it is appropriate to mark its history in milestones.

Essayist and poet Wendell Berry's short verse, which serves as the epigraph of this book, suggests that the road will give way to place with its own distinctive characters. Mountain View has become such a place, along El Camino Real, and its history is shaped by lively personalities who illustrate the transformations of the city. In this story we find a Broadway playwright, a world-class landscape artist, a renowned handwriting expert, the creator of baseball's "spitball," and the Nobel Prize-winning inventor of the transistor. Other, less celebrated people, like Indian Lope Inigo, Doña María Trinidad Peralta de Castro, Chinese merchant Yuen Lung, newspaperman P. Milton "Pop" Smith, and scholar Mary Julia Gates, personify the town's history. Each began life entrenched in a particular cultural tradition and witnessed sweeping social and economic changes over the course of a long life. Each was forced to adapt to the presence of people of different cultures and each found new ways of living and working in the world. The stories of these individuals, along with many others, highlight Mountain View's milestones.

Transportation is the defining theme of Mountain View's history. Many of the town's historical milestones coincide with the introduction of a new mode of transportation—when the Spanish brought horses, California's first stagecoach, the opening of the San Francisco-San Jose Railroad, the first automobiles, airplanes, dirigibles, supersonic jets, and the late twentieth-century light rail projects. While the particular conveyance does not in itself constitute history, the chapters here are titled with each new-fangled

invention symbolizing the larger changes taking place within the community.

The city had its origins as a stagecoach stop at what today is Grant Road and El Camino Real near the edge of Stevens Creek. A local shopkeeper, Jacob Shumway, named the locale "Mountain View" as a commentary on the panorama of the coastal mountains to the west. A few years later when a snow-covered Mount Diablo was visible to the northeast, a ranch hand noted in his journal "when we turned out this morning, the tops of the Contra Costa range of mountains were white with snow . . . Mr. Shumway never knew the like before."[1] On that clear winter's day, mountains could be seen all around.

When the San Francisco-San Jose Railroad was completed in 1864, it bypassed the stagecoach stop, but a new Mountain View Station sprouted up a short distance away near the railroad tracks and today's Castro Street. The station town quickly eclipsed the little stage village, and Mountain View took on an entirely new character.

Second only to the railroad, the most significant influence on Mountain View during its first century of growth came from the divine inspiration of a religious woman. Mrs. Ellen White, one of the founders of the Seventh-Day Adventist Pacific Press Publishing Company, believed it was God's will that the church-sponsored business move from Oakland, California to Mountain View. When Pacific Press opened its doors in Mountain View in 1905, it ushered two hundred workers and their families to a town of just six hundred. It literally changed the complexion of the town and maintained a powerful economic, political, social and religious presence for eighty years.

Unless we reflect on our collective past, many pieces of Mountain View will be lost to history. This story tells about some of those almost forgotten episodes: at one time, Castro Street was taken over each year by a swollen creek, wreaking havoc and even death, on the community; in the 1920s, a doctor established a state-of-the-art maternity clinic and emergency room on El Camino Real, complete with a separate x-ray facility; and for about twenty years beginning in the 1930s, Mountain View had its own airport. Each layer adds color and dimension to the local story, but each has faded into an increasingly obscure past.

One of the most contentious issues facing the town from the very beginning was the manufacture, sale and consumption of alcohol. At one time, Mountain View had eighteen wineries and at least a dozen saloons. An insect infestation destroyed the vineyards, and the temperance movement closed the saloons. To drink or not to drink, whether the most carefully vinted zinfandel or basement-distilled "hooch," was the subject of heated debate for decades.

Mountain View has had a political impact on Santa Clara County and California's state government. Local leaders, such as the Reverend Wesley Gallimore, Frank Sleeper, and Doctor Bowling Bailey in the nineteenth century and Walter A. Clark, Martin Spangler, Sr., and Victor Calvo and in the twentieth, served as county supervisors or state assemblymen. Each brought local concerns to a higher political forum and connected Mountain View to the wider world around the valley and the state.

A 1914 business directory described Mountain View as "situated in the northwestern part of the famous Santa Clara Valley on the coast line of the Southern Pacific railroad, 11 miles north of San Jose, 36 miles south of San Francisco, and 6 miles from Palo Alto and the Stanford University."[2] A contemporary description would surely substitute "Silicon Valley" for Santa Clara Valley, but might otherwise remain the same.

When Stanford University opened in 1891, local real estate boosters used the new institution to market and populate Mountain View. The San Francisco earthquake of 1906 brought displaced city-dwellers. Some came temporarily, but many remained. From the opening of the Naval Air

Shoreline Park

Station—now Moffett Federal Airfield—in 1932, Mountain View became a center of the emerging defense industry. During the Silicon Valley era, strategic connections between science and technology are being forged by the city's people and institutions, giving Mountain View global recognition.

Mountain View was incorporated on November 7, 1902. Today's Mountain View has a population of just over 72,000 residents, encompasses twelve square miles, and its borders touch Sunnyvale, Los Altos, and Palo Alto. The city is also interconnected with places around the globe because its residents hail from every continent on earth. Mountain View's challenge is to maintain its own identity, its history, and its personality in the midst of the breakneck speed of the technological, sociological and demographic changes that have created the Silicon Valley. The celebration of the city's centennial in the year 2002 can encourage attention to community history and prompt questions about the future economy, the environment, and the city's role in the region and the world.

PART ONE

SETTING OUT ON THE JOURNEY

CHAPTER 1

ON FOOT AND ON HORSEBACK

I|MAGINING WHAT THIS PLACE MIGHT HAVE looked like before Europeans began to settle here in the 1770s can be difficult for contemporary Californians. To prod our imaginations, we turn to the diaries kept by a few Spaniards for their perspectives on the landscape and its inhabitants. Padres Juan Crespí and Francisco Palóu recorded their observations, drew sketches, and noted the progress of their earliest days in pristine California.[3]

In 1769 Spain launched *La Santa Expedición* (the Sacred Expedition) from *Baja* (Lower) California in today's Mexico to explore *Alta* (Upper) California for settlement. Spanish expeditionary forces and clergy travelled by sea and by land the length of today's California in search of a vast harbor vividly described by their predecessor, Sebastián Vizcaíno. The explorers did not believe Monterey Bay lived up to Vizcaíno's elaborate depiction, so they continued their search. As the explorers scouted the terrain on foot and on horseback they stumbled upon San Francisco Bay, and were in awe of its mammoth proportions. They forded numerous rivers, creeks and estuaries edging the bay, and their diary notations indicate they were startled by the wildlife that they encountered along the way. They

Drawing of a California Indian by *G. M. Reasserts* who visited the region in 1842 - 1843. It is taken from his travel and sketchbook, *A Sojourn in California*, reprinted by Grabhorn Press in San Francisco in 1955.

also came upon several villages of Indians, who appeared willing to share hunting and fishing grounds.

As the explorers wended their way south along the San Francisco peninsula they camped near a creek they named *San Francisquito*, today's border between Palo Alto and Menlo Park. A few miles further south they came upon another substantial creek they called *Arroyo de San José Cupertino*[4], which was later renamed Stevens Creek. From its source twenty miles away in the Santa Cruz Mountains, it snaked its way in a northeasterly direction across a wide valley toward San Francisco Bay. *Arroyo Permanente* (Permanent Creek), so-called because it did not dry up in summer, was also in the path of the Spaniards. Stevens and Permanente creeks remain important landmarks in what has become Mountain View.

Stevens Creek was edged by great, looming willows, a nesting ground for hundreds of species of birds and waterfowl. The geese were so plentiful that, according to one eyewitness, as they took flight "they would actually darken the air, and

make such a tremendous clacking as to be quite terrific." Black birds were so dense they appeared as storm-threatening "clouds," and giant black condors with a wingspan of nine feet or more, soared overhead.[5]

Prowling across the valley, the explorers had to continually skirt boggy marshes and standing ponds. In the distance, rivers and creek beds were visible only by an outline of thick trees along their banks. Marshy swamps with cattails and tules edged the bay where large groves of willow trees, or *sauzales* as the Spanish called them, stood along the tidal waters. Today's Moffett Federal Airfield was a dense willow grove, and San Francisco Bay, teeming with fish, mussels, oysters, and seals, was the main food supply for the native people.

Heading southeast, the Spaniards encountered an expansive valley of grass and scrub. It was checkered by standing groves of valley and live oak, and hemmed in by coastal mountains. One diary reported the land was "all black, mellow soil, well covered with several sorts of herbs and grass, with many oaks. . . ."[6] Indeed, a dense grove of valley oaks stood over much of today's Mountain View.

Further inland on drier territory, grasslands punctuated by isolated oak groves stretched out between today's Mountain View and the hills near Saratoga. Huge tracts of *chamizales* (chaparral) and bushy manzanita undergrowth, laced with poison oak, provided a haven for bobcats and foxes. There was "no passage except by a few regular beaten roads,"[7] and the surrounding hills were covered by oak woodlands.

Both small and large mammals, from the tiny chipmunk and squirrel to rabbit, fox, deer, mountain lion, and grizzly bear, flourished in pre-Spanish California. Grizzlies were commonplace and dominated the local food chain feeding on deer, elk, and seals that washed up on the shore. Indians did not have the weapons to kill the gigantic bears, but Spanish and Mexican guns greatly reduced their populations. For a time after the Spanish arrived, grizzlies actually thrived because they preyed upon domesticated animals introduced by the newcomers. But by the mid-nineteenth century, grizzlies were almost extinct. Staged bull and grizzly fights and bear hunting had become popular sports, and the Spanish, Mexican, and American ranchers would not tolerate the enormous predator freely roaming about.

The coyote, like the grizzly, also fed on domesticated animals and thrived under the new occupants of the land. But its raids on sheep, pigs, and chickens made it such a pest that the ranchers resorted to traps and poisons to control its numbers. Tule elk abounded in the grassy Santa Clara Valley. Missionary Francisco Palóu described them "as large as the largest ox or bull, with horns similar in shape to those of the deer, but so large that they measured sixteen palms from tip to tip."[8] Palóu also noted hundreds of pronghorn "about the size of a three-year-old sheep" with short horns and short legs. Hunters quickly eradicated both animals from the valley grasslands.

The explorers found at least two Indian villages, which they called *rancherías*, in what today is Mountain View. Rancherías were communities of unrelated families, cooperating for harvest, hunting, religious ceremonies, and for settling disputes.[9] One village was located at what today is Central Expressway and San Antonio Road. Anthropologists who excavated the site at the turn of the twentieth century called it the Castro Mound, and dated human occupation there to 760 B.C. The mound measured ten feet high, 450 feet long, and 290 feet across its widest point, making it the largest Indian mound in the southern part of the San Francisco Bay region. Professors from Stanford University and University of California at Berkeley excavated the mound and found clues to the lifestyle of the native people, including mortars and pestles, charm stones, implements, and seashells. Some of the artifacts can be found today in museum collections at the two universities. The Castro Mound was plowed under to make way for a subdivision in the 1940s.

Another *ranchería*, which the Spanish missionaries named San Bernardino, was located along lower Stevens Creek near today's Moffett Federal Airfield. The village had rounded, thatched huts constructed out of grasses and

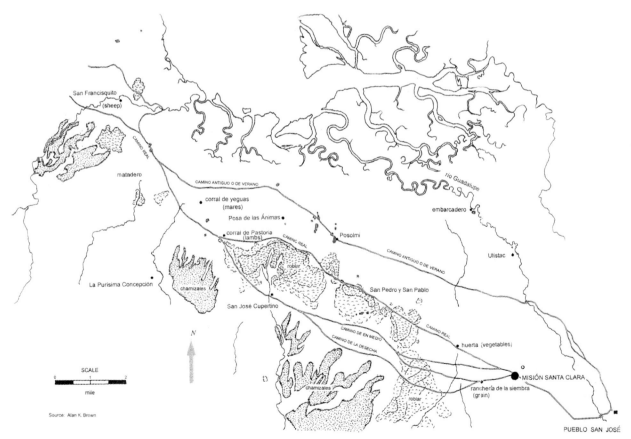

Map showing Upper and Lower San Francisco Roads and surrounding geography by Alan K. Brown. The Camino Antigua o de Verano (old summer road) follows the general course of today's Highway 101. Much of today's Mountain View was covered with an oak forest, fanning out from Arroyo de San Jose Cupertino, later renamed Stevens Creek. Reprinted by permission from *Inigo of Rancho Posolmi* by Lawrence H. Shoup and Randall T Milliken, Ballena Press, 1999.

A decaying **Mission Santa Clara** as depicted in an 1876 publication *An Arboreal Song of The Alameda* (The Beautiful Way) by Mary H. Field.

tule reeds. It was home to over one hundred individuals, making it one of the larger communities in the valley. The skirted women and unclothed men shared hunting and gathering tasks, but the men were the primary hunters. Women gathered berries, nuts and herbs, and wove baskets. The men made rope for fishing and trapping.[10]

Padre Juan Crespí shared a positive, although paternal, impression of the natives when he wrote, there are "large villages of barbarous heathen who are very affable, mild and docile, and very generous in giving what they have."[11] The Indians supplied copious amounts of food to the Spanish explorers. Several entries in the Spanish diaries mention the Indians sharing food.

The Spanish and the Indians had completely opposite attitudes toward animals. The natives hunted for food and had no domesticated animals. The Spaniards introduced many farm animals, heretofore unknown to the Indians, and relied upon animal husbandry for survival in remote California. They considered cattle- or horse-killing a capital offense and punished offenders accordingly. These opposing viewpoints became a major source of contention when Indians killed livestock for food and the Spanish sentenced the perpetrators to death.

Indian land-use practices also differed significantly from the Europeans. The Indians did not engage in formal agriculture like the Spanish and their acorn, game and shellfish diet did not require the cultivation of corn or other vegetables. The natives set annual fires to control the underbrush and stimulate the growth of useful plants. These burnings also reduced the threat of uncontrollable wildfires and allowed more free-flowing springs. When the Spanish curtailed the annual burnings, streams dried up and the underbrush took over.

In 1776, after the earliest Spanish expeditions had already made their way to Alta California, Juan Bautista de Anza arrived in Monterey with a caravan of settlers, including women and children to populate the new *presidios* (military posts), *pueblos* (towns), and missions in Alta California. Their trek had taken them over eight hundred miles from today's Arizona desert. The Anza Expedition settlers were simple, illiterate peasants, and many were *mestizos* (mixed race). The roster included names such as Castro and Peralta, whose descendents became important throughout Alta California and in Mountain View history. Ignacio Castro, a twenty-year-old native of Sinaloa was one of these settlers; he eventually married María Pacheco. Their son, Mariano, married María Trinidad Peralta, the daughter of another Anza settler, Luís Peralta. This couple came to own over eight thousand acres of land from which Mountain View later grew.

The missionaries searched the natural landscape for a good location to build a mission. A site on the banks of the Guadalupe River was chosen and dedicated to Saint Clare by Padre Tomás de la Peña on January 12, 1777. The Franciscans immediately set to work recruiting converts and laborers to build the mission. At the end of the same year, on November 29, 1777, *El Pueblo de San José de Guadalupe*, sometimes called El Pueblo or just San José, was founded as the first civil community in Alta California. Fourteen families from the Anza Expedition were directed to settle the new town.

Mission Santa Clara lands extended from the Guadalupe River on the east to San Francisquito Creek on the west, roughly from today's San José to Palo Alto. Its northern edge was San Francisco Bay reaching south to the coastal mountains. The mission fathers recruited natives from this vast area and beyond, but particularly from seven local villages, including San Bernardino. At that time, the native population in the valley was about three to six persons per square mile. California was more densely populated by Indians than any other region in North America, except central Mexico. The region's native population was a very diverse group of people, speaking at least one hundred different languages.

Two years after its founding, the mission was flooded by the Guadalupe River and was moved to the south. In 1784 a third mission was built even further back from the river. This third site was dedicated by the founder of the Alta California missions, Fray Junípero Serra. Father Serra is widely regarded as the driving force behind California's mission system and has been lauded by many as a saintly man for his relentless missionary zeal. Indeed, he is a candidate for Catholic sainthood. However, Serra has also been criticized for the cruel treatment meted out by the padres to the Indians. Historians remain in conflict regarding Serra.

An adobe church was built and it stood twenty-two and a half feet high, twenty-five feet wide and 113 feet long. The roof had a redwood plank ceiling with adobe tiles and thatch on the outside. The main twin doors were made of cedar and redwood. The church was white-washed both inside and out and the interior walls had painted decoration near the adobe floor and the ceiling. The mission compound included grain warehouses, a residence for padres, a separate residence for the *mayordomo* or overseer, and a large kitchen.

The padres began baptizing natives from Ranchería San Bernardino in 1777.[12] Eventually this village supplied forty-four married adults to Mission Santa Clara. The horse-riding, swashbuckling Spanish soldiers were imposing enough to induce fearful natives to bring their children to the missions for baptism. But a series of epidemics, heretofore unknown to the natives, also scared them into going to the mission. The padres

required families with children to turn them over to the mission when they reach adolescence, where they remained. The mission experiment, intended to last about ten years, supposed that the natives would adapt to Spanish culture. When that occurred, the mission lands would be distributed to them. The experiment did not succeed, the Indians were not free to leave the mission, and any attempts to do so were severely punished.

One particular Indian, named Lope Inigo,[13] serves as a dramatic example of the social transformations occurring in California during the late eighteenth and early nineteenth centuries. He began his long life in a native village, was Christianized by mission padres, worked as a mission laborer and foreman at the mission, and much later was the recipient of a Mexican land grant that he had to defend from swindlers and squatters.

Inigo was born in 1781 at Ranchería San Bernardino. In 1789, sometime after his mother had died, the eight-year-old was baptized at Mission

Portrait of Inigo from a daguerreotype, circa 1850s.
Courtesy Santa Clara University Archives.

Crisanto Castro and his wife, Francisca Armijo. He was the youngest son of Mariano Castro and María Trinidad Peralta, and he took over the operation of *Rancho Pastoria de las Borregas* after Mariano's death. The couple had nine children.

Santa Clara and renamed Inigo in honor of Saint Ignatius. At age ten he began living full-time at the mission; he remained a fixture there for the next fifty years. In the winter of 1794-95, a drought and disease-induced conversion took place among the Indians surrounding Mission Santa Clara. During that winter, over 550 converts, mostly adult, were baptized. Among them was a girl named María Viviana.[14]

In 1797, when Inigo was sixteen, he married fifteen-year-old María Viviana. She mastered domestic chores like roasting and grinding grain and weaving woolen blankets. He worked as a manual laborer, and he participated in two major projects. In 1799, two hundred Indians were used to uproot willows from the banks of the Guadalupe River and transplant them along the path known as The Alameda, to shade the road linking San José to Mission Santa Clara. At about the same time, a three-mile long irrigation ditch or *acequia*, was dug by the Indians to supply water to some mission properties.[15] Inigo was a laborer on both projects, he emerged as a leader, and was made an *alcalde* (in this case a labor foreman) at Mission Santa Clara. Despite his success as a foreman, records indicate that in 1814 Inigo and another Indian attacked one of

the Franciscans at the mission. The Indians were captured and punished, but to what extent is not clear. Nevertheless, for most of his life at the mission, in the eyes of the padres, Inigo was a good citizen.

Inigo and Viviana lived lives typical of missionized Indians. According to anthropologists Laurence Shoup and Randall Milliken, the couple very likely lived in a "family-style adobe" house. They had eleven children together, but only three lived to adulthood. Viviana died in 1828 on the same day that her youngest son, two-year-old José Tómas also died. She was forty-six.

Up until 1822, Spanish land grants to private individuals in California were few and far between. After that year, when Mexico gained independence from Spain, land grants became more common, and over the next twenty years almost eight hundred *ranchos* (ranches) were granted. During the 1830s most of California's missions were secularized, or removed from the control of Spanish-born Franciscan priests and put in the hands of Mexican-born secular clergy. An administrator representing the interests of the new ranchero ruling class known as *Californios* (California-born Spaniards) was appointed to distribute mission lands and emancipate the Indians.

The ranchos granted by Mexican governors that comprised today's Mountain View were *Rancho Pastoría de las Borregas* (literally, the ewe lambs pasture), measuring about 8,800 acres, and Posolmi (an Indian name), which the Spanish also called *Las Positas de las Animas* (little wells of the souls), measuring almost 3,400 acres. One Californio explained about the sheep pasture: "the mission used to keep their sheep there from time immemorial and hence it acquired the name 'Pastoría de las Borregas.'" It is estimated that between fifteen and twenty thousand sheep were pastured there.

To the west lay *Rincón de San Francisquito*, almost 8,500 acres granted to José Peña in 1841, who sold it to the Robles family in 1847. Today's Los Altos Hills was called *La Purísima Concepción* (the Holy Virgin or Immaculate Conception), making up almost 4,500 acres, and the same amount of territory made up *Rancho San Antonio*, granted to Juan Prado Mesa in 1839. At present it is Los Altos.

In 1839 Inigo was officially emancipated from Mission Santa Clara, and he returned to his ancestral land, Posolmi, at today's Moffett Federal Airfield. He petitioned Governor Juan B. Alvarado for ownership of this land and he also requested custody of his twenty-five-year-old son Manuel, who was still under the guardianship of the mission.

Governor Alvarado referred the matter to his brother-in-law, José Ramon Estrada, the administrator of Mission Santa Clara. The government agreed to give Inigo "10 tame breeding cows, 5 bulls, 15 mares with a stallion, 2 yoke of oxen, 5 milk cows, 4 tame horses, 50 sheep, 10 mules, 1 cart, 1 plow. . . ."[17] He was also awarded guardianship of his son, Manuel, and a boy born to one of his daughters, his grandson Casimiro. Inigo built a "rush" house at Posolmi, planted some fruit trees, and raised livestock. In May 1844, after sixteen years as a widower, Inigo remarried. He and his second wife, Eustaquia, had two daughters and a son, but none survived childhood. All this time since his emancipation, Inigo thought the land had been granted to him, along with the livestock and tools.

Mission Santa Clara's administrator José Ramon Estrada was well connected in California. His father, José Mariano Estrada, a native of Baja California, had been in Alta California since the late 1790s. The senior Estrada married Ysabel Argüello and among their children were José Ramon, Santiago and Francisco. The father and at least two sons served in an official capacity at the Monterey presidio.

As administrator, José Ramon Estrada reported to Governor Juan Alvarado, who had been his boyhood friend and was married to his wife's sister. Alvarado, following Mexican policy, directed Estrada to distribute mission properties to Californios in good standing. Estrada controlled over 80,000 acres from San Francisquito Creek and San Francisco Bay on the north, south to the Guadalupe River. It is not surprising that Estrada's family would benefit from his position, even though administrators were prohibited from requesting land for immediate family members.

In 1840 the administrator's father, José Mariano Estrada, petitioned for a grant of two leagues more or less, approximately 8,800 acres, to "establish thereon a rancho in company with my son Francisco." The administrator noted that he was "incompetent to report on the foregoing petition" because the petitioner was his father. But in 1842, Governor Alvarado granted the land "of the extent of two square leagues." Alvarado continued, "I declare the said Francisco Estrada owner" of the rancho. One of the requirements was that he had to build a house there and occupy it within one year.[18]

Francisco had been married in 1839 at Mission Santa Clara to Inez Castro, the daughter of Mariano Castro and María Trinidad Peralta. Both Francisco and Inez were part of the ruling class ranchero families who were gaining huge tracts of land throughout California. When Francisco Estrada received the land grant, he, his father, and father-in-law, Mariano, raised livestock on the rancho. By 1842 they built a small adobe house there, near today's Rengstorff Avenue just east of the railroad tracks.

As Francisco Estrada occupied La Pastoría, he encroached on Inigo's land. In the meantime, his brother was replaced as administrator by his great uncle, Ignacio Alviso. In 1843 Inigo went to Mission Santa Clara to complain that Estrada was occupying Posolmi as well as La Pastoría, but Alviso turned a deaf ear. There was no written proof of a land grant to Inigo; the Indian was told that the records were mysteriously "lost." He suspected that either José Ramon Estrada or

Ignacio Alviso had destroyed the record at the behest of their relative, Francisco Estrada.

When Governor Manuel Micheltorena succeeded Alvarado in 1842, he appointed Father Jesus María Vasquez del Mercado to monitor Mission Santa Clara. The priest believed Inigo's assertions that he was being swindled even though the only existing record indicated that livestock, not land, had been granted to the Indian. Mercado appealed to the new Governor and with Mercado's intervention, Inigo was successful in obtaining Posolmi.

Micheltorena ordered a new survey of the land in question and it was carried out by Antonio Suñol of San José. Suñol discovered that the Estrada land grant contained an area much larger than two leagues or the 8,800 acres originally granted. So the government measured off a portion for Inigo and on February 14, 1844 Governor Micheltorena gave Inigo title to almost 1,700 acres, about half of what he thought was his. It extended "from his [Inigo's] house to the first spring of water inclusive called Las Animas, and from the Sausal to Los Esteros."[19] The Indian also requested custody of his seriously ill daughter, Magdalena, her husband, Simon, and their two children. This family left the mission to live at Posolmi with Inigo. By this time, Inigo had a "very good wooden house with a shingle roof, consisting of a small parlor and a small chamber, and another separate room for his son Manuel and his family. . . ."[20] Inigo secured his land only through determination and persistence.

In 1850 Inigo sold the eastern half his land (almost 850 acres), to Robert Walkinshaw for $2,500. Walkinshaw, a native of Scotland, came to California in 1847 from Mexico as manager and part owner of the quicksilver mine at New Almaden for the firm Barron, Forbes & Company. Walkinshaw was married to a Mexican woman and they built a sprawling home near Inigo's and raised their children. The aging Indian occasionally visited their home, and Walkinshaw was often seen ferrying Inigo around in his buggy. The two developed an unlikely friendship.[21]

Inigo also sold about four hundred acres to Thomas Campbell. Some others occupied Inigo's land without purchasing it and were squatters, including John Whisman, Silas Emerson, and Wesley Gallimore. Robert Walkinshaw died in 1858 while on a visit to his native Scotland, and the land remained in his family until 1882. Subsequent owners of that land were the Curtners, Cunninghams, Holthouses, Hirsch Land Company, and the United States Navy (NAS Sunnyvale, later Moffett Field).

In the meantime, early death would cut short Francisco and Inez Estrada's stewardship of Rancho Pastoría de las Borregas. Inez Castro Estrada died in 1844; Francisco became very ill and died in San José a year later. They left no children. Francisco's father, José Mariano Estrada, who had originally requested the land grant, inherited Rancho Pastoría de las Borregas. In 1845 he sold the rancho to his late son's father-in-law, Mariano Castro. Then the senior Estrada died in 1847.

Mariano Castro, very nearly the same age as Inigo, was born at Yerba Buena (later called San Francisco) in 1784 to María Pacheco and Ignacio Castro, members of the Anza Expedition. Not long after Mariano was born, his parents settled in El Pueblo de San José. As a young man, Mariano served at the presidio in Yerba Buena for a little over ten years. The brown-eyed soldier stood five feet, five inches tall and had a fair complexion with chestnut-colored hair and did not wear a beard.[22]

Upon returning to San José, Castro married María Trinidad Peralta (hereinafter M.T.P. de Castro), the daughter of Luís Peralta (also of the Anza Expedition) and María Loreto Alviso. The Peraltas were prominent in San José; their restored adobe home still stands today in the city's center. When Mariano Castro married María Trinidad, Luís Peralta gave the couple a dowry of cattle.[23] The Castros had nine children, the youngest of whom, Crisanto, was born in 1828. The Castros must have achieved some influence in the pueblo for during the same year as the birth of their youngest child, Mariano was elected alcalde (mayor or justice of the peace).

From the time Mariano acquired Rancho Pastoría de las Borregas in 1845, he lived at least part-time, in the Estrada adobe there and raised livestock. The Castro family, like most Californio families, had Indians working its rancho. According to William Dale, a Mountain View resident since 1850 who was interviewed early in the twentieth century, the Castros had between seventy-five and one hundred Indians living and working on

A portrait of the Peter Davidson family in 1851 by Giovanni Martinelli. According to their marriage record at Mission Santa Clara, Don Pedro Davidson married María Josefa Castro, the daughter of Mariano Castro and María Trinidad Peralta de Castro. Also pictured is the couple's first child, Peter A. Davidson. *Courtesy of the Fine Arts Museum of San Francisco, Museum purchase, M.H. de Young Endowment Fund through Walter Heil, DY54858.*

the rancho. He remarked, "they were somewhat the same position as slaves under a kindly master."[24]

In 1849 Don Castro sold fully half of the rancho to an Irishman, Martin Murphy, Jr. Perhaps in preparation for the sale, Castro commissioned a survey of the rancho, which was carried out by Charles Preuss of San José. Curiously, the Preuss map shows the houses of John Whisman, the Robles family, and Inigo, but does not indicate the Estrada-Castro adobe. However, a map produced in 1853 shows a Castro house, suggesting that it was probably built after the sale to Murphy. William Dale recalled that in 1850, at the same time that Martin Murphy, Jr. was building his frame house, "the roof was not yet on the Castro adobe."[25]

Around 1850 then, Castro built a new house to replace the old adobe. The house was built of a combination of adobe and wood. Its front porch faced to the west, while an outdoor staircase to the attic was on the north end. Mariano Castro lived there until he became very ill in the mid-1850s, and went to his house in San José. From that time on, his son Crisanto, lived at the rancho.

In May 1849, Mariano Castro also bought a small piece of property in San José at San Pedro and Santa Clara streets from his son-in-law Peter Davidson, in exchange for some land. Davidson had married Castro's daughter, María Josefa, at Mission Santa Clara in 1848. Peter Davidson was a native of Austria and had been in California since 1843. During the 1840s, he had a store in

San José and exported hides and tallow. From 1850 until Castro's death in 1856, Davidson acted as Castro's agent and exercised his power of attorney—skillfully and, some of his contemporaries believed, unscrupulously. Years later in court proceedings, Davidson referred to his late father-in-law as "his ignorant and unlettered principal" for whom he managed business affairs.

American emigrants trickled into California throughout the 1840s. When the Mexican War was over in 1848 and with the discovery of gold the same year, the trickle turned into a torrent of new arrivals. The westward movement had accustomed Americans to homesteading, or staking out unoccupied land and paying the government a minimal fee for it. Many did not know about nor adhere to the provisions of the Treaty of Guadalupe Hidalgo, which had ended the war with Mexico. The treaty clearly stated that title to land in California would remain with the current owners. Many Americans became squatters, simply taking over land and livestock and building homes, believing they had legal right to do so. The rightful owners of the land, usually Californios, had to go to enormous expense, hiring lawyers and having land documents translated, just to retain their own property. Most were not successful.

In 1851 the United States Congress passed the Land Act in an attempt to cope with confusion and conflict over property ownership in California by setting up a legal process to determine the validity of land claims. However, it did not enforce the

Treaty of Guadalupe Hidalgo, but put the burden of proof on the land owners. Title records were incomplete, in some cases nonexistent, and very often boundaries were determined by natural objects such as trees, rocks, or streams. When, or if, those objects were moved or changed, the boundaries could be challenged. The whole process was a lengthy and expensive undertaking that enriched lawyers and translators, and took an average of seventeen years to settle. Castro's case took nineteen years and Mariano did not live to see it finished.

Castro had initiated his case in the spring of 1852 when he petitioned the Board of Land Commissioners to verify his claim to Rancho Pastoría de las Borregas. Two witnesses for Castro, Antonio Suñol and José Fernandez, both of San José, had conducted surveys of the rancho in 1843. To prepare his testimony in the summer of 1852, Suñol went to examine the Spanish record that held the survey he had taken to lay out Inigo's land almost a decade before. Suñol was stunned to discover that about a dozen pages, including his survey, had been ripped from the record. He believed that American alcaldes had allowed records to be damaged or destroyed so that some squatters would have a better chance of gaining title.[26]

Edward Dale, an American settler leasing Castro land, appeared as a witness for the United States before the Land Commission. But he could not answer the key question put to him about what eastern boundary to the rancho that Castro claimed.[27] The Land Commission confirmed Castro's title in 1854, but the decision was immediately appealed by the United States government. The process to clear title to the Castro claim was not complete until 1871. In the intervening years, the Castros paid attorneys' fees with portions of land that were then divided and sold.

An attorney named James Jones was hired by Peter Davidson to represent Castro in land dealings. Jones negotiated a lease for land containing the Fremont House, a wayside inn operating since 1848. Cyrus G. Saunders leased one hundred acres with the existing inn, enclosures, and corrals, for $50 per month for a renewable term of two years. He added a ten-room hotel and had the old structures removed to another property for use as a hunting lodge.[28] Saunders was not successful at Fremont House though. He could not keep squatters at bay and in November 1853 he defaulted.

The previous April, Mariano Castro signed ownership of over 450 acres "in consideration of the natural love and affection" to his daughter María Josefa and her husband Peter Davidson. The swath of property, which included Fremont House, buffered Castro's property from Martin Murphy, Jr.'s Bay View. It extended from the San Francisco Road at Stevens Creek to Whisman's. Two months later the Davidsons sold the same land for $5,000 to John Sullivan of San Francisco. One settler recalled Davidson "was almost glad to be rid of the land in order to rid himself of the squatters."[29]

Jones was also instructed to file suits against squatters on Castro land. Among the squatters taken to court by Castro and Davidson were Cyrus Saunders, John Whisman, A. Whisman, T. Creighton, and George W. Moody.[30] For his services, Jones was paid with Castro land, which he then sold. Several years elapsed before anyone realized that Castro paid Jones with land outside the boundaries of his two leagues. In other words, he paid with land that he did not own. In the meantime, Jones sold the land to unsuspecting buyers, who sold it again. Then Jones died in late 1851. Many people suspected Davidson was the swindler, rather than his father-in-law. Davidson admitted the plan a dozen years after Castro's death when a prominent judge, Joshua F. Bullett, tried to buy some of the property but could not because of the tangled title. The court record reads, "Davidson, by his own statements, was at least a party to, if not the author of, the devious plot."[31]

Secundino Robles and his wife, María Antonia García de Robles. The couple had twenty-nine children.

Complicating the transfers of ownership and the succession of land transactions was the fact that most of the principals could neither read nor write and were monolingual. Mariano Castro spoke only Spanish; Martin Murphy, Jr., spoke only English; Inigo spoke Spanish, an Ohlone dialect, and eventually a halting English. None of them could read. Each relied heavily on the counsel of others, and in some cases, that proved their undoing. Castro's questionable counselor was his son-in-law, Peter Davidson. Inigo depended upon his neighbor, Robert Walkinshaw. Murphy made sure his sons were educated at a new school run by the Jesuits, Santa Clara College.

Mariano Castro died in 1856. Peter Davidson witnessed the will and arranged to have it translated in 1857. Castro's widow, M.T.P. de Castro, was named executrix. That same year, one of his daughters, Mercedes, married a native of Argentina, Andrés Calderon. Eventually both of Castro's sons-in-law, Andrés Calderon and Peter Davidson, were appointed appraisers of his real and personal property.

Mariano Castro's estate was valued at $38,200, which represented his remaining 3,500 acres of the rancho at $10 per acre, a San José adobe at Santa Clara and San Pedro streets ($200) with an adjacent lot ($1,000), personal property (furniture, $200), and livestock (sheep $800). The house on the rancho where he had

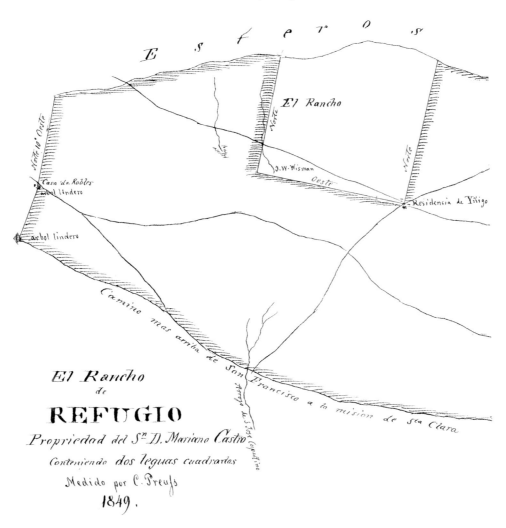

Survey of Castro's rancho, sometimes called *El Rancho de Refugio* (ranch of the refuge), drawn by Charles Pruess in 1849. Note the location of Inigo's house (spelled *Ynigo*), Whisman, and Robles. This map shows *Arroyo de San José de Cupertino* (later named Stevens Creek), and *Camino mas arriba de San Francisco a la mision de Santa Clara* (upper San Francisco Road or El Camino Real). The handwritten text at the bottom reads: "I, Charles Pruess, Certify that I was employed by Mr. Mariano Castro to survey his Rancho Refugio situated in the Valley of the Pueblo de San José, California and have executed the said survey in the best manner according to the Title papers (illegible) to by said Mr. Castro and have made a map."

ON FOOT AND ON HORSEBACK

The Secundino Robles home
Robles and his brother, Teodoro, purchased *Rincón de San Francisquito*, almost 8,500 acres from José Peña in 1847. By the 1880s the Robles family had fewer than 500 acres remaining. The house stood near today's Central Expressway and San Antonio Road.

lived from 1851-1855 was worth $1,000. By the time the estate was closed in 1871 its value had risen to $113,900 which included the lot in San José ($10,000), Rancho Pastoría ($100,000), and almost $4,000 worth of horses, cattle and sheep.[32]

Mariano's son, Crisanto Castro, lived on the rancho along with Crisanto's widowed mother, M.T.P. de Castro, and his unmarried sisters. In 1857, Crisanto married Francisca Armijo,[33] and the couple had seven sons and two daughters. The entire family was important to the next generation in Mountain View.

The disputes over title and ownership continued long after Mariano Castro's death, and the Land Commission continued to call witnesses. The widow Castro marshaled the family for the long, complicated proceedings, despite the fact that she was illiterate (her father, Luís Peralta, did not believe women should be educated and had refused schooling for his daughters). She was no stranger to drawn-out litigation. When her father died in 1851, his $1 million estate was left in considerable dispute. María Trinidad and her sisters sued their brothers for a portion of the estate, since the daughters had been excluded from the inheritance. In what became known as the "Sisters' Title" suit, the women claimed their father had been mentally incompetent when he made his will. But more likely is that his final wishes were in keeping with the policies of his

life—to keep his daughters sheltered, uneducated and dependent. The sisters lost their suit.[34]

Bitter litigation over Castro land continued. The Land Commission reversed its original confirmation to Castro and the land was re-surveyed by the Surveyor General. The case went to the California Supreme Court but was dismissed because it was said to fall under federal law. Later, it went to the U.S. Supreme Court. The Castros ended up with a confirmation of most of their land, but sold huge portions to raise cash and pay for litigation.

These land disputes caused hostility and conflict between neighbors and exacerbated tense relations between native Californians and newcomers. Since 1847 Teodoro and Segundino Robles owned the former Peña rancho of 8,418.21 acres, which represented "virtually everything between the western foothills and San Francisco Bay, from Castro Station on the south to Palo Alto on the north."[35] The Robles hacienda was located near today's Central Expressway and San Antonio Road, and the adobe and wood house was home to Segundino Robles and his wife, María Antonia Garcia, and their twenty-nine children.

Segundino stood over six feet tall and was "a fine looking old Castilian Spaniard, straight and tall, with a fine military bearing-every inch a 'Don'."[36] Despite his formidable stature, he had to defend his land and livestock aggressively. One night he mistakenly corralled his neighbors' animals and was almost lynched for the error. The newspaper reported it this way:

> *Having lost about 100 head of tame cattle a short time before. . . . he went out with some of his men, and unable to see the brand, drove them into his corral. In the morning he saw they were not his, but his neighbors!. . . . The next day, Americans came to his house, insulting his family & said they had come to kill him.*[37]

Don Robles survived the encounter, but it graphically illustrates the cultural conflict of those troubled times.

No one in the environs of Rancho Pastoría de las Borregas was safe from the rising tide of acrimony over land ownership. Inigo, the Walkinshaws, Castro's heirs and vendees, and Robles each had reason to worry how the bitter property disputes would be settled. Very large portions of Pastoría de las Borregas and the surrounding ranchos were sold or traded as lawyer's fees and and in an effort to keep the families financially viable. Ultimately, the Castros received confirmation for 4,200 acres of Pastoría de las Borregas and Martin Murphy, Jr.'s official total was 4,900. Walkinshaw did not live to learn that he was awarded title to the land he had purchased from Inigo. The government confirmed 8,400 acres to the Robles, but it was rapidly whittled away to satisfy debt and to support the huge family.

Life in mid-nineteenth century California took on new complexities with a larger and more diverse population engaged in unprecedented commerce and cultural exchange. The surprising growth of San Francisco and San José as a result of the Gold Rush demanded native and newcomer alike to find new ways to get around the vast landscape of California. The stagecoach, imported from the East Coast, was a welcome improvement over the heretofore reliance on foot and on horseback, or the awkward horse-drawn wagon.

CHAPTER 2

STAGECOACH

TWO PARALLEL ROADS RAN THROUGH CASTRO'S land linking San José and Yerba Buena (San Francisco). The *Camino Antiguo Verano* (literally the old summer road but usually called the Lower San Francisco Road) was the more direct route, which ran very near today's Bayshore Freeway, Highway 101. During the rainy weather, though, this road would often be an impassable, muddy bog. The alternate route, the Upper San Francisco Road or *El Camino Real* (today's road of the same name) became the path of choice because it was dry most of the year. A logical resting-place on the road between Yerba Buena and San José was where El Camino came to Stevens Creek. It is no wonder that a stagecoach stop grew up there.

Early on, the Lower San Francisco Road was more heavily travelled. California's first wayside inn, Fremont House, was established on the lower road in 1847 by George and Sarah Harlan. The Harlans built a "little clapboard redwood house"[38] and christened it Fremont House, in honor of the enormously popular explorer and topographer Captain John C. Frémont. When Fremont Township was created in 1851 out of a north-west portion of Santa Clara County including the Mountain View area, it was named for Frémont as well. In 1848, a gold hungry George Harlan left his wife at home and set out to try his hand at gold mining.

The next year the Harlans sold Fremont House to James Lynn, whose son-in-law, Washington Moody, operated the inn. Then Cyrus Saunders, an innkeeper, farmer, justice of the peace, and county supervisor took over the management of Fremont House, leasing the land from Castro. Saunders built there and generally improved the site, but within two years, he defaulted and filed bankruptcy. The district court of Santa Clara County rendered a judgment against Saunders, ordering him to pay Mariano Castro almost $700. At this time, title passed from Castro to his daughter, María Josefa, and her husband, Peter Davidson. They sold to John Sullivan, and for the entire second half of the twentieth century, the Fremont House was occupied by a Sullivan descendent, Mrs. Mary Murphy O'Connell.[39]

Not long after the Harlans opened Fremont House, forty-year-old John W. Whisman[40] and his wife, Margaret, opened Willigrove Inn on the southwest corner of Inigo's land. They had come overland in 1846 with four children from Missouri. He staked out the land with a ditch that extended around three sides of the property. "Whisman's ditch" became a landmark for surveyors and appears on hundreds of property deeds through the 1850s. They harvested grain, raised livestock, and operated Willigrove Inn, which was likely named for the nearby willow groves.

While Fremont House practically fronted the south side of Lower San Francisco Road, Whisman's was to the north, set back about a half mile. When Harlan contracted "gold fever," the Whismans gained the lion's share of road-weary customers and by 1848, theirs was the most popular inn between San Francisco and San José. An 1849 advertisement gives us a glimpse of Willigrove Inn:

> The travelling public are respectfully informed that a House of Entertainment has been opened under the above name. . . . The Table will be well supplied, the Bar amply furnished with choice Wines and Liquors; while the convenience and beauty of the locality—its excellent water and abundant pasturage, render it a desirable stopping place for those visiting the interior. The Inn is situated about forty miles from San Francisco, and twelve miles from the Pueblo de San Jose.
> J.W. Whisman.[41]

He laid out a neat and inviting drive up to his little inn, where the house and two small out-buildings were nestled among the willows. From the front of the house, visitors could see the San Francisco Bay and Mount Diablo beyond; one visitor claimed that on an exceptionally clear day he could see the peaks of the Sierra Nevada in the distance.[42] Behind the house was a thick growth of trees and fields of wild mustard. Today, the site of Whisman's house is marked with a sign, just outside the main gate to Moffett Federal Airfield.

Guests commented on the quality of the fresh butter churned by Margaret Whisman, a commodity not yet readily available in California. An Indian took care of the livery for guests when they arrived at the inn. In the spring of 1850, one traveler described his trip to Whisman's: "Our host is a true Yankee, and his wife and three or four noisy children transported us back to Yankeeland." He went on to describe his arrival there this way:

> The sun is down, darkness comes on apace, and we push our horses still farther, for the grizzly bears are numerous in this neighborhood and an encounter with them is not to be courted. We have a revolver each and hold them in readiness. We have no moon to guide us by its silvery light and tis now too dark to distinguish the road. We have left the oaks and now come to an open country; trusting to our horses to keep the road, we give them the rein and dash forward into the seemingly dark void. We now hear the bellowing of a herd of wild cattle and before we know it are in the midst of them. Luckily we were not attacked by any of them and after losing the road two or three times came across an Indian Camp and by dint of the little Spanish I could talk ascertained that we were within a half a mile of Wistman's Ranch. We soon arrive there and receive a hearty welcome, gave our horses in charge of the Indian boy to stake them out in the rich grass and sat down to a good supper looking more like home than any thing we have seen yet.[43]

The Indian camp mentioned was very likely the home of Inigo and his family.

Perhaps responding to the requests of travelers at his inn, Whisman started the first stagecoach line in California in 1849 and it ran between San Francisco and San José. Fare between the two towns was two ounces of gold or $32; the trip took nine hours. In 1849, a driver earned $300 per month, but he also made money when people paid him to deliver mail. Since there was no official postal service, individual drivers were asked to make deliveries and allowed to pocket the money.

Whisman's stagecoach venture was short-lived. His rig was "an old French omnibus" pulled by poorly treated "mules and mustangs." Not only was his equipment poor, but the fiercely stormy winter of 1849-50 made the road between San Francisco and San José so muddy that the coach "wheels soon sank to the hubs." Worse yet, his driver was stealing from him. By February of 1850, driver Preston K. Woodside was ordered by the district court in San José to pay Whisman and his partner, a Mr. Jarvis, $676 that he had evidently collected in fares on the stage line. Whisman was represented by attorney James Jones in his suit against Woodside, the same Jones who represented Davidson and Castro.

Whisman thought he could keep his business alive by running his stage between Willigrove Inn and the embarcadero at Alviso, but a competing stage line with better equipment and horses beat him out. And even though the court ordered Woodside to pay his debt, Whisman could not salvage the beleaguered stagecoach line. In the fall of 1850, he sold out to his main competitors, Hall & Crandall.

By 1855 Whisman was drowning in debt and several portions of his property were auctioned at Sheriff's sales. He was also ordered to satisfy a $3,600 debt. Margaret Whisman had died and John promptly remarried. When John appeared to be going bankrupt, his new wife, Mrs. Hannah Whisman, declared herself financially independent and published a legal notice saying: "I intend to carry on, in my own name and on my own account, the business of farming, and the buying, selling, and raising of stock,. . . ." The Whismans, like

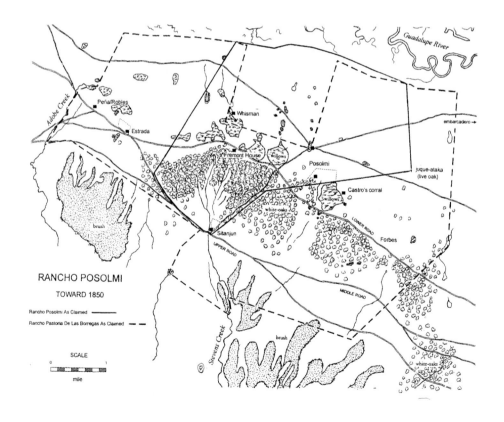

Source: Alan K. Brown

Map of Rancho Posolmi (Inigo's land grant) and *Rancho Pastoria de las Borregas* circa 1850 by Alan K. Brown. The solid line indicates the land Inigo claimed. The dotted line indicates the land the Estradas and later the Castros said was theirs. Eventually about 1,700 acres were confirmed to Inigo, half of the original grant. The box labeled Estrada is approximately where Rengstorff Avenue crosses Central Expressway. The box marked Whisman is the southwest corner of Moffett Federal Airfield. The road labeled the upper road is approximately today's El Camino Real. Reprinted by permission from *Inigo of Rancho Posolmi* by Lawrence H. Shoup and Randall T. Milliken, Ballena Press, 1999.

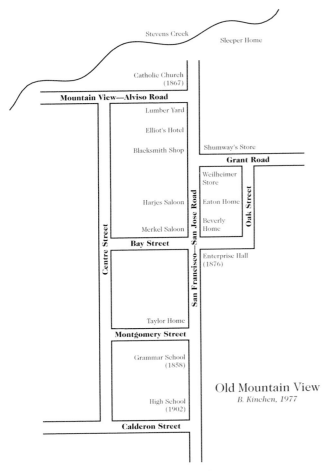

Map of old Mountain View drawn in 1977
by Barbara McPheeters Kinchen.

many couples, were probably trying to protect whatever other property she had owned previously or that she and her new husband owned together from attachment for old debts.[45]

California's first legislature, which convened in San José in 1849-50, established twenty-seven California counties, including Santa Clara County. On September 9, 1850, California was admitted to the Union after over a year of heated and angry debate in the nation's capital over whether the new state would be slave or free. More than a month passed before news of admission reached California shores. When Governor Peter Burnett, California's first American civil governor who happened to be in San Francisco, heard the news, he wanted to deliver it personally to the state capital in San José. He commanded Jared B. Crandall, the proprietor of the Hall & Crandall stage line that had bought out Whisman, to rush him to San José. When another coach driver tried to beat Crandall and Burnett to San José, a

race ensued with the two coaches careening down the peninsula at top speed to spread the news of statehood. Burnett's stagecoach won by a tiny margin, and perhaps not so coincidentally, Hall & Crandall were soon awarded a four-year contract to deliver the U.S. Mail for $6,000. The contract allowed them to reduce San Francisco-San José stagecoach fares to $16, and later to $10, driving any competitors out of business.

On its regular route at a more leisurely pace, the Hall & Crandall stagecoach made a rest stop in the shade of a large laurel tree about a half a mile southeast of Stevens Creek within the city limits of today's Sunnyvale. It had become a natural stopping point to change horses with San Francisco 35 miles to the north, and San José 11 miles to the south. As yet there was no bridge over Stevens Creek, and coaches and wagons had to negotiate the slippery banks and ford the rocky stream.

In the fall of 1852, two New Englanders built a new stage stop west of the creek and added a small hotel, a saloon, and a barn. Over the next several years a tiny hamlet began to emerge around it. Among the descriptions, the most vivid are those written by a young ranch hand, Alfred Doten. Although he earned his keep as a farm foreman, Doten was moonlighting as a corresponding journalist and sent descriptions of California to his hometown newspaper the *Plymouth Rock* in Massachusetts. He also kept a voluminous diary where he recorded his daily activities. In 1856 Doten described Mountain View this way: it "consists of a post-office, hotel, a grocery or so, a dwelling house, a Jew shop,. . . . It is very prettily located on the main road to San Jose, shaded by large, fine spreading oaks. . . ."[46] The post office Doten mentions was run by Jacob Shumway, the hotel belonged to William Elliot, and the "Jew shop" was a general merchandise store owned by the Weilheimer brothers. Perhaps the New England newspaper would not approve of the four saloons Doten neglected to mention.

Elliot's hotel was a saloon and boardinghouse where meals and drinks were served and rooms were let, both to stagecoach passengers and to many locals. One fourth of July Elliot's was full just with the neighbors. "This was a profitable day for Elliot, for a great many folks were there

getting tight—everybody who had any loose change spent it for whiskey."[47] Although Elliot loaned money and helped people out, he would not tolerate an unpaid bar tab. One unfortunate customer left Elliot's without paying, and the hotel keeper pursued him to San Francisco, searched several barrooms before finding the culprit, performed a citizen's arrest and brought him back to Mountain View. Then he hogtied the raucous fellow for a ride to a San José courtroom to extract what he was owed.

A small store stood where today's Grant Road meets El Camino Real. It was run by bachelor Jacob Shumway, usually clad in overalls and a checkered work shirt. In 1854 Shumway was appointed Mountain View's first postmaster and he dispensed postage along with general merchandise and groceries. A postmaster was often assigned the task of naming a locale for the U. S. government. Shumway is credited with naming Mountain View, as Doten wrote, "for the fine view of the coast range of mountains presented at this particular point."[48] Whether or not Shumway had any help in choosing the name, it won the approval of the locals. An early twentieth-century author, Mary Julia Gates, applauded his choice and granted "all honor to the old bachelor who had a fine fitness for words."[49]

Shumway adhered to a strict observance of the Sabbath by closing up shop on Sundays, but could sometimes be cajoled into providing emergency rations. Ranch hand Doten wrote that he "got some grub. . . . from Shumway—Sunday law—had to smuggle the things out of back door."[50] Directly across Grant Road from Shumway's, two German Jewish brothers opened a general store. Seligman and Samuel Weilheimer provided a bit of competition for Shumway because they were open for business on Sundays. Both brothers brought brides to Mountain View during the 1850s and began the families that would be important in Mountain View for almost fifty years.

A blacksmith shop sat just west of Elliot's hotel and across the San Francisco Road (El Camino Real) from Shumway's and the Weilheimers' stores. Evan Jenkins eventually took over as blacksmith, repairing farm implements and fashioning tools of all sorts for farmers in the surrounding country-side. John A. Wright established a lumberyard and mill on the north side of the San Francisco Road. The little town also featured a shoemaker named Douglass, and several Germans settled nearby, including saloon-keepers John Murkel and Richard Harjes. Locals were doctored by Nathaniel Eaton, a combination physician-dentist who also served as justice of the peace. Mountain View's first jail, a two-roomed wood shed, sat near today's Bay Street and El Camino Real. In 1853 the first telegraph line between San Francisco and San José began clicking out messages.

Many families moved to or near the little village. James Washington Mockbee, a forty-

First Presbyterian Church of Mountain View dates to 1851 and was known as the Cumberland Presbyterian Church. Pictured here is the pastor, Benjamin Franklin Whittemore, his wife, Minne, and a daughter. Through the years, the church has occupied four buildings. The first building was completed in 1860 and stood at Church and Castro Streets. A fire destroyed this building in 1911.

niner from Kentucky, married Clarissa Boone, reportedly a distant relative of Daniel Boone, in Mountain View in 1855. They had eleven children, many of whom became important in the town's history. One of their sons, Jake, became a playmate and lifelong friend to Seligman Weilheimer's son, Julius.

In 1852 some parents built a wood-framed, one-room schoolhouse near today's Stierlin Road and the railroad tracks. A single door and three tiny windows lit the small room. Hinged planks hung on two walls for student desks. Among the families whose children enrolled in the school were the Bubbs, the Dales and the Yeagers.

William Bubb and his wife, Mary Ann, came overland to California in 1850 with their seven children. They settled off today's Fremont Avenue on the Permanente Creek. One of their sons, Benjamin T. Bubb, married Sarah J. Smith, and they accumulated 165 acres north of his parents' place. Their modest house stood at what today is Begen Avenue and Leona Lane. The couple had one daughter and six sons. Benjamin died in 1888 in an accident at his farm. One of his sons, William, succeeded him as a farmer.

The Dales originally leased land from the Castros and, in 1864, purchased a ranch on the banks of the Stevens Creek from the Reverend Cornelius Yeager. The Yeagers and the Dales had come overland to California together. Yeager had purchased the ranch from Cyrus Saunders, county supervisor and justice of the peace. Soon after Yeager bought the land, he was willing to sell it for the same price to Edward Dale, but the government stepped in and informed the parties that a portion of the land was government land. After the land was surveyed again, Dale had to pay an additional $1.25 per acre, the standard price for government-owned land.[51]

A few years later, the schoolhouse was "hauled by oxen"[52] to the edge of Permanente Creek and named the Permanente Creek School House. In 1854 the Mountain View School District was formed, and the next year Santa Clara County was divided into school districts. In 1857, Mountain View's grammar school was built at Calderon Avenue and the Old San Francisco Road.[53] The new public school accommodated about forty students.

The first teachers were Protestant ministers, beginning with the Reverend Wesley Gallimore. When the hefty (he weighed almost three hundred pounds) Presbyterian first taught in Mountain View he was also serving as the Santa Clara County Assessor and on the county board of supervisors (at that time called the Court of Sessions). Evidently he meted out rather harsh punishments; after striking the son of fellow minister Cornelius Yeager, he was sorely criticized and found himself without a teaching job.[54] Much later Gallimore owned almost three hundred acres of the Inigo ranch, although he and his family lived on The Alameda in San José. His daughter, Elizabeth, would go on to become one of Santa Clara County's first women physicians, popularly known as "Dr. Bess."

There were several preachers in the environs of Mountain View. Wesley Gallimore, Cornelius Yeager, and John Eusebius Braly were of the Cumberland Presbyterian faith, while Orrin Crittenden was a Baptist. The Bralys had a farm near Lawrence Station on the way to Santa Clara, but they were influential in Mountain View because John E. Braly helped establish the Cumberland Presbyterian Church there in 1851. It was the first Protestant congregation between San Francisco and San José. Braly's open-air revival meetings every summer on Permanente Creek drew very large crowds. Alfred Doten described one this way:

A large brush shade had been built for the occasion and plenty of benches for the multitude, many families are camped here in sheds built for the occasion—There were from two to four hundred people present, I should judge—I met lots of my old acquaintances there—Brawley, Yager, and others preached, prayed & [et]c and the brethren and sisters sang—A long table was set with communion service, of which many partook—about 4 PM the meeting broke up, all hands dispersed to eat supper, which was prepared on several tables about the camp. . . . Everybody, both converts and outsiders, seemed to enjoy the camp meeting much. . . .[55]

Braly and his wife, Susannah, had seven children, three of whom were girls. One son died in 1862 after being kicked by a horse. Their second son, John Hyde Braly, followed in his father's footsteps and was a Cumberland Presbyterian minister in Mountain View where he and his father alternated leading the congregation. The younger Braly was also a schoolteacher, and eventually was the superintendent of schools in Santa Clara County. Another son, James, married John Whisman's daughter, Mary Elizabeth. The Braly's eldest child, Sarah, married Dr. Benjamin Cory, a prominent San José physician.

The Reverend John E. Braly's wife, Susannah, kept a diary for most of her life and it illuminates her perceptions of everyday farming tasks as well as a woman's life in nineteenth-century Santa Clara County. The family routinely rose at 6 a.m. and began the day with prayer. After a morning meal, they would set to farm work. Susannah killed hogs to render lard and to "make a kettle of sope [sic]." Her other farm tasks included picking the feathers from her geese, drying fruit,

The Crittenden Ranch was established by the Baptist minister, Orrin Crittenden (1814-1903), when he arrived in Mountain View from Massachusetts in 1853. The 160-acre ranch was sold to the United States government, a portion of Moffett Field.

Top (left to right): Samuel P. Taylor, Benjamin T. Bubb, Henry Rengstorff; *Middle:* Sophia and Seligman Weilheimer, Hannah Whisman, John Snyder; *Bottom:* Richard Harjes, Clarissa Boone Mockbee, Orrin Crittenden.

and churning butter. Mrs. Braly sold many of the products from the family farm, and hotel keeper and store owner Seligman Weilheimer was a regular customer. She charged $.30 for a dozen eggs and five pounds of butter would bring in $1.70. On at least one occasion Weilheimer bought twelve geese from her for $15.[56]

Susannah Braly hired Chinese men to do domestic work, but she was not successful at keeping them in her employ. Her diaries have numerous references to the "Chinamen" quitting. While she was a full partner in the farm with her preacher husband, she did not partner with him in his ministerial work. When a woman did preach at one of Reverend Braly's revivals near Mountain View, Mrs. Braly recorded, "I was not eddified."[57]

Orrin Crittenden came to Santa Clara County in 1852 and established a 160-acre dairy farm between Henry Rengstorff's land and Daniel Frink's acreage. Besides being a farmer, he was a Baptist preacher, speaking in Mountain View and as far away as Healdsburg and the San Ramon Valley. Crittenden went to considerable expense to defend his claim to this land. He suffered many financial setbacks, especially when Stevens Creek flooded his farm, and in 1880 when the family home burned to the ground.

Early in the 1850s, the Santa Clara County Board of Supervisors directed a committee to lay out a public road beginning at "the New Embarcadero" near Whisman's, to a lime kiln near the west hills. It had been a path that ran from the bay toward the Mountain View stage stop and on toward the foothills. The new road was to be sixty-six feet wide for a distance of 7.76 miles[58] and it ran roughly from the site of Moffett Federal Airfield south to connect with Grant Road toward today's Los Altos. For a time it was called Emerson Road, then later, Grant Road. It became the backbone of Mountain View.

One of the neighbors living on this road was the Kifer family. John Kifer and his wife had attempted to set up housekeeping at least twice before, but were forced to move on when they were found to be squatting on someone else's land. First they were chased off land owned by Martin Murphy, Jr.; then they were evicted from John Sullivan's land. Finally they purchased land on Grant Road for a ranch. Several of their children married children of their neighbors, creating a network of family allegiance along Grant Road. Martha Kifer married John Snyder, Lucy Kifer married William Dale, Shelby Kifer married Isabella Smith and Letitia Kifer was already married to hotelier Samuel P. Taylor.

John and Martha Snyder's homestead consisted of more than 1,000 acres of hillside property just west of today's Highway 280. Today Gate of Heaven cemetery and a retirement community, The Forum, occupy the former Snyder ranch. Wagons heavily laden with hay and grain clambered downhill toward the landings at the bay. Snyder planted grapevines and owned the first commercial vineyard in the Santa Clara Valley. He eventually added a winery and a distillery, and his wagons left the ranch loaded with barrels of wine rather than the grain crop of earlier years.

Two of the Snyder children, Arthur and Sarah, walked three miles from their home to the old schoolhouse. In 1865 the family built a big colonial-style house near the banks of Permanente Creek.

After three more children were born to the family, the house was enlarged.

The younger Snyder children attended the San Antonio School, which was built in 1867 much closer to home. This school was on the southeast corner of William Dale's ranch, and was built with contributions from John Snyder, William Dale, Jacob Shumway, Frank Sleeper, Daniel Whelan, James Laird and S. Weilheimer. The 750 square foot, one-room schoolhouse was built out of redwood.

As one-time teacher Susie Corpstein wrote:

. . . . there was a creek, wandering lazily along through the oak shrubbery, past the school and spreading out on the valley floor below. It made an ideal swimming hole where it skirted the school yard. The children dammed the creek up every year in spring and at noon hour, everyone big and little went in swimming—the teacher included.[59]

William Dale built a teacher's desk that was used for many years in that school and today is exhibited at the Cupertino Historical Museum.

When the children grew up, the Snyder's son, John Henry, owned a livery stable on Front Street.

San Antonio Schoolhouse, built in 1867 on 2.5 acres donated by William Dale. Other early pioneers such as T.F. Grant, John Snyder and Joseph Barton helped in the construction of the little one-room schoolhouse and Dale built the furniture. Grades one through eight attended the school. There were eight rows of desks, one for each grade. Three of the walls were covered with blackboards. A pot belly stove sat at the rear of the room for heating during the winter. There was a teacher's platform and desk at the front of the room. The school was discontinued in 1917 and was later converted into a private residence.

Their other son, Arthur, helped in management of the home ranch and several other properties that his parents had come to own. In 1920, the former Snyder ranch of 1,000 acres was purchased by the Catholic Archdiocese of San Francisco for $150,000 and became St. Joseph's Seminary.

George Grant and his brother, Theodore F. Grant, settled in the foothills near Permanente Creek, the site of today's Deer Hollow Farm. Theodore married Margarite Shaw, and their children also attended San Antonio School. When the schoolhouse was salvaged and rehabilitated as a home during the 1980s, an amazing discovery was made. As the siding was removed for restoration, workers found several drawings and notes by one-time San Antonio School students from a century before. One note was penned by Bella (Isabella) Grant, Theodore and Margarite's daughter. It was written to the young John Snyder, and read: "Dear John, I think the teacher is a longtoed fool don't you? P.S. a long assed one too. I.G." Then in another hand, "Tis true."[60] The long forgotten messages give us a glimpse of school days of long ago. Young Bella Grant died of tuberculosis in 1884, but her parents lived until 1924. Today's Grant Road takes its name from this family.

Early in 1861, hotel proprietor William Elliot died of consumption. Two years later, the fifteen-room hotel was bought by Samuel P. Taylor who was married to Letitia Kifer. The Taylor Hotel continued to serve travelers on the stage line for $2 per night with an extra $.25 for a bath. It became a meeting place for fraternal organizations and Catholic religious services. Letitia operated the inn on her own for several years after her husband's death.

Daniel Whelan, an Irishman, purchased Evan Jenkins' blacksmith shop. He and his wife, Margaret, carried on the business and raised their children in Old Mountain View. Whelan served for a time as Road Master, a local official charged with maintaining the roads. In 1865 he purchased an acre of land adjacent to the blacksmith shop from M.T.P. de Castro for $300. Little did he know his business would remain in his family for the next eighty years, until 1945. In 1960, when Daniel's son, Charles Whelan, died at age 80, the newspaper recalled the passing of an "old time smithy."

Among the settlers occupying the old Inigo land grant was Silas B. Emerson, a stock farmer whose ranch was two miles north of Mountain View's post office. Emerson took great pride in his stock; he raced his horses and sold bulls. His neigh-

The Taylor Hotel of old Mountain View, formerly known as Elliot's hotel at the stagecoach stop. Date unknown. When Samuel Taylor died, it was run by his widow, Letitia (Kifer) Taylor.

Whelan's blacksmith shop, established by Daniel Whelan in Old Town.

bors were the Murphys, Wrights, and Gallimores. In 1857 Emerson bought what he called his "upper ranch," eight hundred acres along Grant Road. When he paid his $195.00 tax bill in 1859, it indicated that he did not have clear title to the lower ranch. Perhaps this is why he put so much effort into the upper ranch.

Emerson hired Alfred Doten as a farm foreman, and Doten's daily diary gives us a glimpse of working a hay ranch. Hay farming was an intensely laborious occupation. It required continual plowing, winnowing, and sowing. Harvest time demanded threshing and sacking over and above the usual chores of "milking, hunting, and serving as housekeeper."[61] Then there was a constant battle to keep wandering cows, particularly from the neighboring Murphy ranch, from trampling and chewing up the crop.

Predators such as coyotes and skunks had to be kept from the stock, and Doten often poisoned scraps of meat to kill them. He applied the same remedy to Inigo's bothersome dogs. He explained: "The squirrels are the grand pest of this valley. They are almost as bad as the locusts of Egypt, or the grasshoppers of Utah, in their devastation on the vegetable and grain crops." Doten advocated strychnine to control squirrels that were more plentiful "than the rats in San Francisco."[62]

After the grain was threshed and winnowed, it was collected in sacks and hauled by wagon to Alviso, where it was loaded on a steamer headed for San Francisco. Then Doten would return to the ranch and take a stage from Mountain View to San Francisco to meet the grain at the wharf and try to find a buyer. While in San Francisco he would often treat himself to a bath and a haircut, have his boots blackened, and take in "a lyceum or other show." The profit margin was very narrow, one trip netting about $35 after paying for shipping, laborers, and haulers.[63]

Peach season called for similar efforts. After harvest, Doten hauled baskets of peaches by wagon to San Francisco to sell them, often peddling them to travelers or innkeepers along the way. On one trip to the city he sold twelve bushels of peaches. On his way back to Mountain View he retrieved empty baskets from his roadside customers.[64]

Fruit culture, for which Santa Clara County eventually became so famous, had its beginnings in these small orchards belonging to livestock ranchers. Farmers focused on grain-growing but were beginning to experiment with fruit trees and grape vines. A report from the Santa Clara County Assessor's office in 1856 indicated that "we are, so to speak, yet in our infancy in the science of fruit growing."[65] The climate was ideal to grow fruit.

But after rainy winters, the summers were scorching dry. "Look in almost any direction in the night," Doten wrote, "and fires can be seen gleaming on the mountain ranges. . . . kindled either by accident or design. . . . a fire has been burning in the coast range mountains for the last six weeks." Driving dry winds also swept the valley, making it difficult to work. One night a frustrated Doten bemoaned the loss of a privy when "the wind blew the old shithouse over again."[66]

Alfred Doten was a Republican, and voted for John C. Frémont for President in the election of 1856. The "Mountain View Frémont Club" was formed, and the twenty locals who came to the meeting chose rancher Frank Sleeper president of the club. They believed Frémont would promote a railroad project from the East to the Pacific. Frémont lost to James Buchanan, a Democrat and a bachelor. Local women also rallied for Frémont with the slogan, "We want no old bach to rule over us!" which they carried on a placard in a pro-Frémont parade. Frémont's wife, Jessie Benton Frémont, was well-known in her own right, and had stayed in San Francisco and San José when her husband was California's first U. S. Senator in 1850. Mrs. Frémont was tirelessly supportive of her husband's political career. Her father, Thomas Hart Benton, was a powerful U. S. Senator from Missouri. The Republicans won in Santa Clara County but did not carry the nation.

The Sleeper family was well known in the community. Frank and Eunice, both New England natives, settled near the edge of Stevens Creek during the 1850s and established a farm. The Sleeper ranch was supplied with water by an artesian well that was five-inches in diameter and 194 feet deep; fifty gallons a minute reportedly flowed from it. The couple raised Mrs. Sleeper's two nieces and a nephew, the Beverly children. Today's Sleeper and Eunice avenues recall this family.

Frank Sleeper had emerged as a leader in the community when he headed up the local Republican club and worked for Lincoln's election. He was elected to the Santa Clara County Board of Supervisors in 1864 and served in that capacity for four years. In addition to his political activities, Sleeper helped Crisanto Castro lay out streets for a development in Old Mountain View, but the arrival of the railroad thwarted some of their plans.

During Sleeper's term as county supervisor, some Mountain View projects were put on the county's agenda. In July of 1867 a request was made for the county to build Grant Road and to construct a bridge across "Stephen's or Cupertino Creek" at El Camino Real because "the crossing is now impassable for loaded wagons with two feet of water. Strangers come to it and turn back while the neighbors make out to get across with considerable trouble."[67] At this time the creek was known by both names and "Stephen's" was still spelled correctly, for pioneer Elisha Stephens. Soon the name was misspelled, and the creek and road became known as Stevens Creek.

The Sleepers hosted musical entertainments, where Mrs. Sleeper played the piano and sang ballads or recited poetry. The family also faced its share of hardship when in 1866, their daughter, Anna, died of diphtheria. Frank Sleeper died in 1872, when he was just fifty years old. His widow, Eunice, was somewhat unconventional, but remained an important citizen in old Mountain View. She was also a devout spiritualist who espoused many religious teachings popular at the time, including the ability to communicate with the dead. For a time she lived in the former Shumway store, which she and her husband had owned. As early as 1870 she was an ardent suffragist and represented Santa Clara County in California's Woman's Suffrage Association. Eunice set up a trust that purchased a building in San José for the Y.W.C.A. and it became known as "Sleeper Hall."

In the early 1890s, by which time Mrs. Sleeper was a venerable old-timer, she had a house built behind Enterprise Hall in Old Town. The Hale family rented it and took in three schoolteachers as boarders. After a very short time, however, the family and boarders moved out, claiming the house was haunted. Supposedly objects moved by themselves, strange noises were heard; the residents claimed they saw a ghost there. These strange appearances were credited to Eunice Sleeper's belief in the paranormal. The existence of the apparitions was never proven, but Mrs. Sleeper would not deny their presence.[68]

When Mrs. Sleeper died she left her property to her nephew, Judge Frank Beverly. The staunch Republican judge, who had been the local justice of the peace for over thirty years beginning in 1881, had presided over most court proceedings in Mountain View. The tall, lanky judge was an affable fellow but he had a persistent tubercular cough that often interrupted his discourse.

Daniel Frink and his wife, Pauline Reynolds, purchased four hundred acres of the old Inigo land.[69] The couple raised six children there. Frink had come to California in 1847 as part of Stevenson's Regiment of one thousand volunteers from New York state. The volunteers were discharged in 1848, and many became political and business leaders in American California. Frink established a successful stock farm, and he partnered with Theodore P. Shirley in 1865 to open the first hotel in Mountain View Station.

The Inigo property became the focal point of a court case involving several Mountain View neighbors. Evidently Daniel Frink had agreed to purchase the land with money he had collected from George W. Moody, James C. Braly, Jacob Shumway, Wesley Gallimore and Daniel L. Moody "on the court house steps," the common practice for land that had been foreclosed. Blacksmith Evan Jenkins contested the unlikely partnership. But Frink's purchase was legal, and

an 1870s map shows the Jenkins acreage adjacent to that of Frink and Gallimore.

Frink was a stalwart Republican and was elected to the California State Assembly in 1879. His claim to fame is his introduction of a bill to prohibit "keeping or the sale of animals with glanders," a highly contagious condition affecting horses and other livestock. For his human constituents he put forward a petition from four women requesting "the removal of political disabilities," that is, asking for the right to vote. That bill was referred to the Judiciary Committee but never acted upon.[70] In 1890, one of Frink's children tried to take over his affairs claiming addiction to alcohol was impairing his mind.[71] In the previous few years, Frink's wife, Pauline, his daughter of the same name, and a grandchild, all had died. Frink died in 1891.

All was not totally peaceful in little Mountain View. Silas Emerson had quite a dispute with rancher Frank Gallimore, the Reverend Wesley's brother, and the two challenged each other to a duel. They never actually fought it, but Emerson had some other conflicts, too. He did not part friends with employee Alfred Doten when he refused to pay his wages. Doten called in arbitrators to force Emerson to pay, and, short of cash in the interim, Doten tried to borrow $200 from the Murphys. He had no luck there, even though he had provided music at more than a few of their

RESIDENCE & DANIEL. FRINK, *Mountain View, Santa Clara Co., Cal.*

Lithograph of the Daniel and Pauline Frink ranch, located on former Inigo land at today's Moffett Federal Airfield from the *1876 Historical Atlas Map of Santa Clara County*, by Thompson & West. Besides farming, Daniel Frink partnered with Theodore Shirley in the first hotel in Mountain View Station. The Frink's son Daniel B. went on to serve on the town's first Board of Trustees after incorporation in 1902.

First Catholic church in Mountain View, named St. Joseph's. It was on the north side of El Camino Real, near the Stevens Creek Bridge. It was built in 1868 on land donated by San Franciscan John Sullivan.

parties. Bar-keep Elliot ended up loaning Doten $100 to help him get by. Eventually Doten repaid his debts and moved to Nevada's Comstock Lode region, where he worked full time as a newspaper man. He became a friend and colleague of another Nevada newspaper reporter, Samuel Clemens, alias Mark Twain. In an interesting twist of fate, from 1896 to 1902, Doten's daughter, Bessie, came to Mountain View from Nevada and taught at the San Antonio School.

Doctor Bowling (D.B.) Bailey (his first name was actually "Doctor"; he was not a physician) had come to California from Tennessee with his brother, Boanerges Bailey in 1850. The brothers became financial successes and each has a street named for him; D.B. in Mountain View and his brother's in South San Jose. D.B. Bailey settled in Mountain View as a stock farmer, and was a school trustee. He purchased land in Mountain View from Sherman O. Houghton and from M.T.P. de Castro, and he eventually owned well over 250 acres.

In 1859, after some stump speeches at picnics and other social gatherings, D.B. Bailey was elected as a Democrat to represent Santa Clara County in the state assembly. He served as chairman of the Committee on Education and in

1860 put forward a bill to establish the University of California,[72] although the bill was rewritten and not passed by the Legislature until 1868.

Late in the 1850s, a German immigrant named Henry Rengstorff bought land in several places in Santa Clara County, including acreage north of Mountain View near the bay. He had come to California during the Gold Rush and after working as a farm laborer for a few years, was able to establish a hay and grain-shipping business. Within a few years, he built warehouses that could accommodate as much as 3,000 tons of hay. Rengstorff's Landing grew into a major commercial enterprise serving the Santa Clara Valley, and was the departure point for schooners laden with tons of fruit, barrels of wine, and bushels of grain crops, as well as lumber from the western foothills.

While Rengstorff's Landing became one of the busiest ports in the state, other nearby landings dotting the edge of the bay also did considerable business. Guth's Landing at the end of Stierlin Road,[73] Jagel's Landing at Whisman Road, and a one named for Inigo to the east, all became shipping points for agricultural goods from the valley to San Francisco and beyond.

For a time Rengstorff worried that the railroad would put his shipping concern out of business, but rail-shipping fees remained higher than what he had to charge. Henry and his wife, Christine Hassler, purchased more land, and in 1867 they built a 15-room Italianate house on Stierlin Road for their growing family. Rengstorff House survives today at Shoreline Park where it was moved from its original site and rehabilitated in the 1980s. The Rengstorffs had seven children, and one of their descendents lived in that house until 1959.

Rengstorff employed several farm laborers to manage his crops, but he also rented out large tracts to other farmers. He partnered with farmer Peter Swall who grew strawberries on land on San Antonio Road, south of Charleston Road. Chinese pickers harvested the crop there. A road leading to the Swall Ranch from El Camino was called Swall Road, but later became part of San Antonio Road.

In 1869 Whisman School District was formed, and in 1871 a one-room schoolhouse was built on an acre donated by Henry Rengstorff near his home off Stierlin Road. Both he and his son,

Henry A. Rengstorff, served on the school board at different times. The younger Rengstorff married the schoolteacher, Nellie Baker. Over the years Whisman School's enrollment fluctuated dramatically, and it struggled to remain open. In 1889, for example, there were only ten pupils.

The bitter and lengthy Civil War plaguing the nation during the 1860s had significant repercussions in the West, and even though they viewed the battlefields from a distance, Californians were not immune to the hostilities. Many who had come to California during the Gold Rush returned to their native states to fight for the Union or the Confederacy. After Abraham Lincoln was elected President on the Republican ticket, sectional allegiance ran high in California and in Mountain View. A total of 557 men sailed out of San Francisco to fight for the Union. Many local militias were mustered to stand ready to relieve troops in the East and to protect California's long coastline. A number of men from Mountain View and Mayfield made up Company C, second regiment which was trained and drilled locally. It was ordered to keep mail routes open in Arizona and throughout the Southwest, and the recruits fought Indians more than Confederates. Sherman Houghton, M.T.P. de Castro's lawyer, captained a local militia whose main activity turned out to be parades.

Old Mountain View residents tried to expand the little community at the stagecoach stop. In 1870 the Weilheimer brothers bought the land that their store sat on, along with eight other lots, for $1,600 from the Sleepers.[74] Samuel Weilheimer, John Kifer and Jacob Shumway hired A. Van Dorn to lay out a large parcel of land south of the Old San Francisco Road (El Camino Real). A main street would bisect the El Camino about a block west of the existing stores and run "from the foothills to the railroad and embarcadero."[75] This subdivision was never built.

In 1867 St. Joseph's Catholic Church was built on land had been donated by John Sullivan on the Old San Francisco Road near the edge of Stevens Creek. Sullivan had been part of the Stephens-Murphy emigrant party, speculated in real estate and was a founder of the Hibernia Bank in San Francisco. He was a major benefactor of the Catholic Church, having donated the land for both Old Saint Mary's Cathedral and Saint Patrick's Church in San Francisco. Although he never lived in Mountain View, he had purchased a swath of land from Peter Davidson and his wife María Josefa Castro de Davidson. Bishop Alemany solemnly blessed Saint Joseph's Church in 1868. The small, white house of worship could hold about 150 people but it was often so crowded that many had to kneel outside during the services. It was expanded during the 1880s to hold an additional 100 people. Mountain View's Catholic Church was serviced by priests from Santa Clara College and therefore considered a "mission" because it had no resident pastor until 1901.

When the storekeeper Jacob Shumway died at age seventy in 1868, Mountain View lost the long-time resident who had given the little community its name. The executors of his estate were also old-timers Evan Jenkins the blacksmith, and farmer Christopher C. Stierlin. Shumway's doctor, Nathaniel Eaton, and Daniel Whelan the blacksmith, had witnessed his will.

The little community of Mountain View was just setting its foundations. Businesses and homes clustered around the stagecoach stop became the nucleus of a community of farmers in the surrounding countryside. Accelerated commerce and a denser population made many Californians demand rail transportation. Indeed, the railroad had been an important political issue as early as 1856 when John C. Frémont ran for President. The public clamored for faster, more efficient transportation both within the state and to the East. But of the dozens of families who put down roots in Mountain View during this era, none could foresee that the construction of the Southern Pacific Railroad, which bypassed old Mountain View, would change all their expectations.

CHAPTER 3

THE RAILS

CONSTRUCTION ON THE RAIL LINE LINKING SAN Francisco with San José began in the spring of 1861. The roadbed was graded, bridges were built, and railroad ties delivered to points along the line. The San Francisco and San Jose Rail Road Company used Chinese labor, predating the practice of the transcontinental railroad. The going wage for Chinese construction workers was a dollar a day, about $27 per month, plus board, meals, and coffee. This wage was much lower than white laborers in mines or factories, and it set a precedent for paying Chinese construction workers extremely low wages.[76] By January 1863 the track was ready for iron rails and later that year, trains began running from San Francisco, south as far as Mayfield.

The San Francisco and San Jose Rail Road Company initiated service all the way to San José on January 18, 1864. Locals showed up in buggies and on foot to witness the first train come through, and 2,000 men and women crammed into the entire fleet of 29 cars for the inaugural ride. Fare on that first day was $3 each way, double the regular fare, for the two hour and ten minute trip. The locomotive *San Mateo* was one steam engine serving the San Francisco-San José run during the 1860s.

An **1876 map** showing both old and new Mountain View, along with the new Southern Pacific Railroad line. Property owners are also mapped. From the *1876 Historical Atlas Map of Santa Clara County*, by Thompson & West.

The railroad company acquired the right-of-way from various property owners along the line, but it did not always procure permission before building. Indeed, M.T.P. de Castro transferred the right-of-way to the railroad through Rancho Pastoría de las Borregas a full six months after the company began running trains.[77] The Castros were paid $500 by the railroad company for the right-of-way, which it estimated to be about seventeen and a half acres of land. The company also promised the Castros a flagstop near their home just off today's Rengstorff Avenue. The Castros and their descendents could travel free of charge on the railroad with just a lift of the flag. The original deed that transfers the right-of-way to the railroad does not mention the flagstop but the promise may have been a verbal one. The family used the flagstop for decades and later, an official stop there was named Castro Station. It remained in operation until 2000. M.T.P. de Castro also deeded five acres to the Cumberland Presbyterian Church in 1861 for a "burying ground and for all religious, moral, civil, and intellectual purposes."[78] In all likelihood, the land was already being used as a cemetery and the deed was simply a formality, since records show burials as early as 1859 and a church occupying the site by 1861. That site is today's Pioneer Memorial Park.

As it had for countless towns across the country, the railroad changed everything in Mountain View. The former stagecoach stop was bypassed, putting an abrupt end to its growth. Soon it became known as old Mountain View, or simply Old Town. A permanent stop was created a half-mile away at Mountain View Station, and a saloon was converted into a small depot. A new village took shape along the tracks. For the next few decades, the two communities were distinctly separate, but eventually they coalesced to become the City of Mountain View.

Within a month of the railroad opening in early 1864, the aged Inigo died. He was buried near his home on the old rancho. One hundred years later, in 1974, the Mountain View Historical Association placed a memorial marker near his burial site, but by 1982 the marker had disappeared, and was very possibly stolen.[79] A number of Lockheed buildings were constructed in the immediate area, and the disposition of the marker and the actual remains of Inigo are still a mystery.

In 1860, the Castros hired San José lawyer Sherman Houghton to defend their land claims. He had come to California as part of Stevenson's Regiment of volunteers from New York during the war with Mexico. Houghton intended to be a farmer, but instead he studied law and joined a law firm belonging to William T. Wallace and Caius T. Ryland, the sons-in-law of California's first American Governor, Peter Burnett. The trio litigated lucrative land claims cases in the chaotic years after the Mexican War, and during 1855-56 Houghton was the mayor of San José.

The shrewd businessman looked the part with his bald head and full, graying beard. During the 1850s, he learned Spanish, and he became a confidant of some Californio families. Houghton represented both the Castros and the Robles through some bitter land disputes and was paid handsomely with land. The small lot with a saloon that became the new railroad depot had come to him from the Castros. In 1865 Houghton sold it to Theodore P. Shirley for $250, where Shirley acted as station agent and bartender.[80]

Sherman Houghton had first married Mary Donner, a survivor of the infamous Donner Expedition. After Mary's untimely death shortly after childbirth in 1860, Houghton married her cousin, Eliza, another survivor and the daughter of George and Tamsen Donner. They had seven children together, and Houghton's daughter with his first wife made eight. The Houghtons were socially prominent, and even visited with President Rutherford Hayes and his wife at a San José event. The Houghtons often hosted lavish parties, and their house stands today at 156 East St. John Street in San José.

A significant portion of the Houghtons wealth was accumulated through the development and sale of Castro land. In 1860, the U.S. Supreme Court heard the Castro case with Houghton representing the family. The major controversy was the dividing line between the Peña rancho (the Robles land) and that of the Castros. The *diseño* (map) drawn of Peña's rancho in the early 1840s shortchanged him of a strip of land bordering Estrada's. At the time, Peña, Estrada, and the government agreed to give Peña an *augmento* (addition) to his land. Suñol's 1843 survey had clearly stated that the "linea del augmento" (line of the addition) divided the two ranchos. Some claimants in the 1860 case who had purchased Peña land (most recently belonging to the Robles), disputed that boundary. They asserted that the Suñol measurement was taken merely to inform the governor, and should not be consulted as an official record. They wanted the Peña land to extend further east into Pastoría de las Borregas.

Houghton got the case dismissed in December 1860, and the subsequent appeal was dismissed in April 1861. As payment to the lawyer, M.T.P. de Castro transferred five hundred acres to Houghton in 1864. The lawyer was well aware

Early view of Castro Street looking north. In the center distance lie the railroad tracks and the white building on the right is a Southern Pacific hay and grain warehouse. At far left is the Carlin Building that was partly destroyed in the 1906 earthquake; one store away is a brick façade that was purchased by Rogers & Rogers and later enlarged. Land on Castro Street sold for three dollars a square foot in 1880. Businesses were confined to the first two blocks of Castro Street for many years, with residences in the third and fourth blocks. Wheat fields and later orchards occupied the rest of the Castro Street area up to El Camino Real.

that it was the very year the railroad would come through the rancho. The value of the land increased dramatically just after the Castros signed it over to him.

In March 1865, Houghton had the county surveyor record a map of a portion of his five hundred acres, which he called the "Villa Lands." The prime railroad frontage extended from the railroad depot down Castro Street to Dana Street, then west to Oak Street and back to Front Street (today's Evelyn Avenue). It included the small lot and saloon he sold for the depot. In 1868 Houghton purchased an additional 150 acres for $10,000. He encouraged Crisanto Castro, who still owned a good deal of land in the area, to lay out the streets in the new town. Mercy Street was named after Crisanto's sister and his daughter, who both bore the Spanish name, Mercedes.

Sherman Houghton was elected to Congress in 1871 representing virtually all of California from San Francisco south. He was chairman of the Committee on Coinage, Weights, and Measures, and got involved in California land legislation. He served two terms, but was not re-elected in 1874. He and his wife moved to Los Angeles in 1886.

After Theodore Shirley bought the Houghton lot in 1865, he partnered with Daniel Frink to build the first hotel in Mountain View Station. It was a spacious, two-story frame building with a second floor balcony. The hostelry offered lodging and libation; the first floor was the saloon that doubled as a railroad ticket office. As ownership of the hotel changed over the years, so did the name. When the Weilheimer brothers bought Frink & Shirley's hotel in 1867, they called it the Bay View House and hired George Wagstaff to manage it. Later it was known as the American Hotel. What remains of that hotel today was moved to 906 Washington Street and converted to a residence.

The Weilheimer brothers decided to open a second store in the budding village along the tracks. In 1870 they built an attractive new store and celebrated the grand opening by hosting a "very well attended" ball. In the fall of 1874, the Weilheimers' businesses were shut down by a lawsuit brought against them by Levi Strauss Company of San Francisco. The newspaper claimed, "their creditors pounced on them without mercy and without a moment's notice."[81] When the brothers paid their debt and the litigation

was settled, they reopened and continued a successful operation.

Within a decade, however, the brothers dissolved their partnership. Samuel bought out his brother's interest in the Old Town store and became the sole proprietor of the original establishment. A fire destroyed the building in 1874, but Samuel promptly rebuilt it. Eight years later in 1882, Samuel and his family left Mountain View for San Francisco, perhaps because his wife, Babette, suffered from mental illness. She died the following year. He sold his Old Town business to William Bogen, and Seligman

Weilheimer Hotel and Farmer's Store on Castro and Front streets, circa 1860s. This first hotel in Mountain View Station was originally built by Shirley & Frink who sold the property to the Weilheimer brothers.

managed all operations at Mountain View Station and became the local Wells Fargo agent.

By 1870 even more enterprises cropped up in Mountain View Station. Besides the Weilheimer hotel and the general merchandise store, there were two butchers (one who doubled as a barkeep), two blacksmiths, a wheelwright, and a doctor who was also a pharmacist. The San Jose Weekly *Mercury* reported, "Mountain View supports five saloons, the supply is more than the demand at present."[82]

In 1872 the schoolhouse on Calderon and the San Francisco Road caught fire and was completely destroyed. A new, two-story grammar school was built, although the second floor was neither finished nor furnished for another two years. Horse stalls were built behind the school, and the privy was hidden by decorative latticework.[83] This four-room school served all the children up to eighth grade; as yet there was no high school in Mountain View.

The small town was also growing religious and fraternal communities. Presbyterian and Catholic churches were already flourishing. The Methodist Episcopal South church was built in 1872 to accommodate a congregation of about 250. The D.B. Bailey family belonged, and sometimes the church building was referred to as the "Bailey Chapel."

A Masonic Lodge was organized in Mountain View in 1868. Its members met at the Cumberland

Presbyterian Church "each month on the Tuesday preceeding the full moon."[84] By the early 1890s there were thirty-five members. Among the officers were the sons of the town's early residents: Julius Weilheimer, Henry A. Rengstorff, and Jacob Mockbee. The Masons used a number of different buildings in town over time, including the Mockbee Building at Villa and Castro streets. The fraternal order took over the American Legion building on Church Street in 1932, and bought it four years later. The Masons still own that building.

In 1876, the Odd Fellows organized a local lodge. It met every Thursday evening at Enterprise Hall in Old Town. The two-story wood building had "secret society" meeting rooms upstairs and businesses occupied the ground floor. By the 1890s, the Odd Fellows had fifty members. Much later the Ugo Mancini family occupied the Odd Fellows building, and then in 1921, Steve Matijasevich bought it and opened Steve's Grocery Store.

The Ancient Order of United Workmen (A.O.U.W.)—a tradesmen's group—began meeting every Saturday night in 1877, and by 1890 had forty-seven members. The Ancient Order of Hibernians (A.O.H.), an Irish-Catholic fraternal order, did not have a Mountain View lodge until 1888. The Irish were the largest foreign group in the county by the 1890s, numbering a little over eight hundred. The A.O.H. convened the first Sunday of each month, and in 1891 had a membership of thirty-one. Michael Farrell, the

former ranch foreman for the Murphy family, was this club's first president.

Successful businesses, popular fraternal groups, and active churchs gave a social and economic structure to Mountain View. Castro Street was the venue for all these activities, and was rapidly becoming an important thoroughfare. But it had one major drawback—during the rainy season, Permanente Creek ran right down the center of the street. Townsman William Garliepp recalled, "the folk used to catch fine trout" right on Castro, and local children "played along the creek, fishing, wading and sailing boats."[85]

Evidently at some point during the 1850s or 1860s, the natural course of Permanente Creek was diverted, perhaps because it flowed near the Castro home and occasionally flooded. Indeed, in 1851 and 1852 there were "terrible floods which caused all the creeks to run wild."[86] The diversion began about a mile and a half to the southeast of the Castro home near the property line of William Bubb and Silas Emerson. It continued in a northerly direction to the Old San Francisco Road, where it made a slight jog to the west. Then it followed the path of what became Castro Street toward the railroad tracks. From there it headed north to the bay, paralleling Stevens Creek to the east. This was not a problem until the railroad came through, and Castro Street became the center of town.

Farmer William Bubb attempted to channel the water along its original course in order to

54

bypass his property, but the Castros objected, sued, and won. As a result, Permanente Creek was not returned to its original bed, and the natural course of the creek remained dry, even though it was twelve feet lower than the new path along Castro Street.[87]

The creek posed a real danger, and William Garliepp was an eyewitness to its unpredictability. On a Sunday in March 1878 a little toddler, Willie Cooper, was playing with his brother along the banks of the creek on Castro Street when both were swept into the swollen current. Garliepp pulled one boy from the swirling water, but was not able to save the other, and Willie drowned. His body was carried almost a mile downstream before it was found and brought back to his anguished parents.[88] The incident underlined the need to remedy the problem of the displaced creek.

The county surveyor submitted a report to the Santa Clara County Board of Supervisors about the nuisance of Permanente Creek running down Castro Street.[89] The surveyor recommended one of two options: either open the ditch that the Bubbs began, or re-grade the San Francisco Road to guide the water to the old Permanente Creek bed.[90]

There is some confusion as to how the creek problem was remedied. One version of the story is that James Mockbee and an Indian teamster, Jim Cahoolee, scraped out a channel that finally diverted the creek. Another source credits the Graham, Ware, and Hitchcock families with filling in the newer channel and returning the creek to its original bed.[91] In any case, by 1880, Castro Street was dry and and residents were finally able to make their way up and down the street at any time of year.

Almost one hundred years later, during the 1950s, Mountain View once again was inundated by a flooding Permanente Creek. New residential developments near the creek made flood control an important issue, so in 1959 a new diversion was built to funnel the overflow of Permanente Creek to Stevens Creek between Bryant and Levin avenues. Residents of Mountain View have struggled many times to achieve a harmonious coexistence with these creeks.

Townspeople enjoyed several recreational diversions during the 1870s. The annual turkey and pigeon shoot held on Thanksgiving Day was a holiday tradition transplanted from the East.

Another extremely popular pastime was a dog race over open terrain, or "coursing." When a "Grand Coursing Match" was advertised in the paper in 1885, it stipulated that "positively no liquor wagons" were allowed. Boxing was also well-patronized in the town, and a "hard gloves" match between Mountain View's muscular blacksmith, Frank King, and "Professor" Young Dutchy, drew large crowds.[93]

Bicycling was a favorite sport at the turn of the twentieth century. Many local men joined the Mountain View Cycling Club and at one point the club boasted a membership of seventy-five. Besides participating in relay bike races and five-mile-dirt-trail excursions, the club members hosted dances and banquets at the Olympic Hall. Hawley's Bicycle Shop supplied the equipment for many of the club members.

In the 1880s, Fremont Township, which included Mountain View and the surrounding area, still boasted about twenty thousand acres of timberlands. But a sweeping change was taking place on the landscape of Santa Clara County. Since large land ownership claims had been settled, financially strapped heirs subdivided and sold their property. At one time, Mercedes Castro and her husband Andrés Calderon owned 1,500 acres. They sold most of it before prices escalated in the middle 1880s and in 1886, Calderon Avenue was laid out "as smooth and level as a race track." And it was used as a racetrack for impromptu horse races.[94] Benjamin F. Gates was the first orchardist on Calderon Avenue, beginning in 1885. For a time the street was called Stoddard, after a man who bought and subdivided a neighborhood there.

Evidently Andrés Calderon lived apart from his wife and stayed in San Francisco most of the time. After his death in 1892, his nephew, Julius Calderon, sued the estate for back wages. In the suit, the nephew claimed that Andrés had mortgaged the Calderon land, lived off the mortgages in San Francisco, and then left the debt to his widow. Indeed, at the time of his death, Calderon owned a scant eleven acres valued at $1,650, but had a $2,700 mortgage on it. Calderon also owed Margaret Whelan's blacksmith shop $120.[95]

Although the U. S. Land Commission confirmed almost 8,500 acres to the Robles brothers in 1868, the vast rancho had been whittled down to a mere three hundred acres by the mid-1870s.

Even that was difficult to sustain. In 1878 Segundino Robles and his wife, María Antonia Garcia de Robles, sold a relatively small parcel of fifty acres to a group of Italians.[96]

Italians left Italy in large numbers in the late nineteenth century because of poverty caused by depleted farmland and over-population. Many departed from Genoa, Naples or Palermo, and sailed to New York, then came by rail to California. California's farm and fishing industries, as well as a climate similar to Italy's, appealed to Italian immigrants. Italians introduced several varieties of vegetables heretofore unknown in the region, including broccoli, bell peppers, eggplant and artichokes.

Vegetable gardening businesses found fertile ground in Mountain View. The fifty acres of one-time Robles land became known as the Italian Vegetable Gardens, and was owned cooperatively and farmed by five partners for sixteen years. It was not always the same five, and one-fifth portions were bought and sold by several Italian immigrants between 1878 and 1894.[97] In 1894 the Italian Vegetable Gardens cooperative proprietors were Giovanni Ratto, Gaspar Morengo, the Arata brothers, and Giuseppe, Giovanni, and Pasquale Semino.[98]

In 1902 Semino leased his portion to a Chinese flower gardener, Mok Hoong. The ten-year lease required Hoong to pay $180 per year and allowed Semino to continue living in his house. Hoong could use water on Wednesdays and Saturdays, and at night. Mok Hoong began a flower-growing business that was later taken over by a Japanese farmer.

Santa Clara County's population in 1884 was 42,500 and Mountain View had 320 residents.[99] During the unstable business climate of the mid-1870s and mid-1880s, many California ranchos were divided and converted to more intensive cultivation. These smaller farms bolstered the growth of the town of Mountain View because commercial farmers needed the shipping enterprises near the bay as well as good rail service at Mountain View Station. Some families suffered losses while others prospered, but all faced uncertain prospects and had to adjust to the rapidly changing conditions of land ownership and commerce.

Beginning in 1884, the changes sweeping the land became obvious and there was a dramatic increase in the number of acres planted in fruit trees and grapevines. Hay and grain fields gave way as thousands of fruit trees were planted, and the San Jose *Mercury* reported that "this part of the valley is undergoing a rapid transformation." The newspaper listed some landowners and the number of fruit trees each planted:

Bubb, Benjamin T.: 50 apple, 10 pear, 30 peach, 6 plum, 5 cherry, 10 apricot;

Dale, Edward: 7 orange, 300 apple, 6 pear, 200 peach, 12 fig, 100 ornamental, and 3 acres of vines;

Delmas, Delfin [sic.]: 300 ornamental, 300 vines.

Erhorn [sic.], Louise: 250 apple, 975 pear, 300 peach, 600 prune, 500 apricot.;

Stierlin, Christopher C. 50 apple, 50 pear;

Rengstorff, Henry: 20 apple, 30 pear

The article went on, "A number of large tracts have recently been subdivided and it is rapidly becoming a district of small orchards and consequent prosperity."[100] Commercial fruit producers conducted diversified operations, growing several varieties of fruits as well as berries and grapes.

Delphin Delmas was the son of a French vintner who had settled in San José. Delphin became a lawyer and he purchased almost five hundred acres near Mountain View (although today it falls

Pioneer Blacksmith Shop on Castro Street at Villa before 1895 when it was destroyed by fire.

Isabelle Grant, circa 1882.

within Sunnyvale's borders) and planted grapes there. His vineyard succumbed to an infestation of phylloxera and was replanted to fruit trees. Delmas gained national attention because he was Harry K. Thaw's defense attorney in his trial for the murder of prominent New York architect Stanford White. Delmas got Thaw acquitted by reason of insanity, and Thaw was later set free. Delmas was very well known in Mountain View.

Louise Ehrhorn was a widow with ten children who had come to Mountain View after the death of her husband in San Francisco. She purchased twenty-five acres fronting San Francisco Road near Church Street. Later, more acreage was added for a total of about forty acres. She had a variety of orchard fruits planted, and managed the farm along with her large family. Her son, Adolph, succeeded her in the orchard business. Another son, Edward, became an entomologist, or as one newspaper put it, a "bug inspector."

Mountain View-area ranchers were quick to adopt improved farming equipment. D. B. Bailey brought in a new contraption called a hay press.

This horse-powered machine pressed down the hay for bailing; men were no longer required to tamp down the hay.[101] Another big improvement was the hay stacker, or elevator, which tossed the hay to the top of the haystack. Henry Rengstorff invented an excavator, or dredger, to open ditches and channels for irrigating, and in the spring of 1885 he was issued a patent for it.[102]

Chinese labor was critical in the agricultural development of the Santa Clara Valley, particularly in its shift from wheat-growing to fruit. In 1877 a bumper crop of strawberries brought, as the newspaper reported, about 1,500 "Chinamen" to Mountain View to pick the crop.[103] In 1884, it was estimated that there were 2,000 Chinese in Santa Clara County, half of whom lived in San José. As railroad laborers they had earned $1 per day, but after forming an informal farm worker union, they were demanding $1.25 per day for agricultural work.[104]

A "China town" began to form at Villa and View streets in Mountain View that played a significant role in the community well into the twentieth century. During the 1870s, many families employed Chinese house servants. The Baileys, for example had a 15-year-old cook named Cheong, and an adult farm laborer, Ah How.[105] The 1880 census records show that six Chinese men lived in town, and there were 167 Chinese living in the surrounding countryside of Fremont Township.

In 1879, 26-year-old Yuen Lung, a farm laborer, arrived in Mountain View from China, and he evolved into an astute businessman. He borrowed $150 from Jacob Mockbee to set up shop. He became a labor contractor, hiring Chinese farm workers for local growers. He diversified to establish a fruit buying and drying outlet. Then he opened a general merchandise store at the corner of Villa and View streets, where he also lived. At the peak of his enterprises, he employed over 100 people. Yuen Lung was a fixture in the Mountain View business community for forty years.

In 1882 the federal Chinese Exclusion Act prohibited entry of Chinese laborers for ten years. It did allow a small number of teachers, students, or merchants to enter the country, but virtually all immigrants were defined as laborers. The law intentionally made it difficult for the Chinese to establish families by denying entry to women. Only twelve Chinese women lived in San José. Chinese men who were already in the country were not allowed to bring their wives to join them. The law's only exception was for the wives of American-born Chinese men. But there were very few Chinese families in America, and their sons were not old enough to travel to China to marry. In 1884 the Supreme Court confirmed that wives of Chinese laborers could not be admitted to the United States.

Charcoal sketch entitled "China Camp" *by Isabelle Grant* (1865-1882), one of a series of original sketches in the collection of the Mountain View History Center. She was the daughter of Theodore F. Grant (1827-1924) and Margaret Shaw Grant (1830-1924). Isabelle had one brother, Theodore F. Grant, Jr. (died in 1958) and one sister, Sarah Grant (1867-1959). These three children were born and raised on the family's four hundred-acre ranch located on present day Grant Road.

Political sentiment against the Chinese was very strong in California. The anti-Chinese movement was fueled both by workingmen's fear of competition from lower-paid labor during hard times, and by racist attitudes toward Asians. Calling Chinese workers "coolies," the British term for the bound laborers they took from China to their colonial possessions, American workers regarded Chinese workers as unfair competition in the labor market. Chinese immigrants were legally excluded from citizenship, and many whites regarded them as unfit for or incapable of assimilation.

In 1886, an "anti-Coolie" Club was formed in Mountain View, and many townspeople joined. Judge Benjamin E. Burns was the chairman; his wife, Mrs. Katie Burns, was elected president; and William Garliepp was treasurer. Regular meetings were held on Friday night at Margot's Hall on Castro Street, and both men and women participated. Monthly dues were ten cents. The club's official papers declared:

Inasmuch as we of the Caucasian race find the presence of the coolie people detrimental to the interests of our country, subversive of the industrial interests of the white laboring classes, non assimilating in the nature, and naturally inclined toward the basest immorality; devoid of Christian conscience; inclined to and capable of the commission of the most inhuman and horrible crimes; and inasmuch as the Chinese or coolies have neither inclination or capacity of becoming citizens for our country's benefit or defense, therefore, we believe it necessary for the common good, for the preservation of public morals, for the safety of our people and the security of the rising generation that we should have no Chinese in our country; therefore be it. Resolved, By the citizens of Mountain View, in meeting assembled, that we demand of Congress the enactment of laws prohibiting the presence of any Chinese in our country. . . .[106]

A statewide anti-Coolie convention was held in San José in February of 1886. The Mountain View club sent delegates to lend political support to the anti-Chinese movement.

In the heat of the anti-Chinese movement, many locals discharged Chinese domestic and farm help, and the local newspaper published names of these "patriotic" citizens. Businesses also let it be known that they did not employ Chinese help. The newspaper reported, "the white laundry seems destined for success." Pres-

sure was brought to bear on businesses that were based on Chinese labor. For example, the San Jose *Mercury* reported that the "brickyard will be run with white labor exclusively when business is resumed on Apr. 15," and later stated that, "The Mountain View brickyard is now running with excellent prospects having all white labor for the first time in its history." Yuen Lung was able to withstand the strong anti-Chinese sentiment in Mountain View, but his enterprise suffered during this period.

Another railroad project promised some work for the Chinese. In 1884, a thirty-mile railroad, called the San Francisco and New Almaden Railroad was planned to run between Mountain View Station and New Almaden by way of Quito Road in Saratoga. Bids were awarded, a crew of about two hundred men was hired, and construction began, but the right-of-way through many properties had not been secured. The Santa Clara County Board of Supervisors objected because Hollenbeck Lane was being encroached upon and so was the Collins School at Saratoga-Sunnyvale and Homestead roads. The Collins School was eventually moved and today is the Cupertino D'Oro Clubhouse on Homestead Road. Owners of the Sullivan land demanded $400 per acre for right-of-way, and insisted that the whole tract be purchased.[108] The project was finally abandoned because of the excessive cost and the inability to acquire some of the land.

The Democratic party often incorporated anti-Chinese sentiment in its platform, but the Republicans had a stronghold in Mountain View. During the 1884 presidential campaign, the candidates were James G. Blaine, and his running mate, John A. Logan, who carried the nickname "Black Jack," because of his dark complexion. A lively rally was held on their behalf in Mountain View, a few weeks before the election. A "torch light" parade greeted the seven train cars of passengers arriving from San José, with a drum corp and honor guard. Some "patriotic ladies"

Home built in 1888 on the east side of Castro Street at Dana by George and Mary Charleston. He died before moving in, and she refused to live in the house. After remaining empty for six years, Dr. C. O. Gates and his family lived in the house. It was moved in 1945.

Memorial Baptist Church at Dana and Hope streets, organized in 1888 under the Reverend Orrin Crittenden.

John Bergin built a fine brick winery, known as the best in the county, at Brookside Farm, two miles south of Mountain View. He had married Francisca (Walkinshaw) Price, the widowed daughter of Inigo's patron Robert Walkinshaw, who owned the three hundred-acre Brookside Farm. At one time it had been owned by George Donner, the son of the leader of the Donner party. When Bergin married Francisca, he planted seventy acres in grapevines and added a winery. In 1887, the acreage yielded 250 tons of grapes. During the 1890s, the vineyard succumbed to a widespread infestation of phylloxera, a root louse, that impacted grapevine production throughout the region. The damage was so severe that most grape growers pulled up withered vines and planted fruit trees. The Bergin's orchards survived, but in 1899, John Bergin died of alcoholism. In 1903, before his estate was settled, Francisca went to Spain to live out her days.[112]

Richard Heney planted a one hundred-acre vineyard in the foothills that he named "Chateau Ricardo." The wine produced from his vines was highly regarded and was even awarded a medal at the 1889 exposition in Paris, France. When the Heney vineyards were destroyed by phylloxera, they were replaced by French-rooted vines resistant to the root louse, and an orchard of prunes, apricots, and walnuts. The Heney winery building was heavily damaged in the 1906 earthquake but survived. It was retrofitted as a three-story building with 16-foot beams and its walls were three feet thick. After the heyday of the Heney ranch, the building's huge wine casks were used to make bootleg alcohol during Prohibition.

prepared a meal for the hungry Republicans. The Mountain View Black Jack Campaign Quartet provided music and a sing-a-long, including some original compositions.[109] Despite the local popularity, the Democratic candidate, Grover Cleveland, won the election.

Wine production was really on the rise during this period. In 1892 the San Jose *Mercury* reported that "there are no less than eighteen wineries and distilleries at Mountain View and in the vicinity, and no section of the county has a more enviable reputation of the product of its vineyards than has Mountain View."[110] Among the wineries were those of John Snyder, John Bergin, Mrs. Salvin P. Collins, Richard Heney, Bernard Distel, and the Jesuit Fathers at St. Joseph's Seminary. As much as 1 million gallons a year was shipped out of Mountain View at this time.[111]

Julius Wielheimer home that was later occupied by the Arthur Free family and then Chez T.J. Restaurant on Villa Street.

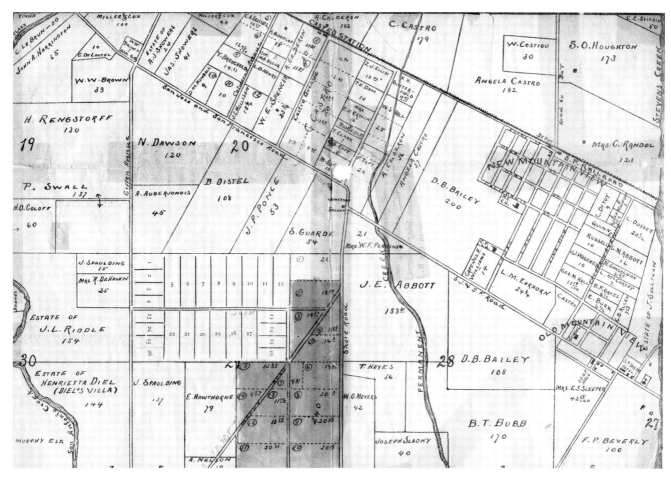

Map of both old and new Mountain View, circa 1891. This map was used in real estate agent Walter A. Clark's promotional literature.

In the 1960s the old fortress was razed to make way for the construction of Highway 280.

Angelia Collins, whose husband, Salvin, had died, owned about 160 acres at what today is Saratoga-Sunnyvale Road and Fremont Avenue. Her husband had been in the saloon and liquor distribution business in San Francisco. Perhaps to supply her restaurants and bars, she built a huge winery with a railroad spur to facilitate shipping. She named the estate Pebbleside Vineyards, and whenever she came to Mountain View to inspect her properties, she convinced her grandnephew, George Swall, to chauffeur her by buggy. At peak production just before the phylloxera infestation, Pebbleside Winery produced 500,000 gallons of wine one year. Angelia died in 1896, and the property was sold to a poultry farmer. The winery building burned down in 1927.

The wine business around Mountain View was successful, at least in part, because of the landings near the bay. John G. Jagels purchased forty acres at the edge of San Francisco Bay of the old Inigo Rancho in 1880. His business became a little community unto itself, with farmers hauling crops to his warehouses to await shipping to San Francisco. Jagels owned two schooners as part of his operation: the *Dreadnaught*, built in 1865, and the *Nellie Rich*, built in 1874. He also owned hay scows, two-masted flat barges with squared bow and stern, which were built to transport hay across the bay.[113] Jagels was stiff competition for Rengstorff.

Blacksmith Daniel Whelan conducted a diversified business in Old Town that flourished as agriculture intensified. In 1882 he advertised "General Jobbing and Repairing Wagons and Agricultural Implements Made and Repaired." Daniel died in 1882, just before his wife, Margaret Whelan, gave birth to twin sons, one of whom also died. Margaret Whelan, who was 38 years old and had seven children to support, took over the business. Within two years she advertised horseshoeing and "all kinds of repairing well and promptly done at reasonable rates."[114] The ads carry Margaret's name as proprietor and imply that she may have been blacksmithing herself.[115]

By 1887 newspapers said Mountain View was "booming." Real estate developments led the way. On a single day, the paper reported, 26 town lots, one 10-acre tract, and one 5-acre tract were sold. Negotiations for the sale of 20 other tracts were pending. "The town is alive with excitement," the newspaper noted, "and many strangers are coming in."[116] The *Mercury* also proclaimed that "no brighter business prospects can be found anywhere in the State than in the rapidly growing town of Mountain View."[117]

> *This quiet little burg has been in a state of commotion for the past few days, caused by the moving of several buildings, but now it has resumed its former calm appearance and the several large houses that have been occupying the middle of the streets have now settled down upon their new sites, leaving somewhat of a vacancy in the center of town . . . .where a new brick block will be built.*[118]

As the village grew, its layout was made more regular, and buildings that had been placed haphazardly in the past were put down in a more uniform pattern.

Mountain View's first newspaper, the *Courier*, was established in 1885 but only lasted about six months. The ads from an August 1885 edition reveal the business make-up of the town. Among the advertisers were the Swall Brothers Meat Market, several saloons, Dr. Caleb V. Jones, W. F. Taylor the druggist, Mrs. Daniel Whelan at Old Mountain View Blacksmith & Wagon Shop, A. Weilheimer harness and saddler, an insurance salesman, a carriage painter, and Charles Guth, the Constable of Fremont Township.

In 1888, the first issue of the Mountain View Weekly Register was produced by Frank W. Bacon and Harry Johnston. Bacon was a journalist with a keen interest in the theatre. He eventually became a playwright of some repute, penning and starring in the 1919 Broadway hit "Lightnin'." At this point in his career, however, he was a struggling journalist. He was working for the *San Jose Mercury*, trying to sell ads to shopkeepers up and down Castro Street. He noted it "was a town of perhaps eight hundred people and twenty-five saloons." Merchant after

John Snyder in his Front Street (today's Evelyn Avenue) livery stable.

merchant refused to buy an ad in the *Mercury*, but one suggested he might consider advertising in a Mountain View paper. Bacon took the idea seriously, and the *Weekly Register* was born.

Setting up shop in Mountain View was a major undertaking, and Bacon recalled when "the press arrived in Mountain View—an impressive monster of wheels and levers. The man who hauled it from the station in an old hay wagon took his pay out in advertising."[120] Bacon's wife, Jennie, edited copy and wrote editorials and the society column. Their stint on the local paper was brief, however. In December 1888, the Bacons' baby daughter died, and this personal tragedy coincided with Frank Bacon's decision to sell the paper, which had not been profitable. Nevertheless, the Bacons remained well-known in Mountain View, even after they moved to San José.

A visitor stepping off the train in Mountain View would immediately see Weilheimer's hotel with its adjacent livery and horse corral that faced Front Street. Julius Weilheimer, eldest son of Seligman Weilheimer, ran the "Farmer's Store" at 124 Castro Street. In 1896, an extension was built on the general merchandise store.

Castro Street was a dirt road with wood-plank sidewalks that offered a few boarding houses, a barber shop and bath house, a doctor's office, an insurance agent, a couple of butchers and two cobblers. A jewelry store in the Olympic Hall building was owned by Phillip Clark, who supplied watches to many townspeople until 1916.

Venturing past Castro Street, visitors could play billiards and buy a drink. There was a Chinese laundry on Hope Street, a sign that the

Southern Pacific Train Depot at Mountain View with wagons loaded with barrels of wine from John Snyder's ranch.

anti-Chinese agitation had not permanently displaced these small businesses. A dozen or so homes clustered near Castro Street; some had water tanks and windmills in their back yards. The new part of town had two churches, Methodist and Presbyterian, and the Memorial Baptist Church was added when it was organized in 1890 under the Reverend Orrin Crittenden.[121]

In 1884 George Swall bought out a butcher business, and four years later built a new building at the southeast corner of Castro and Villa streets. He carried out his own slaughtering, and he ran two wagons supplying meat to the surrounding community. George T. Wagstaff was the proprietor of the Mountain View Tavern and Reading Room and offered fine cigars and liquors "recommended by all respectable physicians."[122] One can only wonder what reading material he offered. Previously, during the 1870s, Wagstaff had managed the Weilheimer Hotel. He built a "large and commodious" store[123] at the corner of Castro and Villa streets shortly after the Wagstaff home had been badly damaged in a fire that began in Mrs. Krumbeck's nearby millinery. After he died at age 59 in 1890, his eldest daughter, Miss Belle Wagstaff, ran the variety store selling cigars and stationery.[124] Mr. Muncy, another blacksmith, was expert at shoeing horses and repairing farm implements.

Office of the Mountain View Register, established in 1888, and an unidentified man standing in front. In 1903, proprietor B.C. Nichols provided space for a lending library.

THE RAILS

He bought the lot adjoining the Wagstaff residence for his blacksmith shop.

Jacob Mockbee, who befriended Yuen Lung, built a home at 190 Hope Street in 1884. He was a blacksmith by trade, but became more involved in finance as time went by. Mockbee leased his blacksmithing business on Castro Street to young William Whelan, whose father and mother had owned a blacksmith shop in Old Town since he was born. In 1892, after William Whelan died, Mockbee briefly resumed the business. He then leased it to McDonald & Burke, who relocated the shop to the 300 block of Castro Street in 1905. Jacob Mockbee joined forces with Aaron Weilheimer to sell Studebaker wagons.[125]

Mockbee, like many other townsmen, was a volunteer firefighter and an original member of the Mountain View Station Hook and Ladder Company, Number 1. Sixty volunteers were organized in 1874 and in 1888 ten more joined. The volunteers practiced bucket brigade fire-fighting procedures, and the press dubbed them the "boys of the buckets and axes." Frame buildings and wood-plank sidewalks made everyone very concerned that a fire might erupt and quickly spread out of control. Indeed, a fire did break out in 1895 on Castro Street, between Front and Villa streets. Evidently it "ate its way

in all directions until only charred remains were seen . . . ."[126] The worst fears in Mountain View were realized, but property owners began to rebuild immediately.

In 1888 a San Jose *Mercury* reporter wrote about a tour of Mountain View he had recently taken with Judge Benjamin E. Burns. The two went by buggy to see Mr. Henry Rengstorff on the road toward the bay. On the way back to town, they called on Christopher C. Stierlin and Henry McCleary "whose orchards are most excellent proofs of how well the pear, the almond and the prune grow on the lowlands between Mountain View and the bay." Upon their return to town realtor Walter A. Clark escorted them south through large orchards and vineyards which extended "from the town line of Mountain View to the tops of the foothills." The reporter was favorably impressed by the town and its environs and he wrote up a glowing report for the newspaper.

As ranchos were replaced by orchards and subdivisions Mountain View took on an entirely new look. One of Mountain View's earliest and most successful boosters was real estate agent Walter A. Clark. The Illinois native arrived in Mountain View in 1885 at the height of a real estate boom in Santa Clara County. Although he did some work in merchandising and banking,

served as the postmaster for a while, and dabbled in politics as a state assemblyman in 1899, real estate quickly became his primary business.

Walter's two brothers—Philip, a jeweler, and Stephen, a druggist—were also merchants in town. Stephen married Daniel Frink's daughter Stella. In 1895 the druggist added a soda fountain to his apothecary and, according to the newspaper, it "now deals out fizz of all flavors to thirsty wayfarers."[127]

Walter Clark capitalized on the opening of Stanford University in 1891 and advertised Mountain View for its proximity to the new university. Mountain View "will eventually be connected with the University by a motor road, so that it will practically have all the advantages of the University town, and yet lands in Mountain View are only one-quarter of the price they are in Menlo Park." He ran large ads in local and some national papers describing the benefits of purchasing near the university. One cautioned, "Now, just one word of advice: Don't buy a small town lot near the University when you can buy *an acre just as cheap.* . . ." Another promotional piece emphasizing the proximity of Stanford stated that those nearby could take advantage of "the benefit of a free education in one of the grandest schools in the world."[128] A Stanford education would not remain "free" for long.

Clark published the *Realty Herald*, a real estate promotional paper carrying advertisements and real estate investment advice. He described

various subdivisions in and around Mountain View. In Buena Vista, which was outside the town limits, purchasers had to abide by certain restrictions: no barns could be built on the streets, and no liquor could ever be sold on the premises.[129] The Platt Subdivision, with piped water, and graded and graveled streets, must have been the most desirable; those lots cost up

Walter A. Clark, assemblyman, realtor, and developer.

Mountain View Grammar School, located on El Camino Real and Calderon Avenue, after 1875. This school replaced an earlier one that burned in 1872. *Photograph by C.C. White.*

to $425. The Garliepp Subdivison had no such amenities, and the lots went for $150 to $250. The Bailey Addition, so named for the D.B. Bailey family, was subdivided. The Beverly Addition in Old Town, land that Judge Frank P. Beverly had inherited from his aunt and uncle, Eunice and Frank Sleeper, was also subdivided.

Clark was also a leading Republican and had helped organize a local "McKinley for President" headquarters. On election night in 1896, when it became clear that William McKinley won, ecstatic Republicans formed a parade and marched to Old Town and back again. The evening was topped off with exuberant dancing in Olympic Hall. President William McKinley visited Santa Clara County in 1901 and was greeted by enthusiastic crowds. Shortly after his visit here, however, the President was assassinated in Buffalo, New York. Theodore Roosevelt, the effervescent Vice President, was sworn into office, and the Progressive Era was in full swing.

In 1891 Howard Streight bought a ranch of twelve acres on El Monte near Springer Road which he called "The Elms." He was a renowned artist, particularly noted for his western landscapes. During the twenty years he lived on his Mountain View ranch, he produced some of his most notable pieces: a large painting of Mount Shasta and a sunset view over the Stanford University hillside. Streight was a spriritualist and sometimes painted during seances held at his darkened studio. The City of Mountain View owns one of his pieces.

The Mountain View Canning Company, a cooperative, opened at Bailey Avenue (today's Shoreline Boulevard) and the railroad tracks. The principals were many familiar names in Mountain View: Daniel Frink, Dr. Oliver P. Askam (soon-to-be Henry Rengstorff's son-in-law), Henry McCleary, J. E. Williams, vintner John Bergin, David T. Bateman, W.A. Nydgh, D.B. Murphy, Judge Benjamin E. Burns, & W. F.

Debord. A report in 1889 noted that Mountain View Cannery was now busy putting up cherries and at its peak employed 75 or 80 people. But it was a short-lived enterprise, lasting about only three years. Eventually an Italian family, the Sanguinettis, took over the cannery.

In the summer of 1888 the cornerstone of the Olympic Hall building under construction at Castro and Front streets was placed with ceremony and prayer. The building was dedicated the following February, complete with a festive ball and a speech by newsman Harry Johnston. A dramatic presentation of *Above the Clouds* was given, and the cast of characters included Dr. Oliver P. Askam, Harry Johnston, Frank Bacon, Jennie Bacon, Miss Stella Frink, and realtor Walter A. Clark.

In 1889 Henry Rengstorff's daughter Helena married Dr. Oliver P. Askam at the Rengstorff house. According to the society column, "the drawing room was decorated in gold and white, the mantle banked with Australian asters and scarlet geraniums. The daylight was excluded and the soft light from the chandeliers made the scene more effective."[130] Although a few doctors were working the area, Doctor Askam who had an office on Castro Street, was the successor to Old Town's Dr. Nathaniel Eaton. The Askams' sons Perry and Earl grew up to be singers and actors. Perry became a prominent actor with the role of "Red Shadow" in *The Desert Song* and also played the lead in *The New Moon*.

In 1888 a new Southern Pacific Depot was built at Mountain View Station at a cost of $4,000. Residents had gathered signatures on petitions and forwarded them to Southern Pacific Railroad requesting a depot. When it was built, it was the only two-story depot between San Francisco and San José. By 1892, ten passenger trains stopped daily at Mountain View Station. As the train traffic increased, so did the number of accidents along the track. Over the years, dozens of people were killed or severely injured as trains overpowered horses, carts, wagons, buggies, autos, and trucks.[131]

By the early 1890s, the Castro Street business district had grown considerably. When Olympic Hall was completed, it was "the most substantial structure in the town."[132] Several restaurants and a new bakery opened. Roadmaster William Garliepp finished a new bridge on Villa Street over Permanente Creek. It measured thirty by thirty-two feet, making it one of the largest in the county.[133]

A "Free Reading Room" was established in 1890 in the Olympic Hall with the support of Seligman Weilheimer and Judge Benjamin E. Burns, a lawyer in town. Burns doubled as the librarian, but he had a hard time juggling his legal work and lending books at the same time. He handed the management of the free library over to the Women's Christian Temperance Union (W.C.T.U.) in the Castro Building next to Olympic Hall. The library floundered for a few years until an association, headed up by Viola Poland, formed to support it. The group was the precursor to a woman's club. She and her husband, Frederick A. Poland, had a fine home built on their Springer Road ranch, which they had purchased in 1888. He was an orchardist and manager of the Mountain View Fruit Exchange with Mike Farrell.

The W.T.C.U. attempted to limit or ban the sale of alcohol in Mountain View as early as 1894 when it issued a report that the eleven Mountain View saloons were actually costing the town money. The group also urged the town fathers to close saloons from 8 p.m. Saturday evening until 6 a.m. Monday morning. Support for temperance was growing in the town.[134]

During the last decades of the nineteenth century many of Mountain View's founders died. In 1882, William H. Bubb met an untimely death at the age of 46; he left his family's 145 acres in the care of his widow, Susan Bubb. His brother, Benjamin, died six years later at age 50, leaving seven children, the youngest only a year old. As Mountain View's founding generation passed from the scene, both their children and new arrivals stood ready to take their places. Some "pioneers" were later commemorated by having schools named after them and the names of others survive as street names. Seventy-five years after his death, Benjamin Bubb Elementary School opened on a twelve-acre portion of this ranch.

Mountain View train depot, circa 1890s.

D.B. Bailey, former Democratic Assemblyman and prominent townsman died in September of 1888, and his wife took over management of the property. The following month Edward Dale died, bequeathing a farm to each of his surviving children who were already middle-aged. Silas B. Emerson, another longtime rancher in Mountain View, died in San Francisco the next year. When James W. Mockbee, the father of Jacob and Jack, died in June of 1891, the paper lamented, the "real cause of death is believed to have been internal injuries received at the hands of a drunken brute who assaulted him on the street, knocked him down and beat him terribly."[135]

The Weilheimer brothers, who had been merchants in Mountain View for almost fifty years, died within a few months of each other in 1899. Julius Weilheimer was executor for the estate of his father, Seligman. Under Julius's direction, the Weilheimer Store in New Mountain View continued to supply groceries, clothing, hardware, medicine and feed— "A Complete Assortment. . . . at the lowest possible figure."[136]

By 1890 there were 14,340 school-aged children in Santa Clara County. Of those, 56 were "Negro," 32 were "Mongolian" (Asian) and one was an Indian. One of Mountain View's schoolteachers was 19-year-old Clara Halsey. In 1892, the San Jose *Mercury* sponsored a "Teachers' Competition" and asked readers to cast ballots for their favorite teacher. By setting no limit to the number of ballots each person could cast the paper invited participants to stuff the ballot box. Between January and April of 1892, almost one million votes came in, and the *Mercury* spent $9,000 administering the competition. Clara Halsey won the contest with over 91,000 votes. The grand prize was a residential lot in Palo Alto, just off University Avenue, worth $150 which Halsey eventually sold.[137] Halsey kept a scrapbook with dozens of clippings about the contest from the *Mercury*. The scrapbook is part of today's historical collection in the Mountain View Public Library.

In 1897 the school district purchased a lot for the high school for $500 from Crisanto Castro, Angela Castro, and Mercedes Castro de Calderon. Shortly thereafter Crisanto Castro faced a lawsuit brought by his sisters, María Josefa Davidson and Angela Castro. The women claimed he obtained rights to large tracts of Castro land from them by

Clara Halsey Taylor, Mountain View school teacher and winner of the San Jose *Mercury* teacher popularity contest. Her prize was a residential lot in Palo Alto which she eventually sold.

false representations. Crisanto prevailed but the suit strained family ties.[138]

In 1901 a local election passed a $7,000 bond issue for the Mountain View School District to build a high school adjacent to the site of the thirty-year-old grammar school on El Camino Real between Calderon Avenue and Montgomery Street. The following year a two-story high school building was constructed by contractor William Bates. There were two classrooms on each floor, cloakrooms, an office and a small library. Samuel McCrea was principal, and Miss Alice Williston was a teacher. On the opening day of school in September of 1902 nineteen students appeared, but when prune season was over a few weeks later, enrollment jumped to twenty-six students.

Although the birth of triplets is not a particularly noteworthy event in the early twenty-first century, such an event caused quite a stir in Mountain View in the summer of 1895. Triplet girls were born to J. Harvey Smith and his wife, Henrietta, at their Fremont Avenue farm. The girls were named for the "kind neighbors who acted as nurses": Mary Agnes Grace (for Richard Heney's wife, Mary Agnes), Margeretta Valentine Grace (for the doctor's wife), and Francisca Chinita Grace (for Francisca [Walkinshaw] Price Bergin). The couple had four children already, and the three new babies added a considerable expense. "They are healthy and perfect, and so near alike that they are marked by red, white and blue ribbon so that one can be known from the other." Their neighbors collected money for the Smiths "to help defray the heavy expenses attendant in this case." Almost forty-five years later, in 1939, the triplets were awarded a trophy for being the oldest triplets at the World's Fair at Treasure Island. The trio dressed alike for that event too.[139]

The Bank of Mountain View, the town's first bank, was organized in 1900 as a state bank with capital stock of $25,000. Within eight years it accumulated deposits worth ten times that amount. It occupied a brick building at 138 Castro Street that is no longer standing. Cashier for the bank was realtor Walter Clark, and an early advertisement for the bank claimed, "You can open the gates of success if you have the keys." The four "keys" were labeled savings, industry, economy and persistence. It also noted, "No limit as to the amount of your check—small amounts paid as cheerfully as large ones."

Mountain View began acting like a town long before the vote for incorporation. Provisions were made for fire-fighting, street-building, and other civic projects. In 1897 citizens bought a Hope Street lot from Crisanto Castro to build a firehouse for hook and ladder trucks. A new jail was slated for the rear portion of the lot.[140] Some business people began to lobby local residents to support incorporation which would give Mountain View its own governmental system and enable it to spend its tax dollars within its own boundaries.

The small community was rounding the first leg of its journey. The surrounding farmers were comfortably supported by merchants, churches, and social and fraternal groups. The only thing missing was a strong structure of local government. The move to create a municipality happened to coincide with the introduction of the automobile, an invention that would dominate the twentieth century.

PART TWO

THE TWENTIETH CENTURY

CHAPTER 4

THE AUTO

The first mass-produced automobiles came on the scene just after the turn of the twentieth century. In the beginning, only the wealthy could afford to purchase one. Among the first residents in Mountain View to own a car was Crisanto Castro, Jr., who entertained locals by driving his new $1,800 Crawford about town.[141] As demand for the automobile increased, prices dropped, making them affordable to more people. In fact, car ownership became more cost-effective than owning and caring for a horse.

The automobile revolutionized urban and rural life in America. It spawned a variety of new businesses, and several opened in Mountain View. Carriage dealers began selling cars, and a vulcanizing works, or tire shop, opened. And in 1915 the Standard Oil Company established a location in Mountain View with four large tanks holding a total of 80,000 gallons. Several years later, other businesses owed their development to the automobile such as motels, drive-in restaurants, and suburban shopping centers.

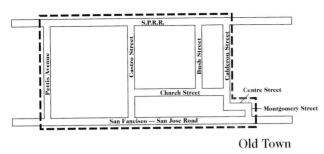

Map of incorporated Mountain View, 1902.

Old Town

Social and political reforms were the hallmark of the Progressive movement early in the century, including a trend toward incorporating communities into cities or towns. An 1883 act of the California legislature allowed communities to incorporate. Palo Alto had incorporated in 1894 shortly after Stanford University opened. Sunnyvale did not officially incorporate until 1912. The local political scene was dominated by a campaign to incorporate the town of Mountain View, whose population was just over six hundred.[142]

The biggest promoter of Mountain View's incorporation was Gustaves K. Estes, an attorney and the owner of the Mountain View *Register*. He pointed out that the total assessed value of property in Mountain View was about $300,000, and the $.40 on every one hundred dollars that local residents were paying the county could go into a town treasury. Estes noted that saloon and business taxes would also stay within the community. He claimed that the town could

expect revenue of $2,200 without levying any new tax. He projected about $1,000 in expenses every year, including the costly but critical water wagons that sprinkled the streets to keep the dust down. At that time, the county was allotting $500 annually for street maintenance and improvements in Mountain View.

Seventy-two local men signed their names to the petition to incorporate. As required by law, copies of the proposal were posted in public places. One was on Olympic Hall near the front door of the post office, another was at the Bank of Mountain View, a third was at Morgan's Blacksmith Shop, and the fourth was on the front of Hawley's Bicycle Shop.

The proposed town was not precisely square, as most new towns were. The southern border ran along El Camino Real from Pettis Avenue on the west to Montgomery Street on the east. The eastern boundary zigzagged to encompass the elementary school property. Then it extended north to the railroad tracks. The unusual configuration may have been designed to ensure that the school was within the town limits, and to include more residents who would support a vote to incorporate, but for some reason Old Town was not included.

Election day was set for Saturday, November 1, 1902. The law required that the polling place, in this case Olympic Hall, be open for voting from 6 a.m. until 5 p.m. Voters were asked to vote "For" or "Against" incorporation, and to

Castro Street at Villa. (Left to right): Mockbee Building, Villa Street intersection, Farmers and Merchants Bank. Directly across the street with the pillars is the First National Bank (built in 1913) and on the right is the Jurian Building. Each of these buildings is still standing.

THE AUTO

choose a five-member Board of Trustees, a clerk who would double as an assessor, a town treasurer, and a marshal.

One hundred fifty-two men voted that day, and 58 percent favored incorporation. The sixty-four naysayers were afraid of higher taxes and thought Estes exaggerated the benefits of incorporation. The election returns were forwarded to the county board of supervisors by Estes, and the board sent official papers to Sacramento where Mountain View was declared an incorporated city on November 7, 1902. The county supervisors directed surveyor C.M. Barker to mark boundary lines and streets in the official town of Mountain View.

Fifteen candidates ran for Mountain View's first board of trustees, and the top five vote-getters took office. Daniel B. Frink won the highest number of votes with one hundred. George Swall, the butcher, received ninety-four votes. Then came Judge Benjamin E. Burns, George Pattberg and Dr. Charles O. Gates. The merchant community was strongly represented on the new town council. Frink was a haberdasher with a men's furnishings store in the Olympic Hall building. Pattberg owned and managed the Pattberg and Ames Automobile and Machine Works in his own View Street building. Swall had a thriving butcher business and Gates was a doctor. The farming community lived outside the new town limits, and although it did not have a representative on the new board of trustees, found sympathy there, too.

John W. Barney, pre-1903. After losing his leg in a timber accident, he was appointed an R.F.D. (Rural Free Delivery) mail carrier. His route was 25 miles long and served 150 families. He resigned his position in 1915 when the postal service introduced motorized vehicles.

Daniel B. Frink's political views were decidedly different from those of his late father of the same name. The junior Frink was a Democrat whose personal philosophy was proclaimed in advertisements for his men's store: "My motto is 'Live and let live.'" The notice went on to promise good value in cigars, tobacco and other notions.

Marshal R. C. Waits who had already been serving as the marshal, was required to be elected under the new laws of incorporation. He won handily, beating two other candidates. For a salary of $30 a month he enforced the criminal code, served civil papers, collected business license fees and property taxes, and rounded up

In 1888, Swall's Meat Market was located at the corner of Castro and Villa streets. The business vacated the lot to make room for the new Farmers and Merchants Bank. By 1906, the shop reopened at 219 Castro Street and featured Swall Hall, an upstairs meeting room. George Swall was the proprietor, and later his son, Lester, took over the business.

Seventh Day Adventist Church, at Dana Street and Bailey Avenue (today's Shoreline Boulevard).

stray animals. He was Mountain View's official night watchman, and some recalled that he kept his vigil seated on a nail keg at Castro and Villa streets beginning at 8:00 p.m.each evening.[143]

The first city attorney was Arthur Free, a young graduate of Stanford Law School. He spent the next seven years working in Mountain View and was appointed postmaster by the federal government. Free set a solid foundation for a long political career in Mountain View and beyond. Free and his wife, Mabel, had five children, including two sets of twins. The family bought the Julius Weilheimer house at 938 Villa Street. Late in the twentieth century, the house became an upscale French restaurant, Chez T.J. Arthur Free later served at the county level and went on to be elected to five terms in the U. S. Congress.

Incorporation sparked a flurry of activity. The trustees purchased eighty street signs that William Garliepp and John Bailey installed.[144] The town was lighted by electricity for the first time that year, and five new electric street lights made the night watchman's job a little easier. The first telephone in town was in Dr. Johnson's Drug Store, where he doubled as a telephone operator. Subscriptions for phone service were initially held by a very few, but grew steadily each year. The Mountain View Municipal Water System, a by-product of the incorporation plan, was established in 1904.

Several new buildings went up on the main street. Julius Weilheimer built a frame building on Castro near Dana Street. Well into the construction, when the roof was partially complete, Weilheimer decided to add a second story. The first floor

accommodated Daniel Farr's farm implement and carriage business. The second floor had a meeting room that was used on Sundays by Christian Scientists; the remainder was a rooming house and home to the Farr family.

In 1902, Professor Daniel T. Ames, a well-known handwriting expert who had been a key witness in several notorious forgery cases, sold his foothills property to Willard Griffin (today's Foothill College campus). He authorized construction of the "Ames block," a two-story brick-masonry building on the one hundred block of Castro Street. He designed it to have apartments upstairs and retail stores and a meeting room on the first floor. By this time, Ames was an elderly man and he sunk most of his capital into this building project. It suffered a delay when a construction worker was injured one particularly windy day. Attempting to place heavy planks upstairs, the worker fell from the second floor and broke his leg. The building was finally finished in 1903.

At the turn of the century, steel industry mogul Andrew Carnegie offered library construction funds to communities across the nation in exchange for a promise from the town to support the library. Historic Carnegie library buildings remain today in hundreds of cities and towns. Mountain View's trustees did not take Carnegie up on his offer, and some citizens thought that decision was shortsighted.

The primary objective of a new woman's club was to establish a public library. The first meeting of the Mountain View Woman's Club was held on April 9, 1904, at Ames Hall at 3:15 p.m. Mrs. Viola Poland convened the meeting and was the club's first president. Some of the original members were Poland, her sister Mrs. Eliza Porter, Mrs. Clement,

Woman's Clubhouse at 440 Castro Street, formerly the Methodist Episcopal Church South.

THE AUTO

Top (left to right): Eliza Farrell, Viola Poland, Elmer Griffin Stricklett; *Middle:* Laura Belle Graham, Elise Rengstorff Haag, Arthur M. Free, Daniel Titus Ames; *Bottom:* Jacob Mockbee, Mary Julia Gates.

Miss Emma Stevens, Mrs. Fannie Ames, Mrs. Katie Burns, Mrs. Krolaw, and Mrs. G. James of Sunnyvale.

Regular meetings were held every other Wednesday at Ames Hall. The initiation fee was $.50, with $1 annual dues. Viola Poland lived only a few months after the club was established, and at her memorial service her husband delivered a moving eulogy urging the women to carry on despite the loss of their leader: "Let your club carry on in its work—do not halt for a moment. She would have felt grieved if she was the cause of sorrow."[145]

Mrs. Eliza Farrell was elected in Poland's place. Farrell, Emma Stevens, and Katie Burns held club office for many years. Other early members of the club included Mrs. Henry A. (Nellie) Rengstorff, who was a teacher at Whisman School, Mrs. Baker, Mrs. Sparks, Mrs. Snyder, and Mrs. Mary Julia Gates. In April 1905 the woman's club opened Mountain View's first public library above Rogers & Rogers store on Castro Street, and hired Emma Hessle as the librarian. A few months later the club handed the library over to the town and it was officially named the Mountain View Public Library. This process

The Ames building after the 1906 earthquake. Daniel Ames is standing in the rear of the building in a heap of bricks.

reflected a typical pattern where women's clubs initiated civic services and then coaxed the local government to carry out the management. The Mountain View Woman's Club also took on projects to help the poor, for the "cleansing of streets," and the construction of a public fountain. Some of these activities were also handed over to the municipality.

Yuen Lung also saw business pick up in the wake of incorporation. However, in the fall of 1904 he was accosted, robbed, and beaten severely by what the newspaper reported as "several Chinamen." Only one, Lem Duck, was apprehended and was positively identified at a hearing before Judge Frank P. Beverly.[146] The perpetrator served a brief sentence, but the others were never caught.

The Yuen Lung Company flourished between 1910 and 1920. The "dealer in groceries" doubled as an employment agency, advertising "first class Chinese servants and Laborers furnished at all times." The Chinese merchant had created an important economic and social niche for himself. The newspaper reported that the Chinese workers spent their pay at local shops. "Wednesday was payday over at Yuen Lung's. . . . all the employees got an envelope with money in it. There were a lot of Chinese boys and men working there . . . . Yuen Lung pays out a lot of money for help every year & as a rule his employees are liberal in spending it around town with our merchants."[147]

Yuen Lung's role as a labor broker to the farming community grew in importance as the fruit industry expanded. A member of the Mountain View Historical Association in 1974 described her memories of Yuen Lung's operation this way:

At prune picking time, in early years, Yuen Lung sent a crew of ancient Chinese men to camp on the ranch and pick prunes. The men walked single file when they left camp to go to the orchard. In the fall after they had

Barney and Juliette Job orchard on Grant Road at Levin Avenue.

gone I would ride my bicycle over the trails they left. Every year the same crew came, with the same cook, whom we named George Washington. This came about because one time when wood was needed he was told to cut a dead cherry tree—instead he cut a live one.[148]

The Yuen Lung & Company Store was at the north corner of View and Villa streets. Four stores, one laundry, a large boardinghouse, and two fruit-packing houses were located in the immediate vicinity. Three other Chinese shops sat around the corner on Villa Street.[149] In 1920, Yuen Lung contracted for $100,000 worth of fruit and had almost one hundred Chinese workers "picking, hauling and shipping."

But by 1922 his longtime Mountain View business network began to collapse. Yuen Lung, who was in his seventies by this time, had to declare bankruptcy because of a downturn in his businesses. The newspaper described him as "square & honorable. . . . we respect him."[150] His list of assets included two spring wagons, one buggy, 2,000 fruit trays, 2,000 fruit boxes, six fruit trucks and four horses, among other things.[151] They were all put up for sale to satisfy his creditors.

In 1903 the Mountain View *Leader* was established by Mr. Halley G. Copeland, bringing competition to the local *Register*. By the end of the next year his sister, Ara Copeland, had taken over as proprietor of the paper. In the meantime, Gustaves Estes sold the *Register* to B.C. Nichols and moved away from Mountain View. Nichols leased the *Register* to P. Milton Smith (popularly known as "Pop"), a young journalist from Palo Alto. A subscription to the *Register* was $1.50 per year with delivery by mail.[152]

It did not take long for Smith to meet his rival, Ara Copeland. But competitive journalism proved even more difficult because after Pop Smith met Copeland he began courting her. By 1905 Smith had quit the *Register* and bought the *Leader*. "Pop" Smith and Ara Copeland married in 1909, and in 1910 the couple bought the other paper, merging the two newspapers. The merger allowed the purchase of new type-setting machines and a power printing press. Headquartered in one of Jake Mockbee's buildings, the *Register-Leader* was co-edited by Ara and P. Milton Smith.[153]

Although incorporation affected the town in many ways, far more dramatic changes occurred as a result of the establishment of a religious publishing house. Pacific Press Publishing of

The double water tower in the background of this photo toppled to the ground in the 1906 earthquake. In the foreground is the parsonage for the Methodist Episcopal Church South built in 1905 at the northeast corner of Villa and Franklin streets.

A postcard of the Pacific Press Publishing Company, Mountain View, California, after the 1906 earthquake.

Oakland, California, had been established by Ellen and the late James White of the Seventh-Day Adventist Church. It published religious reading material, but its real income was derived from a commercial printing business. The religious company wanted to leave what it perceived as the evil influences of urban life in Oakland and relocate to a rural location. The Mountain View Board of Trustees offered to give Pacific Press a little over five acres to set up shop. The press accepted the offer and built a state-of-the-art 60,000 square-foot building complete with an engraving room, a bindery, and a foundry. The new $40,000 plant was dedicated on April 16, 1905.

About one hundred families moved to Mountain View with Pacific Press and built homes on Pettis and Latham streets. These families changed Mountain View economically, socially, religiously, and made their presence known on the political scene as well. Slowly but surely the Adventists settled into local life. Ellen White wrote a letter

of congratulations to the Adventist families in Mountain View when they established the new facility, but lamented their "continued resistance to reducing the amount of commercial work." She wanted the press she had co-founded to devote itself exclusively to religious publications.

During the same year, Catholics built a new church, where it remains today at Church and Hope streets. It was dedicated to St. Joseph and replaced the tiny, wood church in Old Town. The community had been made into an official parish in 1901, and over the years, seven other Catholic parishes were established from a portion of Saint Joseph's territory. A decade later in 1911, the Presbyterian Church at Castro and Church streets burned to the ground. A new church was built in the same block, but closer to Mercy Street, and some of the church property was subdivided into the Oaks Subdivision.

The Farmers and Merchants Bank also opened in 1905. Its $50,000 in capital stock was

Mountain View Fruit Exchange
building after it was reconstructed
following the 1906 earthquake.

held by Jacob Mockbee, George Swall, Julius
Weilheimer, George Jagels, Henry A. Rengstorff,
William Wright, Michael Farrell, C.O. Gates,
Nathan McCorkle, Anna Campen Salyer, and
Miss Edna Lauer (later became Mrs. Roth),
among others. A new bank building was planned
for a lot occupied by George Swall's butcher
shop, at Castro and Villa streets. The officers
purchased the lot and built the building, which
still stands today at 201 Castro Street. Jacob
Mockbee was bank president and remained so
until 1918. His close friend, Julius Weilheimer,
was vice-president, and Wilbur Camp worked as
cashier. Little Mountain View now had two
banks, competing for a limited customer base.
The Farmers and Merchants Bank eventually
merged with the Bank of Italy in 1927, which
subsequently became the Bank of America.

In the early morning hours of April 18, 1906,
an 8.2 magnitude earthquake shook the San
Francisco Bay Area. By far the most extensive
damage occurred in San Francisco, where a
devastating fire raced through buildings that had
managed to remain standing through the temblor.
There was no loss of life in Mountain View, but
many injuries were reported and some buildings
were destroyed or seriously damaged.

The Weilheimer-Farr building, just a few
years old, swayed "fully ten feet" according to
the newspaper. Mr. and Mrs. Farr, their two
boarders, and another couple with a small baby,
narrowly escaped the teetering structure. Two
days after the earthquake the newspaper noted
that the Farr building was "skewed to the south
and is in danger of complete collapse." [154] Within
a month, however, it was rebuilt and ready for
occupancy again.

The town lost its water supply when two
water tanks on Franklin Street, standing over one
hundred feet high and filled with 70,000 gallons of
water, toppled to the ground. Water gushed in all

The Rogers & Rogers building in ruin. The second floor slid off
the first, onto the street. No one was killed.

directions. The three-year-old water works was in serious trouble. Other water tanks and windmills crumpled, and dozens of chimneys collapsed.

Rogers & Rogers General Store, a two-story, brick-masonry building that also housed the post office, fell "into a miscellaneous heap." It was rebuilt using concrete construction, and although the general store went out of business in 1908, the post office remained at this location until 1928. The Olympic Hall, where so many town functions took place, lost its second story in the earthquake. The Neuroth family had owned the building only a short time, and was never able to restore the second floor. The newspaper reported it "was mostly tumbled into the street." The Mountain View Fruit Exchange, a fruit drying yard and packinghouse, was totally wrecked. Damage in Mountain View was estimated at $175,000.

The earthquake left the Ames building extremely unsafe, and it had to be completely reconstructed. In the meantime, Professor Ames used a corner of his barn in the back of the property for an office. The aging scholar noted, "We are all alive and well, and though we have suffered grievously in a financial way, we have plenty of pluck and are going to do the best we can."[155] The woman's club lost the use of the meeting room at the damaged Ames building. After the earthquake the club met at homes of members until Jacob Mockbee built his hall and offered a meeting space rent-free.

The library had to vacate the damaged Rogers & Rogers building and had a succession of temporary homes after the earthquake. Librarian Hessle made her way to the crumbled building and gathered the book collection. "Miss Hessle, with much time and labor, rescued all of our books . . . " A notice ran in the newspaper that there would be "no fines until May 7" because of the earthquake. Hessle moved away shortly after that, and in the following year, the town hired Laura Belle Graham as librarian. Popularly known as "Miss Dolly," she was the daughter of Elizabeth and Isaac Newton Graham (a middle school was named for him in the 1950s). She was librarian from 1907 until 1915, through several library relocations, and when permanent quarters were established in a new Town Hall.

McDonald & Burke Blacksmith. Dan Burke is on the left, with Louis Conti on the right.

Fred Maxwell Jarvis, born in Iowa in 1887, was appointed Mountain View's first chief of police in 1924. In 1927, he served as one of the city's first public works superintendents.

Daniel B. Frink sold his magazine and sundries business of eleven years to William Garliepp. After the earthquake, Garliepp had to move to the skating rink temporarily, but by the end of the year, he was able to establish permanent quarters in the Rogers Building next to the post office.[156] George Swall purchased the Wagstaff property at Castro and Villa streets for a candy store and a pharmacy. In 1913, this property at 206 Castro Street was cleared for the First National Bank building, and the Wagstaff home was moved to Franklin Street.[157]

The earthquake of 1906 dealt a devastating blow to the brand-new Pacific Press publishing plant. Three walls collapsed, and the smokestack fell through the roof. Although its presses ran twenty-four hours a day, no one was injured because the night shift had just left the building and the day shift had not yet arrived. Pacific Press published three expanded special editions of its magazine, *Signs of the Times*, which included lengthy articles about "Mountain View's Experience" in the earthquake.[158] It reported that Pacific Press's losses amounted to between $20,000 and $25,000. The proprietors took this as a warning from God to stop producing commercial publications and dedicate the press entirely to religious literature. Ellen White, in particular, believed that the earthquake had been a message from an unhappy God.

In July of that year, just after repairs had been completed, a fire broke out in the engraving department. The fire was put out, but the next night it re-ignited and quickly spread, engulfing the entire plant. The company's night watchman notified the manager of the water company, who told him to inform the telephone operator. The operator claimed the town's night watchman had

Construction and laying of the cornerstone of Mountain View Town Hall in 1909.

The Glen Moving Picture Theatre was located at 174 Castro Street. It was Mountain View's first theatre and was owned by Frederick (known as Fritz) Campen, Jr.

to sound the fire alarm, but no one could find the watchman. Almost an hour passed before anyone even knew that the plant was burning to the ground.

Pacific Press officials had previously petitioned the city to place fire hydrants near their building, but the city had not complied. Town officials had established the Mountain View Hose Company, No. 2 in 1905, but had not installed any new hydrants. The fire hydrant nearest Pacific Press was 700 feet from the plant, but the hose was only 675 feet long. So the plant burned, and the losses amounted to $200,000.

Pacific Press officials were angry that the city neglected to provide adequate fire protection. A letter to the town's board of trustees said: "Now we are face to face with the question of rebuilding our plant here in Mountain View or moving to some other place. We do not feel like rebuilding

here unless we can have assurance that we will be treated right. . . . " [159] The letter went on to request a five-year exemption from taxes as an inducement for the company to stay in Mountain View.

Ellen White's conviction that Pacific Press ought to quit the commercial publishing business reached fever pitch, but press officials were still reluctant to shut down such a profitable operation. But they bowed to her request, and as a history of the company noted, "to everyone's surprise, it prospered from the start." [160] The next year a new fire alarm box system was installed on the telephone poles at each corner on the west side of Castro Street. When a call came in for a fire, a siren "would wail, the steam whistle at the waterworks would hoot, and the bell at No. 1 would clang." From now on, there would be no mistaking a fire.[161]

Longtime Mountain Viewers and Pacific Press personnel had different work ethics and personal values. The sale of alcoholic beverages was one issue on which there was considerable disagreement. Pacific Press was firmly rooted in its church, and the Adventists believed that the town should prohibit the sale of alcohol. But the idea of becoming a dry town was unthinkable for many who supported the town's seven saloons. Despite opposing values, Pacific Press was viewed as a pillar of the community. From the 1906 earthquake on, the press consistently had representation in local government; at least one person associated with Pacific Press and the Adventist Church served on the city council for the next five decades.[162] Nevertheless, Adventists remained a distinct group, with homes clus-

Parade led by Charles Mills on an unpaved Castro Street. Note the new Town Hall on the right at the southeast corner of Castro and California streets.

The Richelieu Saloon, located on the 200 block of Castro Street near Dana. It opened just before a town ban on new saloons.

Interior of the Richelieu Saloon, with owner Louis Tambini on the right.

tered to the west of Castro Street, near the publishing plant. They had their own elementary school, beginning in 1906, and a high school, Mountain View Academy, opened in 1922. It remains open today on Shoreline Boulevard.

After the earthquake, real estate speculators sprang into action to lure displaced San Franciscans to Mountain View. One post-earthquake development, called "Castro City," sported such highbrow street names as Stanford, Leland, University, and Fair Oaks. The acreage was divided into small, San Francisco-sized lots with a 25-foot frontage and a 100-foot depth, and it was advertised as a "country paradise." But most of the lots were sold to speculators, and very few houses were actually built. Most of Castro City sat empty until World War II.

In 1910, the population of Mountain View was almost 1,200, and there were one hundred students in high school. New classrooms had to be added and additional teachers hired. About sixty-five children attended the old one-room Whisman School, which was completely inadequate for that number. It was torn down and a larger, more sturdy one put in its place.

The earthquake coincided with an overall change in the economy and style of doing business. General merchandise stores, such as Rogers and Rogers, were replaced by small specialty shops.

New forms of mass entertainment appeared. The Glen Theater, a moving picture house operated by the Campen family, opened on Castro Street in 1912. More professionals went into practice in Mountain View, including doctors, insurance and real estate agents, and several lawyers. The newspaper voiced the sentiments of the merchant community in welcoming newcomers to Mountain View. In a 1907 issue it printed a poem by Max Hill:

> So hitch your horses, set your stakes to stay,
> WE welcome you in good old western way,—
> You'll find us simply human and all that;
> Be one among us, prosper and grow fat.
> So here you are, and here's a hand for you,
> Just make yourself at home in MOUNTAIN
> VIEW.[163]

Castro Street underwent major improvements, and in 1909 cement sidewalks replaced the wood-planked walkway. Claude Redwine came to Mountain View from Watsonville, and in 1913 bought the Mountain View Garage that became a Ford agency. Louis Tambini opened the "Richelieu," a saloon on Castro Street.[164] He acquired his city permit just before an ordinance banning new liquor licenses was passed in the 1912 election.

This steel water tank was built after the wooden one collapsed in the 1906 earthquake. The tank was located on Franklin Street and was known as the Mountain View Water Works. It was taken down in the 1950s because the wells in that part of town had gone dry. The corrugated building in the foreground was the Pickle Works, which was demolished in 1960. Photograph by Mountain View Camera Shop.

In 1909 a few hundred people turned out to witness the laying of the cornerstone to Mountain View Town Hall at the southeast corner of California and Castro streets. It was completed the following year, and was a visible sign that local government had become stronger since incorporation. The library took over part of the first floor. The second floor had a courtroom and judge's chambers. The police department, made up of Marshal Waits and Officer Robert Butler, occupied one office. Waits evidently had some personal problems. His wife, Charlotte, filed for divorce in 1911 when a former wife from Missouri showed up unexpectedly. The policeman had also taken up with another local woman who was not his wife. Evidently his personal life had little impact on his professional one since he won the next election by a large margin.

The first municipal election in which women could vote in Mountain View was held on April 8, 1912. California was the sixth state in the nation to extend the franchise to women, and did so in 1911 by a very narrow margin. The first woman to cast a vote in Mountain View was Sarah Leitch, an 80-year-old who waited at the door of Olympic Hall before 6 a.m., ready to vote when the polls opened.

The most controversial local ordinance of that municipal election was: "Shall the sale of alcoholic liquors be licensed in this Town?" Of the 594 registered voters, 89 percent turned out to vote. The tally was 284 to 234; the noes won by a margin of fifty votes. The local ban on new liquor licenses, coupled with similar bans in adjacent towns, created a "dry" zone, twenty miles long and thirty miles wide.[165]

The Mountain View *Register-Leader* ran an editorial three days before the election recommending a vote against licensing saloons because Mountain View was the only town between Redwood City and Santa Clara where alcoholic drinks could be sold. The writer pointed out that the town already had seven saloons, and approval of licensing would increase drinking.[166] Mountain View's choice to deny new liquor licenses foreshadowed national Prohibition, which went into effect eight years later. The board of trustees was confronted with petitions regarding alcohol several times, and it had limited the number of saloons to seven in 1904.[167]

The first woman to hold elected office in Mountain View was Mrs. Eliza Farrell, president of the woman's club. She was elected to the school board in 1912 and served for nine years.

Machine and Cyclery shops on the 300 block of Castro Street, circa 1907. These buildings were moved to Chinatown by Jake Mockbee. This lot was then occupied by Skinner & Pearson Garage

The **1908 MVHS track team** was represented by, from left to right: Top row: Leslie Morton, Earl Adams, Bernard Mason, Bill Goodwin, Bill Garliepp. Bottom row: Joe Urban, Victor Smith, Max Ish, Ray Winnegar.

The first woman elected as a town official was Lillian Peterson, who became the town treasurer in 1914. She was re-elected several times and served until 1924 when she decided to run for city clerk. In that election she was defeated by Charles N. Lake, an official from Pacific Press.

By this time, City Attorney Arthur Free had been elected Santa Clara County District Attorney, purportedly the youngest district attorney in the state. District Attorney Free went on a speaking tour supporting the Republican Party and later ran for Congress. Free enjoyed campaigning and public speaking and in his flamboyant speeches he loved to proclaim, "This is a *Free* country!" [168]

While he was working on a case for the county, Free befriended a young hoodlum in the county jail who had been ill. Free requested that the man be released to the county hospital, and even offered to pay his expenses. After the man recovered and served his sentence, he confided to Free that he had overheard a plot to rob the Pacific Press payroll, murder Free, the Farmers and Merchant Bank President Jacob Mockbee, and Marshal Walter McComb. Free reported the plot and thwarted the plan, and the conspirators were punished. The press and local officials were convinced of the veracity of the report and took precautions against future assaults on the targeted individuals. [169]

Eliza Farrell and her husband, Mike Farrell, were both former employees of the Martin Murphy, Jr. family. She had been governess and and he the ranch foreman. The Farrells bought about 250 acres on the west side of the former Inigo ranch. In 1912 they sold it to Fred Theuerkauf, who developed a dairy farm there. Besides operating his dairy farm and being an officer in the San Francisco Milk Producers Association, Theuerkauf was a Whisman School District trustee beginning in 1918. The U.S. Navy purchased his land in 1964 to build military housing, but somehow spared his old house. Theuerkauf died in 1974, and the following year the house was declared eligible for the National Register of Historic Places. However, the house burned to the ground on July 7, 1976.

Jacob Mockbee served a number of terms on the town's board of trustees and he held positions in almost every aspect of town government: fire chief, trustee, police commissioner, town clerk, water commissioner, and street commissioner. [170] In 1910, while he was still president of the Farmers and Merchants State Bank, he was appointed fire chief for the Hook and Ladder Company No. 1, just in time to combat some major fires.

At the beginning of summer in 1911 the Outside Inn in Old Town, formerly known as the Mountain View Hotel or the Taylor Hotel, was condemned. The establishment had become very rundown and a haven for illegal activities. Proprietor George Allen was charged with violating several county ordinances, not the least of which

The **girls 1908 basketball team from MVHS** were as follows from left to right: Top row: Henrietta Bar, Annette Stewart, Nell Garliepp, Ysabel Morton, Pearl True. Bottom row: Elizabeth Snyder, Fanny Distel, Agnes Urban, Mary Eastwood.

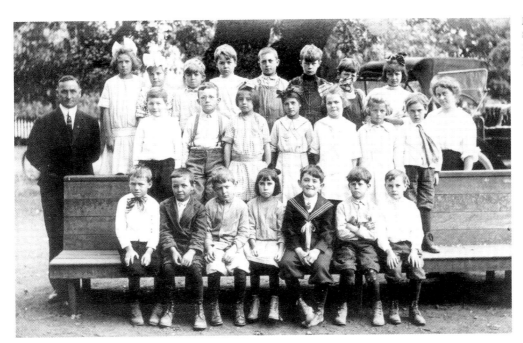

was gambling. The case came before Judge Frank P. Beverly, who was very familiar with the decrepit hotel because he had grown up in the Sleepers's home, just across El Camino Real.

Quite mysteriously, less than a month after the condemnation proceedings, the Outside Inn and its neighbor, Whelan's Blacksmith Shop, were both destroyed by a devastating fire. The smithy was promptly rebuilt and by February of 1912 the newspaper reported that Whelan's new shop "looked like the Palace Hotel." Whether or not the fire was related to the condemnation is unknown. Nevertheless, the Outside Inn was never rebuilt.[171]

Nathan McCorkle came to Mountain View from Nebraska in 1903 and opened a furniture store. As with many furniture makers, he also built caskets. As an undertaker, he opened a funeral parlor on Oak Street near Mercy (later it was on Villa Street). In 1912 he sold the funeral business to W. J. Anway. Then McCorkle ran his furniture store in partnership with baseball player Elmer Stricklett. This enterprise lasted only a few years, and closed in 1915.

Elmer Stricklett was better known for his baseball career than for his brief stint as a furniture store proprietor. Stricklett had played professional ball from 1904 to 1907, first for the Chicago White Sox and then for the Brooklyn Dodgers. He played outside organized baseball for a few years, and despite the effort, could not break back into the major leagues. He is credited with introducing the "spitball" to major league baseball, although some other more famous players, made the spitball well-known. His wife, Mabel Gates, was the daughter of Mary Julia Gates, a local author, and orchardist Benjamin Franklin Gates. Elmer and Mabel eventually took over her parents' orchard property on Calderon Avenue, until they sold it in 1934.

Mary Julia Gates was a writer who sold articles about history, geology and anthropology to newspapers. The Stanford-educated woman was described as "short, plump, dignified with a

Villa Francisca, home of the Castro family, built in 1911 and named in honor of Francisca Armija de Castro. Family members are in front of the home.

warm heart." Besides writing articles, she was often invited as a public speaker and evidently had a loud voice. She was an ardent suffragist who was frustrated that she was not allowed to vote. As a young schoolteacher, she recalled, she had taught a 21-year-old man "all the arithmetic he ever knew. He could vote," she lamented, "I could not." She authored a history of Pastoría de las Borregas that remains today an important source on the history of the rancho.[172]

In 1911 Crisanto Castro, who by this time was eighty-two years old, had a home built on his property very near where the original Estrada adobe had been seventy years earlier. The mission-style house had two wings off a central living area. He named the house "Villa Francisca" in honor of his late wife, Francisca Armijo, who had died a few years earlier. Crisanto did not have much time in his new home because he died the following year.

The Castro legacy, like la Pastoría de las Borregas, was fading fast. Crisanto's estate, valued at $68,000, was comprised of some town lots, the Castro Subdivision, and lots in both Santa Clara and San Francisco. Each of his adult children was mentioned in his will: Marion, Andrew, Joseph, William, Frank and Crisanto, Jr., Mercy and Susie. The previous generation would surely have used their Spanish names: Mariano, Andrés, José, Guillermo, Francisco, Crisanto, Mercedes, and Susana. Castro heirs lived in the

Second location of the Japanese Language School at View and Dana streets. It opened in 1925, was used by the Girl Scouts during World War II, and was torn down in 1962.

house until the 1950s, when it was transferred to the City of Mountain View. In 1961 it caught fire and, although only a portion of the house was damaged, the city deemed it unsalvageable and tore it down. Today's Rengstorff Park occupies the property.

If the Castro estate represented life in the previous century, modern inventions began to dominate future perspectives. Aviation was still in its infancy, but found popularity even in Mountain View. Victor Smith had graduated from Mountain View High in 1910 and gone on to Stanford. Shortly thereafter he quit the university

The Anzini family owned and operated the Junction House. This roadhouse was located in the El Camino Real-El Monte Road area, circa 1906.

Entire Minton Company staff turns out for a portrait. Founder Earl Minton (in suit) is standing fifth from left.

to take up aviation and had "made the world's record for speed in the license test for aviators at San Diego."[173] Unfortunately, in 1912 he crashed and died in an experimental airplane in Palo Alto. Other pilots also lost their lives in Santa Clara County, and the public believed flying was mostly just a daredevil sport.

Beginning in 1912, Chester Awalt was the agent for the Southern Pacific Railroad depot at Mountain View. The second floor of the attractive, yellow, two-story depot became a home for the Awalt family. Three years after they moved in, the family had a bird's eye view of a shoot-out at the station. Evidently a robbery had gone awry and two thieves hijacked a San Francisco-bound train. When the train came to a stop in Mountain View, police opened fire and killed one of the burglars.

Accidents along the railroad were routine and in one incident the newspaper reported that a "railroad engine cleverly bisects a Sedan." Amazingly, the driver, Marengo Gonzales, survived. But shortly thereafter, Southern Pacific was petitioned to install a "wig-wag" at Bailey Avenue and the tracks.[174]

Several businesses around town were owned by Japanese families including a nursery, a florist, a tea and rice shop, and a few billiard parlors. Mr. Yamada, a Japanese laundryman, opened a business on Castro Street. It did not last long, though, because he was cited under a new ordinance prohibiting laundries on the main street.[175] At the turn of the twentieth century there were fewer than three hundred Japanese in Santa Clara County. Within a decade that number increased ten-fold and many Japanese immigrants were employed in agriculture. The

local newspaper noted that Mountain View's Chinatown was growing rapidly in 1919 and had many Chinese and Japanese businesses. Between 1910 and 1913, of the seven business licenses issued to Japanese, five did not use personal or business names. Instead the license simply read "Jap."[176] Immigration legislation passed in the 1920s reduced the number of immigrants and prohibited foreign-born Japanese from owning land. Some families got around the law by purchasing land in the name of their American-born infant children.

Parkinson Brothers Lumber & Hardware on Front Street was purchased in 1911 by Charles C. Minton. At that time, the business employed three workers. Under the direction of Charles' son, Earl, within five years more than twenty employees and four trucks kept the operation going. Minton added a mill to accommodate the demand for house-building materials.

The lumberyard employed several Japanese workers, so the company set up a little school on

Cumberland Presbyterian Church on Castro Street between Church and Mercy streets, 1913.

its property where Japanese immigrants studied English. In 1915 the school moved to the Ogata family home at today's Central Expressway and Shoreline Boulevard and became known as the Haoabese Kabgyage School. By 1920, fifty students came every weekday after public school and on Saturdays. By this time, the instructors taught the children their ancestral Japanese, not English.

Spanish families also did farm work in Mountain View. Early in the twentieth century, tens of thousands of poor Spaniards left Spain, bound for Hawaii, to work in the sugar cane fields. Many were disillusioned with abhorrent working conditions and extremely low pay in Hawaii, so whole family groups moved on to the Santa Clara Valley. One woman remembered farm work this way:

> I started work picking prunes. We were very young, but when I really started working full time, I was fifteen. . . . There were a lot of people working, a lot of Japanese and Spaniards, and everybody.[177]

Many of the Spanish families congregated on the north side of town in what would commonly be referred to as "Spanish town."

Thousands of emigrants also left their homeland in six small republics that became known as Yugoslavia. Several ethnic groups came from this area including Croatians, Montenegrans, and Serbs. Large-scale immigration from this region began as early as 1880 and continued steadily until 1920. War drove large numbers to the U.S. again in the 1990s. The climate of the Santa Clara Valley is similar in many ways to that of the Adriatic region and farming was a natural occupation for many to undertake upon their arrival here. Among the Mountain View families from this region were the Popovich, Vidovich, Jelavich, Viscovich, Glumac, and Kalcic families.

Some Mountain View growers became involved in scientific experiments intended to improve the quality of fruit. In 1914, two women from San Francisco, an attorney and an insurance broker, formed a partnership to operate "Greycot Farm," in Mountain View. Helen Wheeler and Elinor Pratt Lewandowski shipped "consistently high quality" produce, noted a surprised newspaper writer. The two women had only been "book farmers," so their success raised a few eyebrows— as did their lifestyle, two unmarried women living together as partners. The *Register-Leader* felt compelled to assure its readers that the two were "very womanly, very lady-like and charming" while at the same time they had "all of the necessary vim and determination" to be successful in business.[178]

War broke out in Europe in 1914, but President Woodrow Wilson's attempts to remain neutral

This patriotic, multi-cultural play was presented in Mountain View in the late 1910s or early 1920s. Three cast members are identified: Ruth Weaver (to the right of the woman holding the large flag), Charles Moore (between Ruth Weaver and the person in the cassock), and Ella Weaver (to the right of the person in the cassock).

Mountain View Woman's Club minstrel show in 1919. Members are in black face.

enjoyed strong public support. But within two years it was clear the U.S. would have to support its allies. The U.S. entered the war and the Selective Service Act of 1917 required registration for young men across the country.

Three sons of the Robart family of Mountain View served. The third son, Leon, was an infantryman in Company H of the 91st Infantry Division. He was killed in action, becoming Mountain View's only known casualty. The local American Legion Post #248, organized just after the war, was named in honor of Leon Robart. Many others who served carried physical and emotional scars from the war for the rest of their lives. Young Adolph Garliepp suffered from a paralytic stroke as a result of shell shock he received while fighting in France. The newspaper noted, he "was one of the first of our boys to go over and one of the last to come back." [179] He experienced a partial recovery, but died about ten years later. The Cutter family also sent two sons. Allen Cutter came home and served on the Mountain View City Council during the early 1930s.

During the war the woman's club had supported Red Cross efforts to collect wool to be knit into warm clothing and socks. The club also sent care packages to local boys fighting in the trenches of Europe. After the war, in 1919, the eighty-two-member club purchased the former Methodist Episcopal South Church on Castro Street for a clubhouse. Soon-to-be Congressman Arthur Free provided "free" legal advice. The club's fundraising projects included a theatrical production, "Lady Minstrels," where the club members donned black face and sang "All I Want is my Black Baby Back" and "Tuck Me to Sleep in my Old Tucky Home," along with several other popular minstrel songs. Black-face singing and dancing was commonplace and popular among whites in vaudeville acts and cabaret shows during the Al Jolson-era, although today it is considered racist. The minstrel show was very well attended and received rave reviews in the newspaper raising cash for the new clubhouse.

The Vidovich family, circa 1914, whose ten-acre apricot orchard was on Calderon Avenue in Mountain View. Seated in front dressed in white is Anna and her husband, Marion P. Vidovich, is standing beside her.

In the fall of 1919 Congress passed the National Prohibition Act, or "Dry Law," banning sales of alcohol. Despite President Wilson's veto, it went into effect the following January and remained the law of the land until 1933. Temperance workers celebrated, but not everyone in Mountain View was pleased with the new federal law. One resident still bemoaned the election of six years earlier when townspeople had voted their seven saloons "off the face of the earth." He lamented, "we have seven churches in Mountain View, but we have no saloons." [180] Ironically Pacific Press, the most vocal proponent of Prohibition, leased the former Neuroth's Saloon at Castro and Front streets to sell their religious books. [181] Nevertheless, bootleggers quickly set up distilleries to provide "medicinal" and recreational elixers.

During World War I, fruit farmers and cannery managers worried that a labor shortage would put them out of business because so many men were drafted. They were pleasantly surprised when the war actually expanded the market for canned fruits and vegetables. The canneries worked faster and longer than ever before, and turned to new sources of labor, including immigrants and women.

The Sanguinetti Cannery on Bailey Avenue near the railroad tracks, which had opened in 1907 and grown steadily, needed more workers and bigger facilities. In order to attract new employees, including married women, it constructed a bungalow court of ten cottages called Rose Court just off Villa Street for workers' families and installed a playground and a restaurant as well. [182] Those cottages were torn down in the 1990s and replaced with two-story houses.

A few Mountain View growers cultivated sugar beets during the war, and local production continued through the 1920s. About 1,000 tons were shipped out of Mountain View each year. One Japanese sugar beet-grower had a yield of thirty tons per acre in 1920, and earned $14 per ton. By 1938 almost 28,000 tons of sugar beets were harvested from about 1,400 acres near Mountain View. [183]

The fruit industry continued to provide seasonal employment for women after the war. A 1920 advertisement read: "Women wanted to work in fruit at Mt. View Canning Company. Guaranteed steady work until November 20th, nice, clean, healthy place to work. Those who stay until the end of the season will be given extra bonus." [184] Unlike today's "signing bonuses," during the 1920s the reward would have to wait until the work was complete.

California Supply Company on Franklin Street was commonly known as the "pickle factory," and was open year-round. Every year it turned 1,200 tons of cucumbers into pickles and bottled thousands of gallons of catsup. Even into the 1960s, the pungent aroma of the pickle factory reminded the surrounding neighborhood of its presence there. Today it is the site of the police department.

Sanguinetti Cannery, later Richmond-Chase Cannery, located at today's Shoreline Boulevard and the railroad tracks.

During the 1920s, the Clark Cannery employed seventy women during the season and shipped almost eight hundred cases of fruit a day through the South Shore Port. The former Sanguinetti Cannery became the J.W. McCarthy Company and employed about three hundred women and one hundred men. But by the mid-1920s it went bankrupt and was purchased in 1926 by the Richmond Chase Canning Company.

The Panama-Pacific International Exposition was held in San Francisco in 1915 to celebrate the opening of the Panama Canal and to display the city's recovery from the 1906 earthquake and fire. The exposition was wildly successful with nineteen million visitors streaming through the elaborate exhibits.

Mountain View staged its own exposition, mimicking in miniature the international one. The first Mountain View Prune and Apricot Exposition in 1915 became an annual event. By 1921 the affair was held on three consecutive days and drew a crowd of 10,000, quite a feat for a town of 1,800 people. Competitions for the best produce were held for fruits, dried fruits, nuts, vegetables, flowers, livestock, manufactures, home cooking, dressmaking, war and curio exhibits. Children were released from school for a day to participate in the parade. Many came in costume, several little ones disguised as prunes

or apricots. They sang a little ditty to the tune of "Three Blind Mice:"

> *Apricots and Prunes*
> *Apricots and Prunes*
> *We grow them here*
> *We show them here*
> *Three times a day we eat them here*
> *Three times a day we eat them here*
> *Apricots and Prunes*
> *Apricots and Prunes*

Fraternal organizations marched in full regalia behind the bands, and decorated automobiles joined the procession. Grocer Walter Erichsen's Dodge truck ferried three children tossing cereal packages out to the crowd.

Up until 1923, tents provided a venue for the Prune and Apricot Exposition. In 1923 the exposition got a home of its own when a large building was constructed specifically for the yearly fete. The "L" shaped building had a sixty-foot frontage on Castro Street and extended three hundred feet to Bryant Street. Some lumber used to build the huge structure was salvaged from a burned-out auto racetrack in San Carlos. The Mountain View *Register-Leader*, a key supporter, claimed that the "Prune and Apricot Exposition is one of the big annual events of the bay region. It has outgrown the status of a community affair, and almost that of a county affair. It is now the biggest enterprise of its particular kind in the bay region." [185]

The program became more elaborate as the exposition expanded. A queen was selected beginning in 1921, complete with attendants and courtiers, and it became a quasi-beauty contest. In 1927 the "Japanese colony" entered a float featuring men, women, and children in traditional Japanese costume and won first prize for the "best decorated float" in the parade. That year an estimated 25,000 people came to Mountain View for the exposition. However, enthusiasm for the exposition waned as the economy became depressed. The last exposition was held in 1930, and the building was sold to Redwine's Ford Agency. It was razed in 1965.

The Redwine takeover of the exposition building was indicative of the coming of age of the automobile. Redwine's sold Ford cars and trucks and Fordson Tractors. When it purchased and remodeled the Prune and Apricot Exposition Building, it installed a state-of-the-art showroom and garage that extended along Mercy Street to Bryant. June Redwine de Larios recalled, "the building had a large, fenced yard, and my father kept a little Austin there. As kids, when the garage was closed, we'd go there and push each other around in that little Austin. Of course we were too young to drive. It was a lot of fun." [186]

Another indication of the coming-of-age of the auto was the large, electric signs bearing the names of towns up and down the peninsula. Many of the signs were placed at the railroad, but others were also built where main streets came to El Camino Real. An electric "Mountain View" sign was erected in 1915 over Castro Street at the railroad tracks. The huge letters allowed train passengers to identify the rail stop, and local merchants were pleased to have the sign bring customers to their businesses. Funds to build the signs were solicited from individuals and businesses. In 1921, a set of twin electric signs framed the entryway to Castro Street at El Camino Real. They were supported by pillars made of cobblestones that had been collected from the beach at Pescadero. The city purchased land on either side of the signs, and designed a fan-shaped entrance to Castro Street.

A street-paving project was one of the most important tasks facing the city because automobiles required smooth, dry roads. Castro Street continued to be the economic backbone of the town. Since 1918 a "vulcanizing works," or tire repair shop, had operated in the old Farr Building. Mountain View Vulcanizing Works boasted a mold for making "either plain or non-skid retreads" of such high quality that only an expert could distinguish them from new tires. [187]

Even the police were enjoying motoring. During the 1920s, traffic officer Jess Regli faced complaints from citizens because of his noisy motorcycle. The board of trustees asked him to "keep his muffler closed, reduce speed to 35 miles per hour maximum, and that he refrain from controversy with persons under arrest." [188] Regli resigned a short time later. The town purchased its first police car in 1929 when the Mountain View Garage sold it a Ford touring car for $439.

South Shore Port Company, main shipping area for Mountain View, circa 1920s.

"Know The Peninsula" Trip, sponsored by the Mountain View Chamber of Commerce, September 1922.

Charles Pearson, Jr. and Charles C. Skinner opened the Skinner and Pearson Garage, and later it became Pearson Automobile Company. It sold a variety of cars over the years: first Maxwells, Chandlers and Beeleys; then Chevrolets; next Buicks; and finally Oldsmobiles. In 1924 Ugo Mancini established Mancini Motors. Both companies remain in operation today in Sunnyvale.

Even as the public became more enamored with the automobile during the 1920s, progress in aviation and the World War I-induced desire for a strong national defense guided military spending. Nevertheless, most Mountain View residents would never have imagined that a thousand-acre Naval air base with dirigible airships was about to sprout up just to the north of the little town.

CHAPTER 5

DIRIGIBLES & AIRSHIPS

ALTHOUGH THE U.S. WAS ON THE WINNING SIDE at the end of World War I, the intense battles pointed out some deficiencies in American military strategies both under the sea and in the air. Germany outdistanced the U.S. with its U-boats, early versions of submarines, and it rigid airships. The U.S. demanded and received two German airships or dirigibles as war reparations, and American military brass lobbied hard to build up a whole fleet of them. Mountain View would be profoundly affected by these postwar developments.

But just before World War I, the Panama Canal had opened with great fanfare in 1914, and tradespeople the world over believed the new waterway would enhance international commerce. Local merchants were equally optimistic about the economic boom the new canal could bring to California seaports. Many towns around San Francisco Bay jumped on the bandwagon and began campaigning to transform themselves into port cities. The former Jagel's Landing, at the end of Whisman Road, caught the attention of deep-water port promoters. It was purchased by Charles and Clara King and incorporated as the South Shore Port Company to raise $50,000 in hopes of becoming a major port-of-call on San Francisco Bay.

Construction began with a huge dredging project in the summer of 1920, and it cleared a two-mile-long channel culminating at a large landing. Then giant graders were brought in to level the mountain of dirt dredged out of the channel. Plans were approved for warehouses and freight buildings at the edge of a new wharf.

Sunnyvale jockeyed for the spotlight on the port project, and investors from there pointed out that its town boundaries actually extended to the bay, adjacent to the new port. But Mountain View's newspaper noted, "This is essentially a Mountain View project, although our pleasant little neighbor on the south, Sunnyvale, has been rather jealous of the proprietorship. . . . there will be glory enough in the achievement for Sunnyvale and Mountain View, with a generous share left for the rest of the Santa Clara Valley."[189] The local press consistently referred to the project as the "Mountain View port" even though it occupied unincorporated land.

While the port was still under construction, Charles King died, and his wife, Clara M. King, took over as managing partner. The formal opening of the South Shore Port was in May 1923, and a new vessel, the *South Shore*, ferried visitors up the channel to the bay and back. Business picked up quickly, and boats were scheduled to depart from South Shore Port for San Francisco at 5 a.m. daily and the return was scheduled for 5 p.m. The port acquired another boat, *South Shore No. 2*, to accommodate an increase in passengers and freight.[190] A trucking operation also grew out of the port. Its fleet brought produce to the wharf for export.

Although not the astounding success the promoters had hoped, the port drew a fair amount of boat and truck traffic. Fruit crops, sugar beets, vegetables, and grapes were among the crops sent on their way to market out of South Shore Port. Tak Hori, a Japanese-American youngster who grew up in Mountain View recalled the port this way:

> *I cherish my Tom Sawyer days when I and my friends went fishing and hunting daily. There were lots of quail and pheasant on the farms and wild ducks on the slough. We went fishing for shiners and smelt at the South Shore Port, also called Kingsport. It was a harbor where the ships came in from San Francisco and the San Joaquin deltas. It is the present site of Moffett Field.*[191]

Besides the port, the developers built an amusement park and a swimming pool called Kingsport Plunge. It was the largest open-air, salt-water swimming pool in the Santa Clara Valley. The pool measured 50 feet by 120 feet with a depth of from 2 to 9 feet "to accommodate all sizes of bathers," as one ad asserted. The bottom of the pool had colored lights for night swimming. Adjacent to the pool was a bathhouse, several dressing rooms, and a picnic area.

The grand opening of the plunge was in May 1925. Divers from Stanford University and the Olympic Club in San Francisco entertained spectators and the pool was "crowded to capacity" on the opening weekend. High school girls competed in a bathing beauty contest, and the Native Sons and Daughters of the Golden West served hot dogs and ice cream.

But not all was smooth sailing for the new Kingsport Plunge. When the pool was drained after the opening weekend, one of the walls collapsed. Repairs were not complete until after the July 4th holiday. Nevertheless the plunge remained a popular recreation spot throughout the 1920s. Its ad campaign emphasized the health benefits, claiming it was endorsed by many physicians. The pool water had "15 per cent more salt than ocean water" and was "absolutely free from any contagious germs."[192]

Admission to the pool cost ten cents, and an annual pass could be purchased at Knight's Pharmacy for $10. Tak Hori remembered, "that's where I learned to swim; salt water is an aid in floating." He also recalled Clara King, the proprietor. "She charged ten cents for a swimming suit. She was a nice lady."[193]

During 1925 and 1926, the directors of the South Shore Port tried to refinance the corporation so that they could build an extension to the wharf, buy new trucks to support a fledgling trucking operation, and implement regular boating service to Oakland. They asked their stockholders for a $5 per share assessment, but the investors refused to finance the plans. By July of 1927, the South Shore Port Company was in bankruptcy.

The port became the property of a San Francisco dredging contractor who was still owed money. Eventually, the land was sold and became part of Moffett Field.

Mountain View's population had grown to 1,888 in 1920, and although modern, self-service grocery store chains came on the scene, most people patronized small, local shops. Several small grocers had stores on Castro Street or in the immediate neighborhood. Lawson's bought a store from J.L. Fisher & Son and, over time, the store expanded and was called the Blue & White, and later the Red & White. It remained in business until 1960. Small, family-owned grocers were able to compete by offering personal service and free delivery. Some grocers targeted a particular ethnic group. Herrero's Market, for example, had a *chorizo* (sausage) factory. Residents also patronized many other grocers like the Holgueras, Powell Brothers, and Escano Market. Walter L. Erichsen and his brother-in-law, Francis Lawrence, bought Charles Pearson, Sr.'s Castro Street grocery in 1918. Milani Grocery Store, at 295 Castro Street opened in 1927, and remained there until proprietor Charles Milani went to work at Moffett Field in 1946.

Steve's at Old Town and Wagner's on Villa Street, along with a few other merchants, extended credit to customers during the Depression. Fruit farm families often ran a tab at the markets, and paid up at the end of the season after the fruit was harvested. Although Castro Street shops

Prune and Apricot Exposition exhibit held in Mountain View's own exposition building, circa 1920s.

were not open on weeknights, they stayed open on Saturday nights because farm help got paid that day.

Larger chain stores came on the local scene when in 1922 the Sunshine Stores of Redwood City opened it's fifth Grocerteria on the 100 block of Castro Street. It was the first chain store in Mountain View, and five years after it opened, was purchased by Purity Stores. In the late 1930s, Purity opened a new store at Villa and Bryant streets. Likewise, in 1926 Skaggs Safeway opened in a new Mockbee Building on the 200 block of Castro Street. By the end of the decade, the store dropped the name Skaggs and was simply known as Safeway. In 1940, Food City opened on El Camino Real at Miramonte. It was owned by Fred Pieracci and Sam Power, and offered an unheard-of five thousand square feet of shopping space. Later it added a liquor store and expanded even further.

Other small businesses still thrived, though. California Bakery, on the 200 block of Castro Street, was operated by Leone and Louise Arecco and specialized in French and American breads. The bakery, under various owners including the Rosinganas and the Medinas, remained on Castro Street until 1996. Later the Areccos owned Quality Market Grocery, also known as Arecco Market, on the next block. Scarpa & White Meat Market, on the 200 block of Castro Street, "had carcasses hanging there with sawdust on the floor to catch the blood."[194] Swall's was another butcher shop, and "Swall Hall" on the second floor eventually became a gathering place for the Spanish community known as Cervantes Hall. A black man, known only as George, operated a shoe shine shop on Castro Street. The board of trustees approved a "Popcorn License" for a popcorn wagon on Castro Street at $4.50 per quarter.[195]

The Mountain View Chamber of Commerce was established in 1922 and replaced the outdated board of trade and commercial club. It was part of a national organization setting up city bureaus to promote local business. The first president of Mountain View's chamber was realtor William P. Wright. Claude Redwine, auto dealer, was the vice-president and J.J. Taylor served as treasurer. The newspaper reported that "it was reincarnated from the old ashes of the Mountain View

Map of Mountain View, circa 1940.

Dana Street School, open from 1917 until 1959.

commercial club."[196] A more informal group of businessmen, founded by Ormand Newfarmer, called itself the "Breakfast Club" because it met for breakfast at the Silver Seal Creamery to discuss issues of interest to the merchants. Garbage collection was also inaugurated in 1922 for the incorporated area.

The first modern apartment house in Mountain View, the "California Apartments," which still stands today at California and Hope streets was built by Earl D. Minton. It featured six apartments with an "immense oil-burning furnace." Besides operating the lumber business, Minton developed the subdivision Palmita Park (1924). He served on the town's board of trustees as a replacement for his father, Charles Minton, who died while in office in 1914. Later, Earl was elected in his own right, and was the mayor from 1924-1928.

Traditional trades still coexisted with modern enterprises. An old blacksmith shop on the 300 block of Castro Street run by Richard MacDonald and Dan Burke had many local customers. Wally Erichsen recalled, "As a boy I loved to stand in front of the open door and look in and watch Mr. Burke. He would be swinging a hammer over red hot steel, forming and shaping it over an anvil or in a die to make tools and other parts that could not be purchased in a hardware store."[197] McDonald died in 1934, but Burke stayed in business another nine years. He was elected to the city council from 1934-1946 and was Mountain View's mayor from 1937-1942. Watching Burke sparked Erichsen's interest in metallurgy. Years later, he became a metallurgical engineer after graduation from Stanford University.

The growing community also needed new schools. The elementary school was so crowded that another school was opened in a Castro Street house in 1913. Three years later, a $9,000 bond issue passed, and property was purchased on Dana Street to take the place of the Castro Street quarters for the Dana Street School. It opened in 1917 with a kindergarten and first and second grades. Dana Street School's kindergarten was taught by Edith Landels for its entire life: from 1917 until 1959. Another teacher at Dana Street School was Victorine Klein who remained there until 1934. Both women had schools named for them during the 1950s.

Frank Huff had been principal of Mountain View Grammar School since 1899. In 1917, teacher Kenneth Slater took over as principal, and later was superintendent of the school district until 1957. His career spanned forty years.

Victorine Klein

The high school had become so over-crowded that in 1922 a bond issue for almost $200,000 to purchase land and build a high school was passed by a majority of voters. The next year, the school district purchased a twenty-acre prune orchard on Castro Street near El Camino Real and architect William Weeks, renowned for his modern school designs, was hired.

At the official groundbreaking ceremony on March 8, 1923, Jacob Mockbee, who had been a school board member for twenty-six years, shoveled the first bit of dirt. Two months later a cornerstone was laid at a ceremony led by the Masonic lodge. The contents of the cornerstone included membership lists from the Masons, the chamber of commerce, the woman's club and the Parent-Teachers' Association (P.T.A.). When the new building was dedicated in May of the following year, speakers included Trustee Chester Awalt, newspaper editor P. "Pop" Milton Smith, and Mrs. Eleanor Dale, president of the P.T.A. Although the twenty-six members of the class of 1924 never attended the new school, its graduation ceremony was held in the new auditorium.

School started at the new campus the next fall. Two hundred students were taught by thirteen teachers, and Mr. Beverly Nevison was principal. The new facility opened with seventeen classrooms, an auditorium, a theater, and office space. In 1927, the Manual Arts building that had been in William Weeks's original plan was completed, along with a gym and a swimming pool. Later a cafeteria, library, and new classroom wings were added.

Just southwest of the new high school, on a property fronting El Camino Real, stood a large, old house which had been built in 1888 by Joseph and May Williams. The retired sea captain and his wife created a highly visible and productive estate. The forty acres had an orchard of various fruits, fourteen acres of peaches and apricots, and a fifteen-acre vineyard. The estate was

The Army Air Corps flew balloons as well as the Navy from Moffett Field. *Courtesy of the Stocklmeir Library and Archives, California History Center.*

described as "a landmark of ideal California country life. . . . a stately mansion surrounded by beautiful grounds, semi-tropical foliage. . . . stretching back into the town limits."[198]

Ever since the couple died in 1911, it had been rented to a number of different tenants. A doctor bought the property in the early 1920s and turned it into a sanitarium. In 1925 another doctor took over and added a separate building for a maternity ward and for "x-ray treatment." Then Doctor Henry W. Milo, who also had a Castro Street office, bought the property and established Mountain View Hospital and Sanitarium, offering the town its first emergency room. It survived as a hospital until World War II, and today is the site of a fast food restaurant.

The Spangler family came to Mountain View in the early 1930s and bought a mortuary business from the Beardslees. Martin, Sr. and Mary lived above the funeral home on Castro Street and Yosemite Avenue from 1934 until 1962 when they moved to Los Altos. Spangler also was the local ambulance driver, and when he and Mary would go to the movies on Castro Street, he would call the town telephone operator to let her know where he would be in case of emergency.[199] He often assisted Dr. Henry W. Milo, whose office was nearby, if the doctor needed help setting broken bones.

Occasionally a doctor from another town would make calls in Mountain View. One young Japanese girl recalled, "Whenever Mother needed the doctor, she would call Wagner's Rexall Drug store on the corner of Castro and Villa, and leave her name and the person who was sick. I was

Fire fighters' barrel contest, circa 1940s.

really impressed with Dr. [George] Hall. . . . [He made] house calls in Mountain View on Fridays."[200]

The old grammar school took over the former high school building on Calderon Avenue and El Camino until a new grammar school could be constructed. A two-story building replaced the old schools in 1928 and became known as the Highway Elementary School. The two old schools were torn down, and the Highway School became one of Mountain View's preeminent institutions. Its staff educated youngsters up until the 1950s.

The Japanese language school that had begun at Minton Lumber had outgrown its location and in 1924, the school purchased a lot at Dana and View streets for $2,000 to construct a new $7,500 building. The instructors lived in a little house on the school grounds. In 1929 the school was incorporated as the Mountain View Mihongo

Holthouse Ranch, circa 1932. The ranches in the immediate area of the new air base were absorbed into it. *Courtesy of Trudi Odbert and the Holthouse family.*

Gahuen. It had grown to 150 students, requiring the purchase of a school bus.

Saint Joseph's Catholic Church burned down as the result of an arson fire in 1928. Church services were held in the Prune and Apricot Exposition building until the new church was completed. Whisman School, located at today's Shoreline Boulevard and Charleston Road, also burned, and during its reconstruction, the children were bused to the new Saint Joseph's Catholic Church for classes. When Whisman was rebuilt, it was a "modern spacious school" with an assembly hall, a kitchen, three classrooms and an office. Four faculty members taught about one hundred students there.

Several fires during the 1920s indicated how antiquated fire-fighting techniques had become. The volunteer force responded as quickly as it could muster, but structures were very often lost because of inadequate equipment and inaccessible water supplies. Early in 1921, a fire erupted at the Japanese Hot House "on [the] other side of the track," as the newspaper reported. It was outside city limits, and the fire could not be fought because there was no water pressure. It was a complete loss.[201]

When a fire broke out in June of 1924 at the three-story brick warehouse of the Prune and Apricot Association, volunteer firefighters used

Spanish immigrant Benedita Rodrigo, mother of ten, of 460 Bryant Street, picking prunes, 1936.

their new American-La France pumping engine for the first time. In 1928 there was a fire in Minton's box factory and the warehouse for Foothill Cannery on Front Street, today's Evelyn Avenue, just east of the Southern Pacific Depot. The box factory was a total loss, with damage estimated at about $10,000, and the warehouse

Oku home and flower farm nursery, Wright Avenue and Bailey (today's Shoreline Boulevard), circa 1925. (Left to right) Masao Oku, Unosuke Oku (arrived in Mountain View 1902), Leonard Oku, and Yoshie Oku. *Courtesy of Alice Oku.*

full of canned fruit amounted to a loss of about $40,000.[202] It became increasingly difficult to rely on a volunteer fire department.

In addition to their fire-fighting duties, the town's firefighters also sponsored social events. The 200 block of Castro Street was the scene of barrel and hose "musters" where teams of firefighters competed by "putting a barrel in the middle of the street, and shooting water from hoses from two sides. Whoever was the better shot and got the barrel rolling would win."[203] The contests drew crowds of spectators. Fritz Campen, whose family managed the local movie theater, was the fire chief and served on the city council from 1932 to 1940.

The police were no less busy than the firefighters. An overall increase in violence in the 1920s was evidenced by a brutal murder. John H. Mockbee's daughter, Rae, a local beauty, had been chosen to represent Santa Clara County on its float in a parade at the state fair. In 1927, as she and her fiancé, Harry Morgan, were returning to Mountain View after delivering Rae's maternal grandmother to San José, they were forced off Stevens Creek Road near the Heney ranch by some hoodlums who shot and killed Morgan. Rae ran to a nearby ranch for help, but was too late to save Morgan. He was twenty-two and she was just nineteen when the tragedy occurred.[204]

Although Prohibition was the law of the land, Mountain View had its own local "roaring twenties" with get-rich-quick schemes, and the popularity of the speak-easy, or illegal bar. William Seppich, a barber and dabbler in real estate, bought four acres on Dean Street in 1912 to build his home. He was on a personal quest to make a fortune, and, as he colloquially put it, be on "easy street." After a dozen years of failed money-making schemes, he decided the only way he'd ever be on easy street was to name the street himself. The county supervisors obligingly changed the name, and Mr. Seppich could legitimately claim he was on Easy Street.[205]

The Blue and Gold Kennel Club, a euphemism for a speakeasy, bordello, and greyhound dog-racing venue, opened in 1928 at what is today the corner of Eunice Avenue and Porterfield Court. The house had been built in 1924 with seven bedrooms, six bathrooms, two bars and an eight hundred square-foot ballroom. One upstairs bedroom had a small window with a lookout platform near it, equipped with a warning buzzer so that the clientele could be dispersed upon a moment's notice. There was an elaborate distillery in the carriage house.[206]

The newspaper claimed that the club was operated by "Chicago gangsters" and that it was shut down by "revenue agents" in 1938. Its colorful ten-year history was also highly embellished over time. The sprawling house was sold at auction in 1938 to Harold Skinner, who lived there as a recluse until he died in 1962. It became

known as the Wunderman House beginning in the 1960s, for its owner, Irwin Wunderman. He gave tours of the house emphasizing its "harlot history." He found hundreds of bottles on the property and some were labeled "Malt Tonic-Palatable-Healthful-Nutritive, alcohol not over 37%." In 1975 he fought a developer who wanted to build a cul-de-sac for thirteen homes adjacent to his property. Trees that had shielded the house since its Kennel Club days would have to come down. Eventually development surrounded the former club.

Municipal government changed with the times and in 1927, Mountain View's Board of Trustees began calling itself the "City Council." Minutes from council meetings during that year do not indicate the reason for the change, but since the local newspaper also began calling the board a council, it must have been a matter familiar to the public. Higher demand for city services, like police and fire, meant more participation from the council members. Soon they would become boosters of their home turf in hopes of establishing a major American military base.

In February of 1929, *Register-Leader* editor Pop Smith was called over to William P. Wright's real estate office to meet two out-of-towners. The guests were Otto Hirsch of Alameda County who owned several hundred acres of the former Inigo rancho and his real estate agent, Laura Thane Whipple. They had come to Mountain View to enlist the help of Wright in convincing some landowners adjacent to the Hirsch land to sell for a proposed Army air base.

Pop Smith listened intently and was very enthusiastic about the plan. He went before the local chamber of commerce to ask for its support, but some chamber members were skeptical that the Army would actually want the site. John Manfredi joked, "Go on and offer it to them, Pop! If you can put that over we'll send you to Congress!"[207] Chester Awalt, the former Southern Pacific station agent, was president of the chamber at this time and supported the plan.

A small committee, including newsman Smith, went to San Francisco to pitch the Mountain View land for the proposed air base. The San Francisco meeting was a disappointment because the Army had all but settled on a piece of land in Alameda for its base. But the Mountain View contingent learned that the Navy would soon be searching for an air base for its dirigible program.

Toward the end of 1929 when Congress authorized $5,000,000 for a West Coast Navy air base, efforts to woo the Navy began in earnest. Proponents of a site in San Diego offered the land to the government for $1, so a similar proposition was made for the Mountain View-Sunnyvale land. A half a million dollars had to be raised to pay off land owners and get the project off the ground. The deal was backed by San Francisco financiers who came up with most of the money, but Santa Clara County was responsible for raising a formidable $100,000. An all-out public relations campaign was launched to muster support for a local base.

On Tuesday, October 29, 1929, the stock market crashed, and personal fortunes were lost in a day. The impact was not instantaneous in Mountain View, and for a while, conversations still focused on local affairs. Slowly but surely, though, the Depression affected the town. Lean times and little work were the watchwords of the next decade. It was easy to convince locals of the economic value a new air base would afford.

First and foremost, a new base would require five hundred construction workers. A military presence would bring in thousands of personnel who might spend their days off and paychecks in Mountain View. There was very little opposition to the base, and when a film with aerial views of the proposed site was shown at the local theater, it was very well attended. Many people had never seen a film of their own neighborhood, and it caused a great deal of excitement.

In May 1930, Congresswoman Florence Kahn of San Francisco introduced a bill to authorize $4.5 million for a "metal clad dirigible." The behemoth aluminum airships held crew quarters, galley, and walkways for up to ninety men. Twelve enormous helium gas cells kept the ship aloft, and eight 560-horsepower engines propelled it through the air. Water ballast compartments, designed to regulate ascent or descent, were located in the nose. The dirigible was also an aircraft carrier: it held five Sparrowhawk fighter biplanes that could be lowered in or out of the mother ship to engage in scouting expeditions.

The U. S. program to build a dirigible air fleet had begun. During the summer of 1930, a Congressional committee vigorously debated whether to establish the base in San Diego or Santa Clara County. Washington D.C. officials were extremely reluctant to establish an air base in mountainous terrain, as Mountain View's name implied. Even though there were no peaks nearby, the advocates for the Santa Clara County base began referring to the location as Sunnyvale, a more bucolic sounding name.

Rapid Service Station in Old Town, with the Mancini family circa 1930, on El Camino Real near Bay Street. Next door is Enterprise Hall, the Odd Fellows Lodge, and much later it was occupied by Steve's Grocery.

The Sunnyvale base committee had powerful supporters in Washington. Colonel Charles Lindbergh, Admiral William Moffett, and Commander Charles E. Rosendahl each informed the Congressional committee that they believed the Sunnyvale site would make the better base. They proposed that the base be called Naval Air Station (NAS) Sunnyvale. The San Diego site had the support of the Secretary of the Navy.

Congressman Arthur Free, one-time Mountain View City Attorney who represented Santa Clara County in Congress, introduced the "Free Bill" to establish the base and to authorize $5 million for construction. On December 12, 1930, word came that the Congressional Naval Affairs Committee had chosen Santa Clara County for its dirigible air base. The Bay Area-wide effort to lure the Navy had been successful.

At 10 a.m. on that December morning, the loud steam whistle at Pacific Press shrieked, and the water works siren wailed in response. An auto parade formed at Castro Street and the highway which soon grew to a half-mile long. Walter and Bert Erichsen's grocery truck had a "venerable billy goat" wearing a sign that read 'Camp Kearny,' referring to the San Diego site that was not chosen.[208] The fire department joined with police cars blaring sirens and the schools let the children join in the revelry. The parade snaked along the entire length of Castro Street then turned back toward the highway and went on to Sunnyvale. When the parade reached Sunnyvale, more cars and trucks loaded with triumphant base supporters joined as it headed toward San José.

President Herbert Hoover, who was very familiar with the site since he had previously resided at Stanford, signed the Free Bill on February 20, 1931. In July, title to the land, which was held in an escrow account in the name of real estate agent Laura Whipple, was transferred to the United States Navy for $1. Groundbreaking for the base was held in October. "Bulldozers, power-scrapers, pile-drivers, excavation equipment, concrete mixers and scores of other construction units swarmed over the peaceful countryside."[209] A special rail spur running from the Southern Pacific tracks to the air base was installed to transport building material by locomotive to the mammoth Hangar One. Interestingly enough, this same rail spur provided a path for the light rail line built in the late twentieth century. The hangar rose out of an eight-acre concrete slab and at its peak stood 198 feet tall. Ten football fields could fit comfortably in the galvanized steel-sheathed structure. It was completed by the end of 1932, and along with thirty other smaller buildings, cost $2,250,000. A power plant cost $1,500,000, and a laundry was another $50,000.[210] Today it is an architectural and engineering wonder, listed as a Navy Historical Monument and on the National Register of Historic

Places. Back in the 1930s, it was nothing short of a futuristic phenomenon.

Before the hangar was complete, one of the Navy's dirigibles, the USS Akron, was slated to visit the new base. Whisman Road had to be widened to forty feet to accommodate traffic expected for the impending arrival. The dirigible appeared a little ahead of schedule before 7 a.m. on May 13, 1932. It hovered over the Bay Area all day then moored just after 7 p.m. One observer remembered:

> *Parking the sedan in an open field, we all got out and looked to the skies in eager anticipation. We were not disappointed, for in minutes the silvery craft was directly overhead, casting a giant shadow across the place where we stood. To be sure, I had never dreamed that something so large would fill the sky.*[211]

Unfortunately, when the *Akron* departed, it never returned to NAS Sunnyvale. It crashed in an electrical storm twenty miles off the New Jersey coast April 4, 1933. NAS Sunnyvale was commissioned on the 12th of that month and emotions ran high about the shocking loss of the *Akron*.

The brief, official commissioning ceremony began promptly at 11 a.m. Governor James Rolph, Jr. had been scheduled to speak, but state business forced him to remain in Sacramento. Some speculated that the Navy's loss of the *Akron* may have had something to do with the Governor canceling his appearance. As the "Star-Spangled Banner" was played, the colors

Castro City Grocery and gas station was one of dozen neighborhood groceries in Mountain View. It was located in the Castro City neighborhood, near today's Central Expressway and Rengstorff Ave-

were raised for the first time. A moment of silence was called in memory of Admiral William Moffett, and those who had died aboard the ill-fated *Akron*.

The official orders of the day were "Carry on!" Officers were given a special demonstration of Hangar One's gigantic doors. "Thirteen hundred twenty tons of girders and corrugated metal covering were silently creeping along iron rails as the two doors came together," said one news report. By 11:30, U. S. Naval Air Station, Sunnyvale at Mountain View, California was official. The abbreviated thirty-minute ceremony was over, and the five thousand attendees dispersed. A month later, the landing field was named in honor of Admiral Moffett, although the entire base was not christened NAS Moffett Field for nine years.

A farcical comedy "When Men Marry" put on by the Business and Professional Men to benefit local Boy and Girl Scout Troops in April 1935. Note that the entire cast was male.

Happy Landing Café, one of a number of businesses that sprang up along Bayshore Road at Moffett Boulevard, after the establishment of Moffett Field. Many of the businesses bore aviation-related names.

The shifting fortunes of the dirigible program meant that the air base had a precarious existence. The Navy's other dirigible, the *USS Macon*, made its appearance in the local skies in October 1933. The San Francisco *Examiner* headline proclaimed, "Navy's Sky Queen Sights Her New Domain on Western Sea."[212] Over the next year and a half, the *Macon*'s enormous, shadowy presence never ceased to amaze as it floated in and out of NAS Sunnyvale. Its crew took the airship out over the Pacific on maneuvers, practicing long-range reconnaissance and spy tactics. The drills underlined the airship's role as the guardian angel of the Pacific fleet.

That role would be shortlived. While returning to NAS Sunnyvale from maneuvers on February 12, 1935, the *Macon* crashed off the California coast at Big Sur. Evidently some important repairs had been delayed, causing the disaster. Her descent to the sea was slow enough that all but two of the eighty-two crew members were rescued. Dirigible proponents could not convince Congress nor Navy brass to continue to invest in a rigid airship program. The *Macon*'s demise caused the Navy to scrap the dirigible program. The U.S. military never built another rigid airship.

In October 1935, the Navy transferred NAS Sunnyvale to the Army. It became a training ground for the Army Air Corps (later called the U.S. Air Force). In 1941, a private named James Stewart arrived at the base for basic training. As a civilian, he was a popular Hollywood movie actor and his occasional visits to Castro Street

businesses caused a stir. By the time he wrapped up his military service at the end of World War II, he achieved the rank of Major General. The base remained under the jurisdiction of the Army until 1942 when, once again, the Navy needed it as a base for offshore air patrols.

Construction of the Great Bayshore Highway had begun in 1924, just south of San Francisco. The course of the road was surveyed and built, piece by piece, in a southerly direction much as the railroad had in the previous century. It was 1930 before the highway reached the Mountain View area, and when the deal was struck to establish NAS Sunnyvale, the projected route of the Bayshore Highway had to be shifted to the south. The new route skirted the proposed base, but it would cut through a more populated area than previously planned, with small farms and homes at Terra Bella Acres.

Construction of the Bayshore was not complete in time for the grand arrival of the *Akron* in 1932, so a temporary road was paved to guide traffic around a loop to prevent a massive traffic jam.[213] Sunnyvale and Mountain View each wanted to be the first with an arterial street to the base. Mountain View succeeded and officials were quick to assure citizens that acquisition of the land to build Moffett Boulevard would not raise taxes and estimated the total cost for the portion of the road within city limits at $7,500.[214] Mountain View dubbed Moffett Boulevard "the gateway to Mountain View" and in the fall of 1933, a new neon road sign was hung over the Bayshore Highway at Stierlin Road with an arrow pointing to town.[215]

Both the establishment of the air base and the construction of the Bayshore Highway brought whole new array of businesses to Mountain View. Happy Landing Coffee Shop provided a hot meal and friendly service, while the Base Hotel, (formerly the Hotel St. Anne) on the 800 block of Villa Street offered basic accommodations. Some bars and brothels sprang up and their rougher clientele demanded more police activity. Other more legitimate businesses capitalized on the new base including the Air Base Cleaners, the Air Base Creamery, the Air Base Garage, and the Air Base Shoe Shop, just to name a few.

Many residents found employment at the base, but its influence on Mountain View was not only an economic one. It also had a profound social impact with servicemen frequenting churches and social functions in town. Many marriages resulted from military men matching up with local girls. The community quickly developed a keen allegiance to the base and to the Navy.

It is not surprising then, that when the *Macon* crashed and the Navy pulled out of the base, there was a psychological ripple in Mountain View. High hopes and expectations that people had harbored for the new base were dashed. Business slumped, the air base-named enterprises either changed their names or moved out of town, deepening the Depression.

In 1932, Republican Arthur Free, the five-term California Congressman who had been a vociferous supporter of the air base, did not win re-election. He and many Republicans were ousted when Franklin Delano Roosevelt was elected President. Under the Democratic New Deal, federal funds for public works projects supported jobs programs.

One Works Progress Administration (WPA) project in Mountain View was the construction of a small community building on Moffett Boulevard just north of the railroad tracks. The Junior Chamber of Commerce also contributed some money toward the building and hoped to be able to host events there. A city engineer designed a reinforced concrete building with an adobe façade, and workers made the adobe bricks on

site. A contest to name the building was held and high school student Kenneth Frick won, calling it *"La Casa de Monte Vista"* (the House of Mountain View). That name never caught on, and it has always been called the Adobe Building. This 1930s California mission-style building, commemorating the rancho days that had long since vanished, hosted many civic and social functions. During World War II it was used by the USO as an entertainment venue for Moffett servicemen, and later it was known as a teenagers' dance spot called Eagles Shack.

Despite the crash of the *Macon*, enthusiasm for flying gained momentum. Mountain View Airport was opened in 1936 at today's San Antonio and Middlefield roads, on the unincorporated outskirts of the city. It was owned and operated by Ted Simonic as Progressive Air Service. It was a flight school which offered flight instruction and aircraft maintenance and repair. Some locals took flight lessons there, and in August 1936, Manuel Nunes was the first student to complete his training and earn a pilot's license.[216] On May 19, 1938 the first and only airmail flight out of Mountain View took off for Mills Field, a tiny airfield that became San Francisco International Airport. The plane carried 1,002 pieces of mail that day, with Simonic at the controls.[217] The town of Mountain View had been allotted only one thousand 6-cent airmail stamps for the promotion of "National Airmail Week" in May of 1938. The airport was

Mountain View Fire Station, and Mountain View Water Works, 140 Franklin Street, 1927.

Left to right: Ugo Mancini, Chester Awalt, P. Milton Smith, Kenneth Slater.

sold in the early 1950s and transformed into a residential subdivision.

Newspaper editor Pop Smith had been chronicling Mountain View for over thirty years. He had written about incorporation in 1902 and about the new Pacific Press plant in 1904. He lived through the 1906 earthquake and witnessed the post quake development boom. He saw the town through a world war and the establishment of the South Shore Port in 1923. Then he helped usher in the U.S. Navy.

In many ways, Smith was the narrator of the town's history. He wrote a series of historical articles during the 1930s about local ranches and businesses. The articles that Smith wrote remain among the best descriptions of that era in Mountain View's history. He employed a cub reporter, Alan Cranston, and sent him out into the community to come up with stories. The 1932 graduate of Mountain View High School went on to become a U. S. Senator from California.

In 1932, Smith wrote an article about old Yuen Lung. The aging merchant returned to his native China at the age of eighty-five, and died only a month after his arrival there. Soon his former store was razed, and Mountain View's erstwhile Chinatown sunk into deep decline.

One article highlighted the Bubb ranch, almost 170 acres of orchard property cultivated by Benjamin Bubb's grown sons William and Charles. In the first thirty years of the twentieth century, the ranch's fortunes waxed and waned with the demand for fruit and effects of the weather. Smith predicted that the ranch would be subdivided and sold for homes in the near future.[218] Indeed, the First Presbyterian Church, whose membership included the Bubbs, built here in 1959 and sold its downtown church to the city. A school also occupies the former Bubb ranch.

While the automobile had been very popular early in the century, it began to be viewed as a necessity. Auto-related businesses found plenty of customers. Tito Fanucci, a native of Italy, purchased a two-hundred-foot frontage on El Camino of the Graham property to open a garage and service station in 1922. He was an enterprising sort, and in 1925 began to operate bus service from Mountain View to Oakland over the brand-new Dumbarton Bridge. During the 1930s, Fanucci expanded his operation, and by 1937 opened a new service station and an auto dealership. The family lived on the second floor of the premises. During the 1950s a new showroom was added and the Carl Simpson Buick Company opened on that site.

Redwine Auto, occupants of the former Prune and Apricot Exposition building, sold to Mark Tuban at 492 Castro Street. Redwine continued repairing tractors, and Tuban sold cars. Rollie Petty, who had been working for his father-in-law, Samuel Redwine, at Redwine Motor Company, was appointed postmaster in Mountain View in 1933. Nine years later he was given the post for life. Petty served as Mountain View's postmaster for thirty-one years.

In the mid-1930s, the garage portion of the exposition building was taken over by Pearson Automobile Company, a Chevrolet dealer that had been at California and Castro streets since 1919. Then in 1939, the whole operation was taken over by Pearson Auto, selling Chevrolets and outfitting fire trucks. In 1964, Pearson Chevrolet moved to El Camino Real in Sunnyvale, and the former exposition building was razed.

In 1940 Ugo Mancini, the proprietor of Mancini Motors, a De Soto and Chrysler dealer, bought a huge automobile exhibit that was part of the 1939 Golden Gate International Exposition World's Fair at Treasure Island from the Chrysler Corporation. The fifty-two foot high tower, topped with a huge, revolving globe bespoke the grand style of business Mancini sought to carry out. Mancini sold a portion of the exhibit for scrap, then transported the steel, twenty-ton tower and the two hundred-pound globe to Mountain View. It halted traffic on the Bay Bridge and took a crew of eight highway patrol officers to direct traffic. The tower was a distinctive Mountain View landmark until it was demolished in the mid-1970s. Mancini Motors remained in Mountain View until 1971 when it moved to Sunnyvale.

The fruit industry was hard hit during the Depression. Farmers tried to eke out a living. Although their profits were low, they had to hire workers to harvest the fruit. Many workers were "Okies" who had been displaced from the south central states by a devastating drought. Some farm workers came from Mexico. Hundreds of Filipinos were also employed in the valley during the 1930s. They had come to California because of poverty in the Philippines and promises of farm work here. Although they were American nationals, these young, single men faced great hostility and prejudice because many American citizens felt the Filipinos were stealing their jobs. One Filipino farm worker struggled to keep up with the demanding work: "In picking pears we got twelve [pickers] or more. All Filipinos. But in picking tomatoes we are thirty. And it happened that I am the slowest picker. I pick only forty boxes a day because it is too heavy. And I almost cry."[219] Many Filipino farm workers lived in Mountain View's former Chinatown, at Hotel Tabalaya. It was rundown boarding house, but a better alternative than camping in the fields.

Some Japanese families in the Mountain View area worked their own land or farmed as sharecroppers. One Mountain View resident, Rin Abey, described her farm work during the 1930s:

> I used to go out to the farm at seven o'clock in the morning. My husband, who was working outside on his own to supplement our income, came home at five o'clock. Then he helped me with the sorting of the raspberries and took them to the Sunnyvale Natureripe Association. I had six children at this time, but because they were all going to school, I didn't rely on their help. I hired workers.[220]

And a Japanese man said,

> I think the most difficult time was around 1933 to 1935, during the Depression. Every year I used to get six Filipino boys to work for me. It was a problem to have enough

money to pay their wages. I was raising beans, celery and other vegetables. The times were tough but I couldn't farm by myself, I needed workers. They worked for ten cents an hour, ten hours a day. It was very hard to meet the payroll.[221]

The effects of the Depression were felt more dramatically by some than others. Local bank officials knew that plans were in the works to expand Moffett Field so they would not loan to farmers leasing that land. They believed the farmers would be forced off the land before harvest time and therefore would not be able to pay back a loan. Italian immigrant Lorenzo Cerutti was one of those tenant farmers, and his home at Central and Moffett Boulevard was foreclosed by the Bank of America. Cerutti took out his frustration by creating a bomb out of ten sticks of dynamite and blew up the old stone bank on an August evening in 1938.[222] The explosion inflicted serious damage to the bank, but since it was closed, no one was injured. Cerutti was sent to San Quentin, and he lost his home and family. Eventually he became the warden's personal gardener, and upon his release, he returned to Italy.[223] Today the Mountain View Historical Association has a piece of marble from the blown-up bank in its artifact collection.

Canneries attempted to buy fruit from farmers at the lowest possible price in order to keep themselves in business. Canneries reduced wages to stay afloat, which did not sit well with workers. Several attempts to unionize cannery workers were made during the 1930s. In February 1933, a series of open-air meetings was held in a vacant lot north of the railroad tracks on Stierlin Road. Matt Huotari and Elizabeth Nicholas, an ardently pro-union cannery worker, spoke at one of the meetings. The newspaper identified both Huotari and Nicholas as "reds," and the columnist referred to "that Nicholas woman," leading two hundred men, women, and children in a hunger march to demand more work and better pay.

When Officer Fred Jarvis saw the growing demonstration, he attempted to arrest Nicholas and Huotari. According to the newspaper, a "free for all" broke out, with "members of the city council, Deputy Constable Shanklin and a number of citizens" participating.[224] A Mountain View high schooler, Bob Kankel, who got caught in the melee, was stabbed. The constable ordered the fire trucks to bring hoses to disperse the crowd. Five arrests were made, including Huotari and Nicholas. The two hundred demonstrators slowly dispersed before the water was turned on.

Despite the grueling orchard work and uncertain employment at the canneries, the orchard era in Santa Clara County is often fondly remembered. Roberta Bubb Sweeney later recalled, "The orchard was so beautiful when the trees were in bloom in the early spring. There was a different beauty in the late summer, when the prunes turned purple-ripe and dropped to the ground. . . . [and] the fragrant smell of fruitwood when the pruning was done in the fall and winter and the debris was burned in little piles throughout the orchard."[225] Farmers and merchants alike believed that fruit farming would remain the mainstay of the region's economy.

But Mountain View was approaching another milestone. Along with all of Santa Clara Valley, it was about to leave the orchard era behind. Even though the air base did not appear to be much of a success at the end of the 1930s, its accessibility to the Pacific would make it a strategic necessity during the war. Construction of Hangar Two and Hangar Three, at a cost just over $4.4 million, was completed in record time to house patrol blimps protecting California's coast. The base, along with the presence of a new space agency and Stanford University, tipped the scales toward a technological future instead of an agricultural one.

CHAPTER 6

THE SPACE AGE

THE SEEDS OF THE SPACE AGE WERE PLANTED when Congress allotted $10 million for an aeronautical research center and Ames Research Laboratory was established in 1939 next to Moffett Field. The National Advisory Committee for Aeronautics (NACA, later known as NASA), named the facility for the former NACA chairman, Dr. Joseph Ames. It immediately began making advances with its wind tunnels in flight and turbulence techniques. Within a decade, the work there enabled a pilot to fly faster than the speed of sound.

While work at Ames picked up speed, next-door-neighbor Mountain View remained a slow-paced little town of about 4,000 residents. In recalling that era, Mountain View City Historian Barbara McPheeters Kinchen recalled, "Everything you'd ever want was within a few blocks. Up until the 1940s, Castro Street had everything you needed—stores, city hall, high school, pool halls, liquor store, drug stores, garages, banks, theatre, hotel, and professional offices. You did not have to go anywhere else to get what you needed."[226]

NACA-Ames Laboratory, 1940 (later it was renamed NASA-Ames). National Aeronautics and Space Agency (NASA) absorbed NACA and the Space Age was officially launched.

Although Ames and Moffett were becoming influential in the local economy, Pacific Press still maintained a strong foothold. The mayor from 1942 until 1944 was Pacific Press's Charles Lake. After he retired from the Press, he was City Clerk from 1950 to 1951. An invisible, but real line still divided Castro Street: the west side had an Adventist influence where no liquor was sold, and on the east side non-Adventists lived and worked.

But the small-town atmosphere was about to change. Many businesses did not survive the Depression. At the onset of World War II, Walter L. Erichsen closed his grocery store and went to work at Moffett Field managing Navy supplies. Charles Milani also went to work at Moffett and family-owned grocery stores gave way to chain stores like Purity and Safeway that had been growing in popularity.

In 1940 the Mountain View Police Department had four officers, commanded by acting Police Chief Art Excell who had been with the department for eight years. "He built it from a three-man small town force to a well organized police agency," reported a history of the police department.[227] Arthur Nielsen joined the force in 1941 and was paid $125 per month. That year the police department purchased a Chevrolet Master Delux sedan from Pearson Automobile Company for $610. An AM radio was installed in it so officers did not have to keep visual contact with the red light on Castro Street, but could receive alerts while patrolling other areas. In order to make a report, the witness or victim still needed to call the Mountain View Water Department on Franklin Street. The water department in turn called the Palo Alto Police Department with the message. The Palo Alto Police Department broadcast the message, but it was received in the patrol car only if the AM radio was tuned to the highest band. There were no two-way radios in Mountain View police cars until 1948, and police call boxes were installed at two Castro Street locations in 1952.

One of the department's most important jobs was to protect the Moffett Field payroll. Sometimes as much as $1 million in cash was sent from San Francisco on a Southern Pacific rail car and unloaded at the train depot. The government provided no armored car or other security. Mountain View police officers loaded the moneybags onto small carts and pulled them from the station, down Castro Street, to the bank. When the Navy picked up its payroll, it provided armed guards with jeeps to transport the cash to the base.[228]

World War II was a harbinger of change for Mountain View. Pearl Harbor, home of the U.S. Pacific Fleet, was bombed by the Japanese in a relentless barrage on Sunday morning, December 7, 1941—a day, as President Franklin Roosevelt proclaimed, which would live in infamy. On that Sunday afternoon, after hearing the news, Mountain View High School's Dean of Boys, Irval Carter, rode his bicycle to his school office and counted how many students of Japanese descent he had on the roster. He worried about retribution against the 107 Nisei—Japanese Americans born to immigrant parents—who were students at Mountain View High School—fully one in seven students. Later Carter recalled, "They weren't foreigners. They grew up here."[229]

President Franklin D. Roosevelt issued Executive Order 9066, an official proclamation ordering the evacuation of all West Coast residents of Japanese ancestry to internment camps. Irval Carter's worst fears were being realized. Fremont Township Constable Chris Madsen strictly interpreted the order and aggressively "apprehended" Japanese aliens. It was a confusing time when non-Japanese Americans were torn between compassion for their neighbors and fear of sabotage from "enemy aliens."

A Mountain View Japanese American recalled that:

One evening, our house was shot into and the bullet missed my father's friend by inches. Many restrictions on our movements began to inconvenience us. We were ordered to leave Mountain View on May 22, 1942. We left the farm in the hands of Louis Pia who took care of it for the duration. We were fortunate in that we were able to come back to the farm in 1946.[230]

A few local Japanese families were spirited away to Utah by local Adventist sponsors. Appar-

The Cinema Theatre was located at 892 Dana Street and was owned by Antonio Blanco. This theatre began showing Spanish language movies in the 1940s.

ently the Mountain View Seventh Day Adventist Church members, because of their pacifist beliefs, searched out and found Mormons living on Utah ranches to host Japanese families. Some Japanese evacuees spent the duration of the war working on private ranches rather than in the government-run internment camps. One beneficiary of this church plan was Dorothy Kobayashi. "We didn't go into camp. My parents pulled us out of school one day. . . . We left everything in charge of the two steady Filipino

Mt. View Theatre, Mountain View's movie house, 1957, and a view of Castro Street looking south.

workers, Bautista and Abayone. They were instructed to finish the harvest and take care of the ranch. They stayed for four years."[231] Dorothy's family found their property intact when they returned.

Most Japanese families did not find private sponsors. Of the thirty-eight students in the grammar school graduating class of 1941, twelve were ordered to camps with their families.[232] On May 22, 1942, trains departed from Mountain View Station destined for Southern California for transfer to internment camps in Arizona, Wyoming, Colorado and Utah. Mountain View High School students sitting in class could hear the train whistle blast as the cars pulled out of the station full of families from the community. The Japanese language school was disbanded and the property was used by the Girl Scouts.

American-born Japanese youths in internment camps were drafted into the U.S. Army even as their families remained interned. At least one Japanese American Mountain View High School student was killed in action: Staff Sergeant Iwao Yamaji died at Anzio Beach in Italy. Nineteen other Mountain View young men also lost their lives fighting in World War II. A plaque was created to honor all those who lost their lives in the wars of the twentieth century, and it has become part of today's City Hall Plaza.

On the home front, the war effort required rationing of food and commodities that were in short supply. The Mountain View Ration Board was part of a national network of rationing over-seers. Mountain View resident Edna Thompson, who worked for the ration board during the war, described the policies and procedures of the Mountain View Ration Board at 215 Castro Street. It had a counter across the width of the office that was staffed by at least two clerks. The ration board consisted of a chairman and a vice-chairman and four 4-person panels who made decisions about whether to approve particular requests. The work of the ration board was very labor intensive. Each ration stamp or book that was issued was registered in a ledger that was reconciled with the supply of books and stamps at the end of the day.

Small booklets with coupons or pages to be stamped that were issued for gasoline, meat, dairy products, coffee, and other items such as tires and shoes. Gasoline was a coveted commodity, and each car was issued an "A" book. A "B" book would allow for more gas. Farmers were issued a "T" book to fuel tractors and farm equipment. Toward the end of the war even clothing was rationed. Grocery stores were required to honor food rations stamps, but restaurants were not. As Thompson recalled, "The government allowance to wives of GIs was $50 per month, which would hardly pay rent."[233] Building was all but halted during the war years because materials were consumed by the war effort.

Residents supported the Red Cross, planted victory gardens, and managed to go without pantry staples that, until recently, had been plentiful. High school students made model airplanes in class to help learn to spot particular enemy aircraft. A tank at Camp Beale was christened *Mountain View*. USO dances at the Adobe Building were the social highlight of an otherwise serious era.

News from the battlefield was sketchy, and families nervously awaited news of their loved ones. Marine Sergeant Harry Pinto, a young man from Mountain View, found himself as one of the "Battling Bastards of Bataan," or BBBs as they were known. The appellation was roughly translated to mean the men had "no mama, no papa and no Uncle Sam." As a Japanese prisoner of war, he endured the Bataan Death March. Pinto contracted malaria, scurvy, hepatitis and dysentery while his legs were covered in ulcers. Ultimately he survived, but his experiences and those of his comrades were so horrific that only once could he be cajoled into speaking publicly about them, when he gave a presentation to the Mountain View Historical Association. After the war, Pinto worked as assistant to the county recorder.

On V.J. (Victory in Japan) Day, August 14, 1945, all business firms and taverns were ordered to close in celebration of the long awaited announcement and in an effort to maintain public safety. Mayor C. Newton Higdon issued a proclamation which was printed in the *Register-Leader*. It read:

With the cessation of hostilities in the far Pacific but a matter of hours, and in accord with action taken by other communities throughout the country, I hereby proclaim a period of 24 hours be set aside for a joyous celebration of conclusion of hostilities on all fronts. Business houses generally will observe this day-long period by remaining closed. Taverns will comply with the request of state officials that their places of business likewise close and citizens generally will join the nation and world in giving thanks that all aggressor nations now have been overcome and our officials be given power to make peace as they have made war. C.N. Higdon, Mayor.[234]

Even after the war, the Navy continued to have a strong presence in Mountain View. In 1944, the Navy leased Dr. Henry W. Milo's Mountain View Hospital and home. The surgery center was remodeled into a duplex at a cost of about $30,000, while the outbuildings were turned into bachelor officers' quarters.[235] Today a Taco Bell sits on the site of the former Mountain View Hospital.

After the war many Japanese families returned. Some had lost everything, but most tried to pick up where they left off before the war. Mountain View flower grower Roy Ozawa recalled, when we came back "we found a place in San José and were there for three years. . . . Then we came to Mountain View. . . . we grew and shipped our own chrysanthemums in the beginning, but later on we just became the growers."[236] Several Japanese families established flower farms, and were the first customers to the Meyer family who came to Mountain View and purchased Pritchett Electric in the late 1940s. The flower growers hired Meyers to wire green

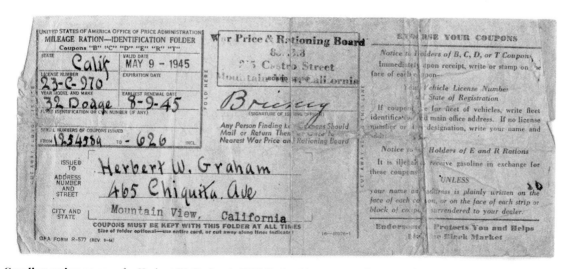

Gasoline ration coupon for Herbert W. Graham's 1932 Dodge. Many commodities and food stuffs were rationed throughout the war, and ration stamps were required to procure these products.

houses, and to install lights and fans to warm carnations and mums.[237]

Ethnic diversity was always a conspicuous characteristic of Mountain View. However, the San Jose *Mercury* said it was an unattractive trait: "Mountain View is an old community. . . . and there has long been one complication tending to obscure a little of its character. . . . This complication is the presence of an extraordinarily large number of distinct nationality groups."[238] Individual ethnic groups formed social and religious clubs and organizations that provided a community network.

Mountain View's mix of racial and ethnic groups was most visible at the high school. Martin Spangler, Jr., who was a student at the time, recalled, "You went to school with Spanish, Okies, Slavs, Japanese, and Portuguese."[239] His list includes immigrants, native-born Americans, and newcomers to California. He emphasized that the young people of many backgrounds associated at the school and were able to get along together.

But everyone did not view the mix of cultures so positively. During the war, Mexican men had been brought to California as farm workers. The *Bracero* (literally, arm or laborer) Program was implemented by both the U.S. and the Mexican governments. While some California farmers welcomed the new labor pool, many American workers resented the presence of the Mexicans. The so-called "zoot-suit" riots erupted in Los Angeles in 1943 between American military men and Mexican youths, and the disharmony extended throughout the state. The youth were called "zoot suiters" because of their distinctive broad-shouldered jacket and tapered pants. In Mountain View, there were conflicts between "zoot suiters" and local Caucasian juveniles. In 1944, Police Chief Art Excell requested a new jail because the number of arrests had increased with this problem. "Hotel Excell is full to overflowing," the newspaper noted.[240]

There was a significant increase in Mexican immigration during the 1940s. Many were farm workers or cannery workers. A Mexican woman described the farm work her family did before they found a home in Mountain View:

I was eight years old. Before that we were regular fruit tramps. . . . We went to the vineyards and then cut apricots. I didn't do it myself, but my mother and my sister did before my mother became blind. They cut apricots, peaches, and pears. . . . We had to stabilize somewhere. We came to Mountain View.[241]

Another recalled,

Mountain View has always had its pockets of poverty, and that's where Mexican families tended to congregate. I remember during the harvest season it was not unusual to visit a family at their campsite because they would come into town and make friends. At one time we were the campers, and now we lived in town.[242]

Club Estrella, formed through Saint Joseph's Church, was one of a few social and religious Mexican groups established in this era. It organized festivals and marched in parades, and celebrated *Las Mañanitas*, (literally, the early morning celebration) the traditional celebration of the feast of Our Lady of Guadalupe.

When former migrant workers came back from the war, they sought out other kinds of work.

When the war was over, my brothers did not want to go back to migrating. They wanted to work in jobs that were more reliable. At first, they started to work in canneries. After the canneries, they branched out and started working in other industries.[243]

As a teenager, Martin Spangler, Jr. worked at the Martin Jelavich family ranch where he hauled fruit, drove a tractor, and worked as a tag checker. He hole-punched the tags hanging round the necks of the Mexican farmer workers for each bucket of apricots they picked. The Jelaviches also had twenty or so Russian women and children come down from Russian Hill in San Francisco to work the orchards and cut 'cots. The babushka-wearing women set up makeshift tents for themselves and their children in the orchard for the season while their husbands remained in the city to work. The end of the season was celebrated with a big party for the Russians, complete with lamb shish kabob.[244]

Martin Jelavich's son, William, operated Robleda Packing Company with his wife Doll. It was a small fruit packing business that specialized in hand-packed and gift-wrapped dried fruit. The local press called the operation "the spiritual descendent of the once numerous firms which sold the lush fruit and nuts of the Valley of Heart's Delight."[245] William Jelavich also was Mountain View's mayor from 1968-70 and held a council seat for almost thirteen years.

A large number of Portuguese immigrants settled in Santa Clara County and Mountain View. Many worked in the canneries, as farm workers, dairymen, or owned orchards themselves. An annual religious festival, *Irmandade de Festa do Espirito Santo* (Brotherhood of the Festival of the Holy Ghost or I.F.E.S.) was celebrated in private homes in MountainView beginning in 1926. By 1929 the crowds were too large for a home, and a club was formed to buy a property at 432 Stierlin Road. The newspaper reported that this "organization which has its own buildings and ground now just north of the railroad on Stierlin Road, is the original Portuguese religious organization here."[246] Eventually there were two Portuguese societies in Mountain View; one on Stierlin Road and another on Villa Street. The annual celebration of the feast of the Holy Ghost, which continues today, includes a religious service, music, dancing, a parade, and an elaborate meal.

Mountain View's Chinatown had been in serious decline for years. In March 1946 several buildings there were engulfed in flames when a fire raced through a laundry, a boardinghouse, one store, and a restaurant. The Mockbee-owned properties at View and Villa streets had become very rundown and burned easily. The newspaper reported that more than sixty people, most of them Chinese, were displaced by the fire. Portable kerosene heaters in the recently condemned structures caused the blaze.[247]

In the postwar era, the nation's burgeoning suburban middle class enjoying new-fangled consumer products such as television, dishwashers, and frozen foods. In retrospect, the 1950s can appear a bucolic era of simpler, slower-paced, and less conflicted times. At the time, however, people's sense of security was overshadowed by the Korean War, a heightened threat of nuclear war, mean-spirited anti-communism campaigns launched by Senator Joseph McCarthy, and every parent's fear—polio. Locally, as in other communities across the country, the postwar suburban trend was supported by the employment of married women. In 1950, thirty-one percent of the labor force in Mountain View was female.

For Mountain View, the 1950s brought the most rapid and dramatic changes of any decade in the twentieth century. The small, working-class multi-ethnic town that was so heavily

influenced by the adjacent Navy base at Moffett Field had 6,500 residents. By the end of the decade, its population would multiply to 31,000.

An economic survey that the City of Mountain View compiled in 1953, included a list of retail and service businesses in the city. There was one fix-it shop, one heating contractor, and one taxi. There were twenty-one grocers, eleven barbershops, and fifteen service stations. Between the two were more modest numbers of clothing stores, ice-cream parlors, jewelers, and lunch counters. The eight real estate agents were a significant increase from William P. Wright's office that had handled most business in town. Products manufactured in Mountain View in the early 1950s were religious books and pamphlets, lumber, building material and playground equipment, light machinery, chemical fumigants, and window blinds. In addition, agricultural products were flower seeds, vegetables, fruit, catsup, and pickles.[248]

The economic backbone of 1950s Mountain View was Moffett Field, with between 5,000 and 6,000 personnel and an annual payroll of $24 million. Ames Laboratories came next, with 1,200 employees and a $6 million payroll. Pacific Press Publishing employed 190 people with a payroll of $550,000. Other important employers were Hunt Foods which had purchased the California Conserving Company, familiarly known as the "pickle works," Teasdale Packing Company, and

the Gemello Winery which produced 50,000 gallons of wine a year and sold all of it in its own retail store.

Mountain View's persona was solidified by some of its popular small businesses. Linda's Drive-in Restaurant, Mancini Motors, Meyer Electric, J.C. Penney, and Monte Vista Drive-in and Mt. View movie theaters, gave the town its character. In 1953 there were seventeen churches in Mountain View and sixty-one civic

Label from Mountain View's Gemello's Winery

Monte Vista Drive-In, circa 1950s, on Grant near El Camino Real. Local families play on a merry-go-round before dark when the movie would begin at the drive-in movie theatre. Photograph by Raymond's Studio.

A building boom gained momentum throughout the 1950s, and in 1959 a new record was set for the number of building permits issued for new construction and remodels. The value of these projects totaled over $19 million dollars. Six million dollars was slated for construction of El Camino Hospital on Grant Road. A 1956 election instituted the formation of El Camino Hospital District. R. Edwin Hawkins was named hospital administrator and held that position for the next twenty years. In 1959, twelve industrial permits were issued along with twenty-six for commercial buildings. Residential construction kept pace: ninety-eight permits were granted for apartment buildings and ninety-nine for homes in Mountain View.[251]

The postwar population explosion in California induced many communities to rewrite their charters and set up municipal governments with professional city managers hired by elected city councils. Sunnyvale did so in 1949, followed by Palo Alto in 1950. In 1952 Mountain View became a chartered city. A fifteen-member board of freeholders led by James Cochran, formerly of Pacific Press and over eighty years of age, drafted a city charter. Approved by the citizens in January of that year, it expanded the city council to seven members and established the position of city manager. Chosen from a large pool of applicants, Mountain View's first manager was James Thomas, who had already been administering the city for six years as the public works director. His title became official with the new charter, and he served as city manager until 1954.

groups or clubs. A Buddhist Temple was built on Stierlin Road in 1957.

Realtor Bill Henderson, a towering six foot six inches, was the president of the chamber of commerce during the early fifties. The chamber operated out of a small building funded, in part, by the late Mary Rose Sladky, who bequeathed $5,000 to house the chamber of commerce. Henderson convinced the business community and local government to form a parking district to make Castro Street merchants easily accessible to the public.[249] At the same time, a parking lot was built on Hope Street for the Castro Street's branch of the Bank of America. In order to make way for the lot, a large, two-story house that had been built by real estate developer Walter Clark at the turn of the twentieth century was torn down.[250] The old house had been the Garliepp home and been in that family from 1911 until 1950.

One new commercial development downtown was very promising for its retail tenants. Palm Plaza, a modern strip shopping center, was built in 1956 on Castro Street not far from El Camino Real. Among its tenants were Yorkshire Clothes, a men's clothing store, United California Bank, Sprouse Reitz, a variety store, a barber, and a Lucky grocery store. Surprisingly, the center had a relatively brief life, from 1956 until 1987. Today, Kaiser Permanente medical building and parking structure occupy the site.

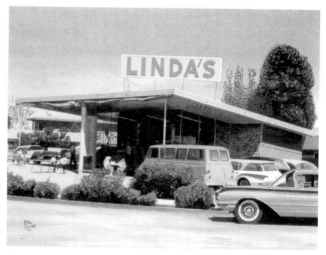

Linda's Drive-in on Escuela Avenue at El Camino signaled the beginning of car culture in Mountain View.

Officer Nielsen was promoted to police chief in 1952 and held that position until 1971. During his tenure, the department grew from 10 to 81 people. In 1951, voters had passed bond issues for construction of new fire and police stations at Franklin and Villa streets. The new station, completed in 1952, had a municipal courtroom, judge's chambers, and seven cells. A modern teletype machine was installed, improving communication with other departments throughout the state, along with its new two-way radio dispatch system.[252] There was not much violent crime in Mountain View and it was not until 1969 that a suspect was fatally shot by police. A man had taken an officer's gun and shot him. In response, other officers shot and killed the suspect. The fire department had five firefighters on payroll with twenty-eight volunteers on call. The department used six trucks and shared facilities and some equipment with the county's Fremont Fire District.

Martin Spangler, Sr., funeral director and one-time ambulance driver, was on the city council for ten years and was mayor of Mountain View from 1950 to 1952. It was a decade of staggering population growth and unprecedented land annexations. In 1961 he was appointed to the Santa Clara County Board of Supervisors as a replacement, and the next year, elected in his own right. Controversies about road construction and sewage treatment confronted him during his tenure as supervisor. His colleagues on the board held Spangler in high esteem and named a county school for the handicapped in his honor.

The city council race in 1952 was the first one where a woman was a candidate. Anita Sanborn listed her occupation as housewife, and launched a viable, albeit unsuccessful campaign for office. City Manager James Thomas suffered a stroke and resigned his position late in 1954. Philip Lawlor was hired to replace him, but was fired in 1958. Lawlor was perceived by some as not aggressive enough on growth. By the 1958 city council election, the platform of three candidates was for "progress" (meaning growth) and to

Ferry Morse Seed Company, circa 1950s.

demand the resignation of Lawlor. The three candidates—Carl Hansen, Jesse Nelson, and Harry True—won by a comfortable margin. Just after being sworn into office, they requested Lawlor's resignation. Lawlor declined to offer it, and the council voted to fire him. Then 29-year-old former finance director John O'Halloran took over. The San Francisco native served for fifteen years of extremely rapid growth. Mountain View's new city slogan was "A Planned Community with a Balanced Economy."[253]

Right after the war, many U.S. corporations opened West Coast branches of their businesses, creating great job opportunities. In 1951, San Francisco-based Ferry-Morse Seed Company established its West Coast headquarters on seventeen acres in Mountain View. It was the largest flower and vegetable seed mill in the world, with about two hundred employees and a $1 million annual payroll. But most of the new companies coming to Mountain View were not related to agriculture.

In 1953 Sylvania Corporation opened a small facility on Whisman Road snuggled in among the fruit orchards. Sylvania wanted to capitalize on Stanford's electrical engineering department, and that first year put thirty workers to the task of developing microwave tubes. The facility became the West Coast headquarters for Sylvania. A year later it built another laboratory as an electronics

division. Both were engaged in classified defense work for the federal government, and employed about 250 people developing special reconnaissance systems and electronic warfare equipment. In 1959 GTE Corporation bought Sylvania Electric Products, and the company became known as GTE Sylvania. By the early 1960s, it had five buildings and was the largest employer in Mountain View with 1,570 workers.

One of GTE Sylvania's more distinctive buildings was a nylon-inflated structure, known to the workers there as "the bubble." Its purpose was to provide a workspace to test and tune antennas. Initially thought to be a temporary

Governor Earl Warren is welcomed to Mountain View's Harvest Festival in July of 1950 when the city held a Harvest Festival which depicted 100 years of Mountain View and California history.

The "United Nations" was the theme of a pageant of 1,000 participants celebrated the contributions of the Mexican, Spanish, Filipino, and Japanese communities in a performance called "Quest for Golden Glory," 1951. Miss Mary Blasquez was crowned queen of the festivities and was prominent in the parade and ball. The parade, "Salute to the United Nations", had 4,000 participants and over 20,000 spectators. Old time Mountain View residents were feted and honored. Besides a public barbeque, there were softball games, soap box derbies, and dancing under the stars.

building, it served its purpose well enough that the company replaced the nylon exterior three times over its lifetime. "The bubble" was dismantled when the property sold in the 1990s.

New industrial developments required city services and utilities. Cities were reluctant to extend services to county residents, and saw an opportunity to reap tax benefits by annexing large areas of land. When it came to annexing property, San José was the most aggressive city in Santa Clara County. Its city manager created a team of annexation managers, which was nicknamed the "panzer division" for the speed with which it plowed through orchards and farms and annexed huge tracts to that city. Sunnyvale was also very aggressive and became the first city in the county to designate certain tracts of land specifically for industrial development.

Mountain View was more reluctant and joined the trend toward annexation later than either San

José or Sunnyvale. City Manager James Thomas claimed that annexation proceedings should be initiated by the residents on unincorporated land rather than by the city. But by the middle of 1952, Mountain View was also actively seeking to annex hundreds of acres without waiting for residents to initiate the process.

A promotional brochure proclaimed, "Mountain View is making its way, not necessarily as a distinctively industrial city, but as a city with enough industry to give it a balanced economy." Voters passed a $225,000 bond issue for a sewer system that would open up hundreds of acres of land for new residential subdivisions and industrial land sites. The sewer system became a crucial component in enabling Mountain View to annex a site at Evelyn Avenue and Mountain View-Alviso Road where Sylvania Corporation built. Sunnyvale was also trying to annex the property and claim Sylvania for itself. The Palo Alto *Times* reported a "tug-of-war" between the neighboring communities and noted that Mountain View was attempting to "fight fire with fire."[254] Industrial land prices in 1953 were from $3,500 to $5,000 an acre.

City Manager James Thomas appointed Dean Haug as a special assistant to facilitate annexations. He became the city's spokesman and he tried to convince residents of the advantages of expanding the city. A brochure titled "What Annexation Means to You" boasted of many benefits, including lower fire insurance premiums for those within city limits. County dwellers would have to pay the extra fire tax charged by the county.[255]

The availability of jobs spurred demand for housing, and residential real estate developers responded with subdivisions of new homes. While some of the city's new residents lived in brand new houses on land that had always been part of the city, others lived in areas that were added to the city during the process of development. The city tripled in size in just a few years. In 1953 and 1954 most of the unincorporated gap between Mountain View and its western neighbors, Palo Alto and Los Altos, was eliminated.

Joseph Eichler, a prolific home builder during the postwar era in the Santa Clara Valley, purchased forty acres on what had formerly been the Mountain View Airport south of San Antonio Road near Middlefield to build almost 175 houses. Palo Alto threatened to annex the property, but an agreement was reached between Eichler and Mountain View that led to the annexation of the development and surrounding acreage.[256] The distinctive layout and design of the Eichler homes, utilizing redwood and featuring atrium cores, has endured and the houses are considered significant examples of postwar California architecture.

A new subdivision built near Central Expressway and San Antonio Road required leveling the ancient Castro Indian mound dating from 760 B.C. Two Stanford University professors had examined and reported on the mound in the 1890s after reading in the local newspaper about a Mountain View schoolboy bringing a skull to school for show-and-tell. Over time the mound had been vandalized, but it was not destroyed until it was plowed under in the late 1940s for Mardell Way, Nita, Dell, and Aldean avenues.[257]

In the summer of 1953, five hundred acres to the west was added to Mountain View, including a haphazard area called Castro City. It had been laid out just after the 1906 earthquake, but by 1941 many lots were lost to delinquent taxes.

Mountain View Mayor William Jelavich (left) and City Manager John O'Halloran flank then Governor Ronald Reagan.

During World War II, some real estate agents bought the lots at low prices and moved cannery worker shacks onto the lots for wartime housing. At that time, a buyer could purchase a property for $150, with $10 down and payments of $5 per month. That neighborhood went through a period of deterioration during the 1960s.

In 1954 the largest annexation to date occurred when the Whisman annexation was approved: seven hundred acres between the Bayshore Freeway (Highway 101) and the Southern Pacific tracks and bounded by Moffett Boulevard on the west and Bernardo Avenue on the east were added to the city.[258] It enlarged Mountain View by between one quarter and one third. The area included land where Sylvania had just built new facilities. It was anticipated that this addition would comprise Mountain View's industrial center. It also included the former Swall ranch, 140 acres fronting the Bayshore Freeway and stretching down Whisman Road. Many entities wanted to purchase the land, but offers were rejected. Nellie Swall Wright, the widow of realtor William P. Wright, and her sister, Ada Swall McPheeters sold to the Industrial Land Corporation, a company made up of Mountain View businessmen. It is not an exaggeration to say that Silicon Valley mushroomed up from the Swall ranch. Indeed it

Permanente Creek flooded in 1955 and this new nearby neighborhood was inundated.

became the site of Fairchild Semiconductor, and much later Veritas Software.

Farmers voiced opposition to the annexation of the Whisman area because they feared that new city regulations would interfere with the operation of their farms. Mayor David Tripiano tried to assuage their fears, telling them that their farms would "not be disturbed" by the annexation. Tripiano had been elected to the council in 1952 at age 31, the youngest councilman to date.[259] His brother, Frank, was serving as chief of the Volunteer Fire Department at this time.

Dean Haug, assistant in the city manager's office, pointed out that some farmers in the area

Rex Manor neighborhood under construction during the 1950s. Note the prices on the sign: $6,975 and $7575.

actually supported the annexation.[260] Although the city was required to get signatures from twenty-five percent of the area's registered voters, it is doubtful that was done. Ralph Tracy, a Whisman Road farmer opposed to annexation, accused officials of gathering signatures primarily from renters and ignoring the wishes of the property owners. One advocate for annexation was Arthur Walker, a resident in the Whisman area and a builder by profession. He claimed if Mountain View did not proceed with the annexation, "we could find ourselves sitting in a ghost town."[261]

San Antonio Road had long been considered the unofficial boundary between Palo Alto and Mountain View. In the summer of 1954, Mountain View started annexation proceedings in the area of San Antonio Road and El Camino Real crossing the supposed boundary and infuriating its neighbor. Later, both Sunnyvale and Mountain View attempted to annex Moffett Field into their respective cities. Neither was successful and today each city's boundaries skirt the federal property.

Despite all the territory added to the city in 1953 and 1954, it was not until 1955 that the borders of Mountain View crossed Highway 101. Mountain View annexed a narrow strip of property running along Palo Alto's eastern boundary from the Bayshore to the bay. Strip annexations were commonplace at the time because state law held that any property directly contiguous to city boundaries could be annexed, avoiding costly court delays. Cities found that a strip of land would allow them to add a much greater area than annexations conducted parcel by parcel. Palo Alto claimed that Mountain View annexed the four-mile-long strip to the bay simply to stop Palo Alto from expanding to the east. City Manager Lawlor denied he was in a contest with Palo Alto.

In 1955 Mountain View Union High School District had added a second high school campus called Los Altos High School. Up until this time, Los Altos students had attended Mountain View High School. But in 1959 Mountain View and Los Altos were engaged in what the press labeled a "bare-fist" war over forty acres at Oak and Truman avenues, where a third high school was slated to be built. The third high school was named for Chester F. Awalt, who had been a school board trustee for forty-one years. The 1961 completion of Awalt High School, which served 1,500 students, made it possible for the

Bayshore Highway (today's Highway 101) looking east toward Moffett Boulevard before the overpass was built, 1957.

buildings at Mountain View High School on Castro Street to be completely remodeled and retrofitted for earthquake safety. During that year, the juniors and seniors attended classes at Awalt. Mountain View High reopened to students of all grades in the fall of 1962. A girls' gym was completed in 1949, and a new pool was built in 1979 and was named for long-time physical education teacher Anthony Calvelli who died that year.

More schools were needed for families moving into dozens of new residential developments. In 1953, 1,355 new homes were under construction in eleven new subdivisions with a price range of $10,200 to $18,000. Besides those houses, more than seventy apartment houses were available "for those non-gardeners who like to live near the country"[262] on what had been very carefully tended farms. Two hundred new homes were built at Rancho Village near El Monte and El Camino Real by Blackfield Construction Company. One resident nearby, in the Permanente Oaks neighborhood on the former Ira Higgins ranch, noticed: "Gradually the orchards disappeared. In back of our house was a strawberry patch which was removed and a cherry orchard was planted there. Then it was sold and we realized you can get much more money for a cherry orchard than a strawberry patch. That is 'progress.'"[263] In 1953 that neighborhood became part of Los Altos.

The schools could hardly keep pace with population growth. Whisman School District expanded by adding a school for the first time since its inception seventy-five years earlier. Crittenden School, which opened in 1949, was named for Albert M. Crittenden (1861-1958), a longtime district board member. He had been a staunch supporter of Whisman School, and in hard times took in boarders to keep the school open. Although he moved to Los Gatos, he remained active in Mountain View organizations and as a supporter of the school.

By 1953 over 1,000 children crowded into Whisman School's five classrooms and four pre-fabricated additions. In the fall of that year, both Powell and Theuerkauf schools opened, and Whisman went back to a comfortable three hundred students. The new schools were named for long-time district board members, Ernest Powell and Fred Theuerkauf.

Edith Landels School on Dana Street was built on the former Marion Peter Vidovich orchard and was dedicated in 1959. The elementary school was named for kindergarten teacher Landels, who had taught in Mountain View for forty-four years, all but her last year at the Dana Street School. Another longtime Dana Street School teacher, Victorine Klein, had a school named in her honor. Her thirty-two year teaching

Aerial view of intersection of Castro Street and El Camino Real, circa late 1940s. Castro Street runs from the middle left to the top right. El Camino Real runs from top left to bottom right. Mountain View High School (top) fronts Castro Street. Just to the south at the intersection of the two major streets is Fanucci & Sons automotive services. Diagonally across the street, the Mancini tower is in front of the car dealership. The other quonset-style building next to Mancini is Food City grocery store. Monson Drug Store fronts El Camino just above Food City.

Demolition of the Old Highway School at El Camino Real and Calderon Avenue in 1962. The Highway School, a 22 classroom stucco building, was opened in 1928. The two story school was located at El Camino Real and Calderon Avenue. The Highway School was condemned as unsafe in 1955 but it was used as the first campus for Foothill College until 1958. Foothill adopted the Highway School's mascot, the Owl. Finally, the building housed part of Lockheed Missiles and Space Company's growing operations.

career ended in 1934, and the Victorine Klein School on Ortega Avenue opened in 1966. Incredibly, Klein School remained open just a little over a decade. It was occupied by the Community School of Music and Art until 1987 when it was torn down. Today it is Klein Park. Few are the communities who can afford to build and staff a school for just ten years.

At the same time, as new schools were built to accommodate the increasing population, the Old Highway Elementary School property was condemned in 1955 because it was not earthquake-safe. For a while, Lockheed Missiles and Space used the former grammar school. Then, after some remodeling, the new Foothill Community College occupied the building. The former grammar school had a statue of an owl on the roof, depicting its mascot. Evidently the college took a liking to the owl and adopted it as its own mascot. In 1962, after Foothill Community College opened its permanent campus, the Old Highway Grammar School was torn down. Two Worlds commercial and residential development was built there and remains on the site today.

Religious groups also established new schools. Saint Francis High School, a Catholic institution for boys, and Holy Cross, its counterpart for girls, both opened in 1956. The schools merged into a coeducational high school in 1972. Saint Joseph's Catholic Church also opened an elementary school in 1952. When the parish became too large, it was divided in two, and Saint Athanasius Church was established with a school in 1959. The Seventh-Day Adventists maintained their elementary school, which had been in operation since 1906, and their high school, Mountain View Academy, which was established in 1922.

As the population exploded and communities in the valley tried to provide housing, schools, and services, the Silicon Valley was coming to fruition (most people would not even hear the words "Silicon Valley" for another twenty years). In 1955 William Shockley, a Stanford University alum and the co-inventor of the transistor, established Shockley Laboratories at 391 San Antonio Road in Mountain View. The fledgling company occupied the bare-bones building which had only a concrete slab floor. It was at Shockley Laboratories that silicon was first used in electronic components in 1956. That same year, Shockley and the other two inventors of the transistor,

Victorine Klein School, remained open just a little over a decade.

Walter H. Brattain and John Bardeen, were awarded the Nobel Prize in physics for their 1947 invention. Shockley hired several young engineers and scientists and worked out of Mountain View until 1961 when he moved his operation to Stanford Industrial Park.

Evidently Shockley did not manage his staff very well. In 1957, while still in Mountain View, eight of his employees quit and formed Fairchild Semiconductor, a pioneer microchip-maker and the West Coast subsidiary of Fairchild Camera & Instrument. Dubbed the "traitorous eight" by Shockley—Robert Noyce, Gordon Moore, Victor Grinich, Jay Last, Jean Hoerni, Julius Blank, Eugene Kleiner and C. Sheldon Roberts—played important roles in the evolution of Silicon Valley. William Shockley remained controversial throughout his life, particularly because he espoused the idea that whites were intellectually superior to blacks. His former employees' company, Fairchild Semiconductor, which opened in Mountain View, soon marketed the first commercial integrated circuit. The state-of-the-art research carried out there led to profound milestones on the way to the computer age.

When Fairchild decided to locate in Mountain View, the city welcomed the company of 350 employees with open arms. The company's building at 350 Ellis Street, became popularly known as the "rusty bucket" because of its color and overall appearance. Unfortunately, the term rusty may not have been simply a metaphor. At the time, the city did not impose any economic or environmental conditions on Fairchild and, after twenty years, the water in the surrounding neighborhood had become severely contaminated. Nevertheless, in the early days, no one anticipated toxic runoff, and many Silicon Valley spin-off companies had their genesis in that "rusty bucket." Today the nineteen-acre site has been transformed to a campus for Veritas Software.

The Wagon Wheel restaurant at Whisman and Middlefield roads became a popular hangout for Fairchild and Lockheed employees, frequented by CEOs and assembly line workers alike. There was so much conversation about work there, that many executives worried that trade secrets would slip out. "The leaks [of information] got so bad that top brass at Fairchild finally tried to prohibit his people from going there." But such socializing was an intrinsic part of the work culture of the valley. Two decades later, when the Wagon Wheel was shut down and the inside completely dismantled, one frequenter noted "is another part of the soul of the community lost too?"[264]

Left to right: Harry Pinto, Iwao Yamaji

Technology industries evolved so quickly that spin-off companies formed overnight. In 1967 GTE Sylvania expanded its Mountain View facilities and formed a laser technology division called the Electro-Optics Organization. That same year, Fairchild Semiconductor's general manager, Charles Sporck, quit to launch National Semiconductor. The next year, Robert Noyce, Gordon Moore and Andrew Grove left Fairchild to start Intel Corporation. In 1969, after W.J. "Jerry" Sanders was fired from Fairchild, he started Advanced Microdevices. A decade later, in 1979, Schlumberger Limited, a French company, bought Fairchild for $352 million.

Stanford Industrial Park was officially established in 1954. This novel approach to industrial development was dreamed up by Frederick Terman, a professor and Stanford's provost and dean of engineering. In 1951, Stanford University began leasing land to companies that had emerged from its electronics and engineering departments. The companies won Pentagon funding largely through Terman's efforts.

Mountain View Industrial Park was modeled on Stanford and developed by a San Francisco real estate firm. Brochures claimed the park was "strategically located on Bayshore Freeway and Stierlin Road. . . . the center of the San Francisco Peninsula." Building sites from a half an acre to twenty acres were available along Terra Bella Avenue near Middlefield Road, very near Terra Bella Acres that had been split by the construction of the Bayshore Freeway. Today it is home to research and development and pharmaceutical firms.

IBM wanted to build a large facility south of El Camino Real on what had been the Gest ranch, across from today's Saint Francis High School. The planning commission, chaired by Victor Calvo, hesitated to approve IBM's request inciting a lengthy political battle over the issue that resulted in IBM withdrawing its proposal. Calvo recalled that he supported "planned progress." He went on, "I know that sounds idealistic, but that's how I viewed it. I didn't think we should take every offer that came along. . . . it didn't hurt Mountain View, either. It focused our development plan."[265]

Calvo was the son of Spanish immigrants and had been raised on his family's farm near San

El Camino Hospital (center), circa 1960s. Photo taken from the Franklin Street water tower. Saint Timothy Episcopal Church complex is in the foreground, and Cuesta Park was developed on the open space between the hospital and the church. *Courtesy of Vivian Schultz.*

Antonio Road. After his term on the planning commission, he was elected to the city council. He served as mayor three different times during his council years from 1962 to 1968. Calvo went on to be elected to the Santa Clara County Board of Supervisors, and later served in the state assembly and the Public Utilities Commission.

In 1960, Mountain View had a population of just over 30,000 people and covered 8.3 square miles. The transformation of the landscape from farm town to suburb continued at a accelerated pace. "Two years ago, Mountain View's California Street was lined with cherry orchards. Well over a dozen delux-type apartment houses now stand where the trees once grew,"[266] noted the local newspaper.

In October 1957, the Soviet Union surprised the world with the successful launch of Sputnik I, a basketball-sized satellite that orbited the earth. The "space race," or rush to dominate outer space, had begun. In response, the U. S. launched its own small satellite, *Explorer* 1, and Congress created the National Aeronautics and Space Administration (NASA) to replace NACA. The space race, coupled with tense U.S.-Soviet relations, contributed to the development of the military-industrial complex. It was a complicated

web of contractors supplying the demands of the Pentagon in the interest of national defense. The space and aeronautics industries implemented many private sector electronics inventions in their supersonic and hypersonic projects. Research projects at NASA-Ames addressed planetary atmospheres, space exploration, and aeronautical issues such as turbulence and noise abatement.

The Vietnam War escalated through the 1960s and as it became more complicated, it cost far many more American lives than anyone had anticipated. Large-scale anti-war demonstrations took place throughout the nation, particularly on California's college campuses. Despite the concentration of defense industries in Mountain View, anti-war sentiment was not very obvious. In one incident in 1969, however, anti-war protesters firebombed the Army's recruiting office at Evelyn Avenue and Hope Street. The arsonists smashed windows and threw a full gasoline can rigged with a wick into the building.

The United States elected its youngest and first Roman Catholic President, John F. Kennedy, in 1960. His plans for a "new frontier" inspired tens of thousands of Americans. In Mountain View, where one-third of the population had moved into their houses in the previous twelve months, citizens embarked on their own "new frontier," literally and figuratively. During the 1960s, the postwar taste for "newness" that swept the country was manifested in "urban renewal." Both officially—with federal financial support—and unofficially, the trend was to demolish old buildings to be replaced with new, modern, and more usable structures. In many communities, entire downtowns fell to the wrecking ball.

The city promoted a "rehabilitation program" that called for city inspection of all buildings to determine public safety. Building inspectors and firefighters carried out the inspections, which began in 1961 and continued through 1964. If the inspectors determined that a building was beyond repair, the city would require the property owner to demolish it.

The rehabilitation plan was also required for the Castro City neighborhood, home to 130 families. The lots there were smaller than the current city standard of 6,000 square feet. They measured about 25' by 100' and commanded rents of about $30 per month. Rents in other neighborhoods were about $100. The city turned down federal urban renewal dollars for Castro City because it would have required razing all the houses and relocating the families, most of whom could not afford rent in other neighborhoods.

Displacing the residents was too high a price to pay for federal funding. Planning Commissioner Victor Calvo remembered, "We thought we could do better on our own than having the federal government telling us what to do."[267]

Mountain View's main business district remained intact, although many old structures, some of them with local historical significance, were torn down. The 1888-vintage Evelyn Avenue train depot was in serious disrepair, and the city council was increasingly frustrated that Southern Pacific Railroad was not taking action to remedy the problem. The railroad company initially wanted to improve the building, but the council wanted the rat-infested eyesore torn down and replaced. The city condemned it in an attempt to force the railroad to take action. Finally, Southern Pacific informed the city council of its intent to tear it down in 1959. In a thirty-day waiting period, there was almost no response from the voting public. Some commuters were dismayed that the station would be closed, but there were not many who wanted to save the building.

Southern Pacific submitted plans for a sheltered waiting area to replace the station, but the planning commission rejected the plan because it did not include restrooms. The council approved the plan, with one dissenter. Councilman Harry True said it was "the cheapest building they [S.P.] possibly can build. There is no other station

Hunt Foods processing plant, commonly known as "the Pickle Works" pickled cucumbers and produced catsup. The corrugated building was demolished in 1960.

Eleanor (Mrs. James) Dale with her beloved redwood trees in the background at the dedication of the Emporium Capwell Department Store on former Dale ranch.

department, the former social hall for the church behind the new City Hall. The fire destroyed many civic records. Then the old 1909 Town Hall that had been outgrown was razed to make room for a bank. Later the bank was converted to a restaurant and then was torn down in 2001.

Mercedes Castro, the last Castro to live at Villa Francisca, transferred the property to the city in 1958 to be used as a senior center or a historical museum. It was estimated that it would cost $39,000 to rehabilitate the old Castro home. City Manager John O'Halloran and other city officials were not enthusiastic about renovating the building. They did not have to ponder the fate of the building for long, because in March of 1961 a fire of suspicious origin burned the villa and gutted the first floor of the west wing. The second floor and the entire east wing remained undamaged. The fire inspector was never able to determine the cause, but he noted that whoever started the fire in the house locked the door behind him when he left. The inspector did not believe that a transient or negligent teenagers would bother to lock the door. The city manager recommended demolishing the building rather

between San Jose and San Francisco as cheap. I don't see why MountainView should be treated differently than any other city."[268] Ultimately, the hallmark of nineteenth century railroading, the hub of Mountain View Station's merchant community, and the former Awalt home, was bulldozed in 1959. Ironically, today's transit center, where light-rail and Caltrain converge, will be the site of a replica of the torn-down depot. In 2001 the city considered either buying a vintage station from a Central Valley town or having an exact replica built. Certainly preserving the former station in 1959 would have been more cost-effective than the $1.8 million set aside to begin to develop what will be called Centennial Plaza. Actual costs will likely be much higher.

In 1957 the congregation of the First Presbyterian Church on Castro Street sold its church and an adjacent manse to the city and purchased property for a new church at Cuesta Drive and Miramonte Avenue. In 1959 city offices were moved from the old Town Hall to the former church and used for council chambers and offices. There was a fire in 1959 in the planning

Mecedes Castro, daughter of Crisanto and Francisca Castro, last resident of Villa Francisca in 1963 at age 92. She died two years later.

THE SPACE AGE

than repairing it, and it was bulldozed. Rengstorff Park now surrounds the former site of the Castro home.

The home built by Letitia Kifer Taylor, the widow of hotel builder Samuel P. Taylor, in 1880 on El Camino Real was razed in 1960. It had been near the hotel and the old stagecoach stop, and the house had remained in the Taylor family for its entire existence. The Colonial Mortuary was built on the site of the old home.

Henry Rengstorff's former home at 1735 Stierlin Road also faced an unpredictable future. The last of the Rengstorff heirs to live in the house were Henry Rengstorff's grandson, Perry Askam, and his wife, Frances. After its purchase by the Newhall Land and Farming Company the dilapidated house was rented out. In the early 1970s, the Newhall Company tried to trade the Rengstorff House to the city in exchange for a zoning variance on three hundred acres north of Bayshore. The land company wanted to build town houses, but the city did not want residential development there.

The Rengstorff house was placed on the National Register of Historic Places in 1978. Mayor Richard Wilmuth favored spending $10,000 to begin restoration, but Councilman Matthew Allen thought the idea "complete folly."[269] In 1979 the City of Mountain View purchased the Rengstorff house for $1 and moved it out of the way of development and onto Shoreline Park land. In 1986 it was moved further north in

Shoreline Park to its current location, where it was restored. Today it is used for weddings and other events, and the second floor is administrative offices.

But by the end of the 1960s, perhaps in response to increasing demolition, a new historical consciousness emerged. Some buildings were designated as historical landmarks and listed on heritage inventories. Local promoters boasted that Mountain View had not abandoned its downtown and only focused on the suburbs, as its neighbors had. The city never used federal urban renewal funds, which would have required the demolition of old buildings.

In the rush to build more housing, city officials approved the construction of new apartment buildings right next to some of the city's oldest homes. The hodgepodge combination did not accomplish the city's goal to spruce up the old neighborhoods. It just made them confused and mismatched with high-density housing checkerboarded with single family homes. Even the forty-year old electric "Mountain View" signs marking north and south entryways to Castro Street were dismantled in this era. City officials felt the signs gave Mountain View the feel of a "small town," contrary to the modern city they sought to build. Some citizens wanted to transplant the signs to Rengstorff Park, but the parks and recreation commissioners declined.

Suburban growth was not an unmixed blessing for Mountain View, and while new homes were built and public services expanded, shopping areas built in outlying areas pulled the lifeblood out of Castro Street. San Antonio Shopping Center had been built with a Sears, Roebuck department store and Purity Grocery Store on San Antonio Road near El Camino Real. It was the first shopping area to compete with the traditional downtown. "Mt. View started to become a ghost town," recalled merchant Richard Meyer, "and lost its elegance. Luckily the bankers didn't move out."[270]

In 1966, a suburban shopping center was completed at San Antonio Road where Central Expressway turns into Alma Street at the Palo Alto border. Mayfield Mall was touted as "America's first venture into a fully carpeted, air-conditioned shopping center."[271] The three-level shopping mall had 407,000 rentable square feet "linked by silent, smooth running escalators." Some of its tenants were transplants from the old downtown shopping district, including J.C. Penney, Hart's, and Kitty O'Hara's, a woman's dress shop. The shopping mall was dedicated October 6, 1966. It survived less than twenty years.

Initially the planning department denied a permit to Emporium because of traffic problems, as well as the city's intention to keep major retail outlets on the west side of town between Mayfield Mall and San Antonio Shopping Center. Ultimately the council relented and unanimously approved the construction of The Emporium.

A four-level, $8.5 million Emporium department store, opened in 1970 on what had been the Dale family ranch. "The new store rises even higher than the 57-year-old oak tree planted there when he [Dale] owned the land that now adjoins Stevens Creek Freeway." The oak and a redwood were "all but lost among the tons of concrete," and the 1,250 parking stalls. Eleanor Dale attended opening day ceremonies, but "almost broke up the proceedings" because she was worried about the old trees. "I think they could use some water," she insisted, and waited for the chagrined officials to comply.[272]

The Old Mill Specialty Center was built not too far from Mayfield Mall, on the other side of Central Expressway and the railroad tracks. The three-story indoor shopping mall occupied thirty-six acres, featuring specialty stores that mimicked miniature, European-style streets. The grand opening was held in December 1976 after the movie theaters had been in operation for several months. A huge water wheel churned water into an imitation creek running down the center of the first level. The retail stores and theaters pulled the shopping and theater-going public away from Castro Street.

A plan to revitalize Castro Street began to be implemented in 1962. The $850,000 beautification project was funded by property owners, a state gas tax, and some storm drain and water bond funds. The street was widened to four lanes, new street lights were installed, intersections were signaled, and trees were planted. Individual property owners were also asked to give their buildings a "face-lift" to give the street a more modern look.

Meyer Electric took over the Penney's building at 278 Castro, which had been owned at one time by the McConnell sisters, Mrs. Earl D. Minton and Mrs. Alvin Brunhofer. "Mountain View has always had a strong banking infrastructure, willing to invest in downtown. The bankers had a lot of faith in the merchants."[273] But the chamber of commerce touted Mountain View as "the heart of the busy San Francisco Peninsula!" and exaggerated that "the 20 square-mile city of Mountain View has 3000 acres of undeveloped land."[274]

Seal of the City of Mountain View

Flying low over 101 at rush hour a P-3 approaches its landing at Moffett Field.

Downtown development continued through the 1960s. In 1964, a chamber of commerce building was built, where it remains today, behind the Wells Fargo Bank fronting Castro Street. A new addition to the library opened in 1966, with 28,000 square feet and room for 150,000 books. Pioneer Memorial Park was developed on what had been the Mountain View Cemetery. The park was built over the graves of early nineteenth-century settlers on land once owned by the Castros and deeded to the Cumberland Presbyterian Church which maintained it. When the city widened streets in 1930, it levied an assessment that the church was unable to pay, so the church transferred the land to the city in return for a verbal promise that the graves would never be disturbed. Years later, when the city wanted to put a street through the cemetery to access the Masonic Temple, no one could produce any documentation of the promise. Eleanor Dale, president of the historical association and whose husband's ancestors had been in Mountain View since 1850, appeared before the city council and accused the city of reneging on its commitment to maintain the cemetery. The street was never built, but in 1966 city workers built Pioneer Park, gingerly hoping against hope that they would not uncover any graves.

One particularly innovative development quickly became the town's "white elephant." The new International Environmental Dynamics (IED) Building, slated to be built at Castro and Mercy streets, was an eleven-story high-rise, making it the tallest building in the city. At a groundbreaking ceremony on October 8, 1969, one hundred civic leaders posed with shovels for the camera. The building design called for a process of building from the top down. Each of eleven floors was constructed on the ground then hoisted into place, starting at the top. It was, as one engineering journal quipped, "the house that jacks built." The innovative construction process was billed as a cost and time-saving method, and the unusual building was projected to cost $5 million. Watching the construction, from the top down, became a spectator sport in Mountain View.

But construction on the building was halted in 1971 because the contractor defaulted on loans on the property. The mortgage company foreclosed, but courts found that it had no foreclosure clause in its loan to the IED developers. Litigation on the property stretched out almost eight years, while the deserted skeletal building sat incomplete, and with a very dubious future. It was nicknamed

The International Environmental Dynamics (IED), later known as the Mountain Bay Plaza Building, was constructed from the top down beginning in 1969. It ran into financial problems and was not completed for a decade. Today it is the Mountain Bay Plaza and is fully occupied.

citizens and elected officials kept some measure of control as to how Mountain View would look as it was buffeted from outside forces, is remarkable in itself.

The space age had come into bloom, promising a rich harvest for many years to come. But the yield of the space program, the military industrial complex and high-tech industries, did not come cheaply. Plentiful jobs made local officials begin to focus on more earthbound concerns such as where the space age workers would live and how they would get to work.

the "dog house" because guard dogs were its only tenants.

The stalled project did nothing to attract new or lively development to the struggling merchants on Castro Street. "For a while it was just a big hole in the ground," merchant Richard Meyer recalled. He tried to put together some investors to buy the building, but found that "no one took Mountain View very seriously because of all the empty space on Castro Street."[275] Since its uncertain beginning, the building has undergone several remodels, including a brief stint as a makeshift City Hall while a new one was under construction. It was renamed the Mountain Bay Plaza, and as of the summer of 2000, was one hundred percent occupied.

The hallmark of this era was the rate of growth for Mountain View—the fastest ever. On the national level, it was a socially and politically turbulent time. As Victor Calvo stated, "the city, as we know it today, took its form then."[276] That

CHAPTER 7

LIGHT RAIL

BY THE EARLY 1980s, THE EXPLOSIVE GROWTH OF
the previous decades forced city and county officials
to examine alternative methods of transportation to
alleviate automobile traffic congestion. Plans were
drawn for connections to San José's Guadalupe Corridor
Light Rail Line, operated by the Valley Transportation
Authority (VTA), running from Great America in Santa Clara
to the Almaden Valley in South San José. A connection to the
west, called Tasman West Light Rail Transit (LRT), was
proposed as a 7.6-mile extension by way of some of the
valley's largest employers, including Lockheed in Sunnyvale
and NASA-Ames at Moffett Federal Airfield. County voters
agreed to a sales tax hike, but $240 million of federal
funding made the project a reality.

Construction was initially delayed because Bay Area Rapid
Transit (BART) officials insisted that a BART connection to
San Francisco International Airport should be built first.
After some disputes, they relented, and the project went
forward until it hit another formidable—and familiar—
hurdle. Both Sunnyvale and Mountain View demanded to
become the line's terminus. In a controversial vote in 1991,
the Santa Clara County Board of Supervisors decided that
the light rail extension should end in Mountain View.

Printed circuit board line workers at Sytek, a Shoreline Industrial Park high technology company in 1985. Many assembly line workers in Silicon Valley of the 1970s and 80s were immigrant women.

Sunnyvale sued, claiming that the environmental impact report minimized the effects of narrowing two Sunnyvale streets in Moffett Industrial Park. Sunnyvale lost the case, the line was built to Mountain View, and it opened in 1999.

Today there are five light rail stations in Mountain View, ending at a confluence of a Caltrain station, Central Expressway, and the Castro Street entryway to Mountain View's main business district. A century ago, merchants chose this spot because of its proximity to the railroad. The Weilheimer Hotel, Rogers & Rogers mercantile store, and the Mockbee and Ames buildings drew customers from Mountain View and the surrounding neighborhood because the train station made this spot the center of local commerce. The transit center, officially named Centennial Plaza in honor of Mountain View's 2002 centennial, reaffirmed the choice location laid out by the town's early settlers.

As commercial development has been enhanced because of convenient transportation, whole new neighborhoods called transit villages have emerged along the line. Whisman Station sits on forty-five acres of the former GTE site, and has almost six hundred townhouses or single-family homes clustered around a light rail stop. The light rail line completely changed Evelyn Avenue, from Castro Street to Pioneer Way. The street was widened, several traffic lights and parking lots were added. The Tech Farm office buildings were built along Evelyn because of transit. The one-time mill for Minton's Lumber Company was razed to accommodate housing along the train tracks.

Not since the establishment of Moffett Field during the 1930s has anything had such a major influence on Mountain View. The light rail line follows the old rail spur installed to build Hangar One and it has sparked the redevelopment of the heavy industrial areas, commercial projects, and residential neighborhoods. Events and people from the 1960s and 1970s paved the way for the modern transportation system's entry into the city.

Administrators attempted to keep up with technological change in the 1960s. In 1966 Mountain View's Finance Department took possession of its first computer, a National Cash Register (NCR) 590 with a memory of four hundred words. It could not read punch cards, but it could interpret punched tape that was printed with magnetic ink. The computer cost $90,000. It was supposed to have a life expectancy of about ten years, but Finance Director Dan Doxtator predicted that "it will probably be obsolete before it's worn out."[277]

Planning Director Robert Lawrence was hired during the 1960s, and he recognized that "at ultimate development, Mountain View's residential areas are expected to be only about 20 percent single-family houses and a whopping 80 percent apartments." Lawrence favored converting three blocks of Castro Street into a pedestrian mall, diverting traffic to streets to loop around the main street. He also supported citizen participation in planning. But in Mountain View, he lamented, "few citizens ever turn out to have their say on the way the city is run, unless a proposed project will involve tearing down their houses."[278]

John O'Halloran, who had been city manager since 1958, was the only top city administrator to remain on the job throughout the turbulent 1960s. All of the others left to take positions in larger cities or were fired.[279] The unprecedented growth of Mountain View, along with political controversies led to an unusually high turnover in city administrative positions in the early 1970s. A new police chief, city attorney, public works director, parks and recreation director, and library director were appointed.[280] Police Chief Arthur C. Nielson, who resigned in 1971, was replaced by Assistant Chief Robert Schatz. In 1973 City Manager O'Halloran resigned to become general manager of the Santa Clara County Flood and Water District. By the end of his tenure, according to a San Jose *Mercury News* article, "60 per cent of the city's residents are largely apartment dwellers, the result of unbridled growth in the late 1950s and early 1960s. . . ."[281] A whopping 150 candidates applied for O'Halloran's position. The new city manager was Richard DeLong, former city manager of Milpitas, but he remained at the post for just three years. In 1976, City Attorney Bruce Liedstrand was hired as city manager and he was ardently pro-development.

In 1980 a new state-of-the-art emergency services police and fire building was constructed at Villa and Franklin streets, half a block from the former police headquarters. The structure was designed for solar heating and cooling, and it had a large public meeting room. The new building took two years to construct, and cost $4.2 million. The building did not prove to be as energy-efficient as expected, and racked up $2,000 per month in utility bills. Evidently, the twenty-four-hour-per day use was not taken into consideration when utility use projections were first made. The interior was adorned with historic photographs of Mountain View, hearkening back to the once small town.

A major fire occurred in October 1995 when Minton's lumber company suffered a six-alarm blaze, and the flames were visible for ten miles. At one time, Minton's had covered three blocks, with 300,000 square feet and three hundred employees. Much of the land had been sold by the time of the fire, and the cause of the fire, which did about $8 million in damage, was never determined.[282] The buildings were cleared, and new construction allowed the lumber company to get back in business.

Planning Commissioner Joe Perez became the first Mexican-American to serve on the Mountain View City Council and as mayor. Both he and his wife worked for Hewlett-Packard, and wanted to be role models for Latino youth. After chairing a committee concerned about the racial and ethnic imbalance at Mountain View High

Aerial view of Mountain View's Civic Center while the Library was under contruction (top).

The Landings, a commercial development on Charleston Road north of Highway 101 built in 1986 directly adjacent to farmland.

School, Perez ran for city council and won. Three years later in 1976-77, his colleagues chose him to be mayor. Unfortunately, early in 1978, Perez discovered that he had cancer, and the popular councilman died on Christmas Day of that year at age fifty. A courtyard at the Two Worlds complex on El Camino Real and Calderon Avenue was named Plaza de Perez in his honor and a memorial plaque was placed there. Perez's replacement on the council was Planning Commissioner Marilyn Perry. She and other women began moving into elective office in the 1970s.

In 1968, Mountain View resident Judith Moss called the city clerk to inquire about the process of running for political office. The clerk offered to mail Moss some forms. To Moss's surprise, the next morning's newspaper reported that she was running for city council. Moss recalled, "No one ever heard of me. I came out of nowhere. It was a new concept: a professional woman and an apartment dweller" running for Mountain View City Council. She did not win that election, but in 1973 when she ran again, Moss became the first woman city council member. In 1975, she became the first woman mayor. Ever since, there have been women on the Mountain View City Council.

Moss's eight-year tenure on the city council coincided with national media attention focused on Santa Clara County as the "feminist capital of the United States" because of the number of women holding elective office. San José's mayor, Janet Gray Hayes, elected in 1974, became the first woman mayor of a major U.S. city. The first time the county board of supervisors was headed by a woman was 1976 when Geraldine Steinberg was chosen as chair.

Moss's views on Mountain View's development were controversial. The vote to approve the Old Mill was the first action of her tenure on the council. Moss voted yea, but later regretted it "because it could have been the perfect site for a high rise building surrounded by a green belt near the train." Other council members strongly disagreed and told her, "If you want high rises, go back to New York."

Moss campaigned to correct the abbreviation of the city's name on signs, headlines, and letterheads. The often misused abbreviation "Mt." actually means "Mount." The correct abbreviation for "Mountain" is "Mtn." Moss reasoned that since the city is not named Mount View, it should be written correctly as Mtn. View.[283] To this day, official reference to the city uses the abbreviation Mtn.

In 1980 Marilyn Perry won election to the city council, and in the spring of 1981 was chosen mayor by her colleagues. Councilwoman Pat Figueroa was named vice-mayor. For the first time in the city's history, two women held top political positions. Another councilman, Richard Wilmuth, resigned after six years to devote more time to his business. He explained that the council position often required twenty hours per week, and in consequence, his business had suffered.

Angelo Frosolone, a native of Italy who had lived in Mountain View since 1958, served eight years on the city council in the late 1970s and early 1980s. He was a self-proclaimed maverick, and seemed to thrive on casting dissenting votes on issues supported by other council members. He claimed his philosophy was simply to vote for "the most good for the greatest number of Mountain View residents."[284] Frosolone was stridently opposed to government spending and accused the federal government of "sovietization" and interfering with free enterprise when it awarded federal grants, including the one awarded for Shoreline Park.

In the meantime, Mountain View landed an "unheard-of federal grant of $1.2 million for land acquisition for Shoreline Regional Park." City Manager John O'Halloran was considered a "whiz" at landing federal and state grants, and his efforts resulted in the biggest U.S. park grant ever given to a government agency—$1.2 million for the bayside park north of Highway 101. Victor Calvo also vigorously supported the park plan. Shoreline Park, a five hundred-acre regional park, was a joint venture between Mountain View, the county, and the U.S. Department of the Interior. To get cheap fill for the marshy park site, the city won approval for a plan to accept San Francisco garbage "when nobody else wanted it."[285]

When it came time to renegotiate the fees that San Francisco paid Mountain View to take its garbage for landfill at Shoreline Regional Park, Mountain View raised the fees. San Francisco refused to pay a higher price. Mayor Moss set up a meeting with Diane Feinstein, who was then serving as president of the San Francisco Board of Supervisors. "Feinstein was very friendly," Moss said. Evidently Feinstein expected it to be a simple conversation and Mountain View would accept an extension of the current price. Moss held firm to Mountain View's demand for higher fees: "We will have a bigger park or a smaller park," Moss asserted, "it doesn't matter to us. But we will not come off the price." Feinstein gave in, although according to Moss, she was not happy about it and "stomped out" of the room.[286]

County Planning Director Karl Belser wanted to create a chain of parks along Stevens Creek, seventeen miles long from Stevens Creek Dam to the bay. Councilman William Jelavich chaired a local committee looking into the possibility and was an enthusiastic supporter. County Supervisor Martin Spangler, Sr. believed it was too late and that too many homes would have to be condemned.

Mountain View Art and Wine Festival.

Shoreline Amphitheatre, the world's largest tensioned-fabric stage tent.

The proposal caused a great deal of debate, and the county board of supervisors nixed Belser's plan because of the cost of purchasing land from private individuals. Later, one section in Mountain View from Bryant Avenue to the bay, did become a park; the county used its flood control easements and some state land, and made a few private purchases. When Victor Calvo was a county supervisor, he was an advocate for parkland acquisition.

In 1991, the 3.5-mile Stevens Creek Trail opened to the public. The original 1960s plan for a creekside park the entire length of Stevens Creek was renewed, but major legislative and eminent domain obstacles remained in the way. Although the process to build the trail was a lengthy one, supporters tried to be optimistic about the eventual twenty-mile trail from the bay to the mountains. In 1999 the third phase of the trail was completed, with bridges over Central Expressway and the railroad tracks. In 2001, the city council approved the addition of another mile to the southern portion of the trail, and

plans for its extension from Yuba Drive to Mountain View High School began.

In addition to Shoreline Park on the north and Stevens Creek park to the east, another large park to the south, framed Mountain View. The Mid-Peninsula Regional Open Space District acquired Deer Hollow Farm in 1975. The former Perham Ranch, and long before that the Grant Family farm, is a nature-study recreation area, and part of the Permanente Creek Preserve.

The chamber of commerce has evolved since its inception in 1922. Today, eighty percent of the chamber's members are small businesses, and the other twenty percent are large corporations. The chamber sponsored the first Mountain View Art and Wine Festival in 1971. Forty artists gathered on a Castro Street that looks very different from the one today. At that time it had many vacant buildings and several empty lots, and the IED building stood empty. By the late 1990s, over 200,000 people came to the two-day event held the weekend after Labor Day and over six hundred artists display their work.

Mountain View and Sunnyvale were still trying to come to an agreement as to the exact location of their respective boundaries. The many annexations had prevented both cities from determining precise city limits. A county commission called the Local Agency Formation Commission (LAFCO), set up to analyze and mediate boundary disputes, incorporations, and annexations, tried to get the two communities to arrive at some agreement. Throughout the 1970s, LAFCO held hearings about dozens of small parcels of unincorporated land that the cities attempted to annex.

During the 1970s, Santa Clara Valley became known as the Silicon Valley because of the number of high technology-based businesses here, including computers and peripherals, semiconductor components, and companies dealing in telecommunications, aerospace, and biotechnology. The largest employers in Mountain View during the 1970s were Fairchild Camera and Instrument with 5,000 workers; Fairchild Semiconductor's 3,000; and Sylvania with 1,809. Both Moffett Field and NASA-Ames employed 4,600 and 1,917 respectively. A cadre of service companies emerged to support electronics and software firms, and an emerging venture capital sector.

A new "gold rush" was on in the last twenty years of the twentieth century, where thousands streamed into Silicon Valley to reap quick money from technological discoveries. In 1983 Sun Microsystems, a one-year-old computer workstation company, headed by a 29-year-old CEO and president, Scott McNealy, came to Mountain View with 125 employees. A year later there were 518 employees on the payroll. During the same period, annual sales jumped from $9 million to $39 million. By 1987 Sun occupied nineteen buildings in Mountain View totaling more that 500,000 square feet. Over one-third of its employees—1,600 of its total workforce of 4,500—worked in Mountain View. In 1988 it became a $1 billion company with large, corporate campuses in Santa Clara and at either end of the Dumbarton Bridge in Menlo Park and Fremont.

In 1982 Jim Clark founded Silicon Graphics (today's SGI), which specialized in computers that manipulate three-dimensional images. Its major customers included the Chrysler Corporation which used the system for car parts, and Levi Strauss which used it to design blue jeans. Hollywood movie moguls such as George Lucas used Silicon Graphics computers to create cinematic special effects. The company received national attention in 1993 when President Bill Clinton and Vice President Al Gore paid a personal visit. A year after the company was founded, Silicon Graphics had $10 million in sales. Just four years later it topped $86 million, and in 1993 it became a billion-dollar company. Clark left to start Netscape the following year. In 2001, SGI cut one thousand jobs, reflecting the national economic downturn.

For a while, older firms continued to thrive alongside successful start-ups. GTE Sylvania continued to expand, and in 1980 it occupied over 900,000 square feet of industrial space in Mountain View.[287] But eventually GTE sold land that now has been redeveloped into a transit village. Microsoft Corporation's Silicon Valley headquarters was in Mountain View on a campus built over landfill. In 2001 it opened a new technology center, in conjunction with Compaq Computer and Unisys Corporation, where other companies could come to test the compatibility of their hardware and software programs with Microsoft products. Company founder Bill Gates appeared at the dedication ceremony for the $10 million facility and over one thousand people attended.

After decades of dizzying growth, city council members were nervous about the rapid rate of development in Mountain View, and about the pro-development stance of City Manager Bruce Liedstrand in particular. Plans were underway for construction of a new city hall and a community theatre. Liedstrand facilitated a Castro Street revitalization and a clean-up campaign for El Camino Real.

In 1987 Liedstrand said, "We are trying to do more than revitalize downtown. We are trying to give this city a sense of place."[288] While Mountain View residents differed about how to plan a livable city, all agreed that what Mountain View needed most was a distinct identity, amid the freeways, industrial parks, and housing sprawl across the entire Santa Clara Valley. Even as some observers lamented the loss of community since the development of Silicon Valley, the lively public debate over Mountain View's future sustained a sense of place and made this locality meaningful to recent arrivals.

But when Liedstrand lobbied for three 18-story buildings north of Bayshore in 1988, the council did not approve and requested his resignation. He claimed that his efforts had been to make "Mountain View the best small city in the Bay Area,"[289] although he acknowledged that the pace of development had been faster than the council desired. When Liedstrand left Mountain View, he became the city manager in East Palo Alto, and Ralph Jaeck took over as Mountain View's city manager.

Shoreline Park and a concert amphitheater came to fruition under City Manager Liedstrand's tenure. They had been constructed on the landfill of San Francisco's garbage, and featured a man-made lake for sailing and wind surfing, and a $19-million Bill Graham Presents concert venue. The park was dedicated in the summer of 1983. During construction, the amphitheater was often called the Graham amphitheater, but other names were also considered, including "Mountain View Meadows" or "Shoreline Music Center." It was officially named "Shoreline Amphitheater at Mountain View," pleasing local officials who wanted the name of the city to be very prominent. On opening night in the summer of 1986, singer Julio Iglesias performed in the world's largest tensioned-fabric stage tent.

Maintaining a park on a former landfill posed unexpected challenges. The first seasons were plagued by an overwhelming odor from methane gas exuding from the decomposing compacted garbage under Shoreline Park. Engineers were able to vent the land to let the gas escape, reducing the unpleasant aroma. The city council voted to change the names of Bailey Avenue and Stierlin Road to Shoreline Boulevard in 1988. A small portion of Stierlin Road kept the original name, hearkening back to Christopher Stierlin, whose farm was such an important place along that byway.

Even as the population climbed to 58,655 in 1980, Mountain View-Los Altos Union High School District faced a seriously declining enrollment. Ten years earlier, the district had hit its all-time high of 5,200 students. By 1980 it was down to 3,500; enrollment was expected to continue to decline to 2,300 during the late 1980s. After eight months of study and community discussion, Superintendent Paul Sakamoto recommended closing Mountain View High School on Castro Street by June 1981. Among the reasons he chose that school over the other two in the district— Awalt and Los Altos High—were that Mountain View was the smallest of the three high schools, that it had severe parking problems, and that the facility was the least adaptable to modernization. The San Jose *Mercury* noted, "District officials have been looking at the possibility of closing a school for several years in hopes of restoring racial balance in the district while dealing with the problems of declining enrollments and shrinking budgets."[290]

Another important factor was that the land that the fifty-five-year-old school was sitting on was more valuable than the sites of the other schools. Later, in 1983, Sakamoto suggested that the city acquire the property as a historic building. But at that point, although the city council had designated it an historic building,[291] it adhered to the recommendations of its Neighborhood Subcommittee to purchase only the gyms and pools.[292]

The last year that Mountain View High School on Castro Street was used for regular classes was in 1980-81. There were 1,200 students there that last year. At the final graduation ceremony, two hundred blue and white balloons were released as a symbolic farewell to the school. Sunnyvale High School also closed that year; Palo Alto's Cubberley High had closed the previous year.

Students from the closed school were sent to Awalt and Los Altos high schools, depending on where they lived. Miramonte Avenue was the dividing line; further north the line followed Bailey Avenue and then Stierlin Road (today's Shoreline Boulevard). School district officials acknowledged that combining the two schools would bring a new racial and ethnic mix to the predominantly white Awalt and Los Altos high schools. Mountain View High School had been racially and ethnically mixed for many years and during the 1960s was known as a rough school.

Mountain View found itself without a high school bearing its own name. Under public pressure, the school district changed the name of Awalt High School to Mountain View High. At the same time, it transferred the older school's eagle mascot and colors, blue and gray, to Los Altos High, giving each surviving school something from the former one.

The one-time high school buildings were used for adult education classes for a time then stood vacant, encouraging rapid deterioration. The school district wanted to sell the high school property to get on solid financial ground. During the first four years of the 1980s, its expenditures exceeded its budget by between $250,000 and $500,000 annually. It asked the city to rezone

Mountain View High School. The 1925 school designed by architect William Weeks. It was torn down in 1987. The solid sixty-year old building proved very difficult to take down and repeatedly resisted the wrecking ball.

the property for residential and commercial use, to encourage developers to buy the land.

The plans to build a new civic center had been underway at the same time that the city was considering the future of the Mountain View High School property just one block to the south. California state law, by virtue of the Naylor Act, gives municipalities the right to purchase, for recreational use, up to one-third of a school property for one-fourth of its market value. City officials did not take advantage of this law.

While negotiations were going on, the city leased the swimming pool and two gyms from the district. Although the city would have preferred to keep the pool, which was almost brand new, developers argued that if it remained where it was, the property value would drop. So the pool was demolished too. The city ended up purchasing only seven acres behind the school site, at Bailey Avenue and Church Street, for a park with a new pool and recreation center. The city council voted to name the park "Eagle Park" in honor of the mascot of the former high school. Discussions that were held between the city and the developer about saving some of the school structure and incorporating it into the new construction came to naught. Instead, eleven acres of the school

site were sold to Prometheus Development for almost four hundred residential units, 40,000 square feet of retail space, and 160,000 square feet of office space.

In 1986, just before the school buildings were demolished, a farewell party was held at the site. Former students gathered to reminiscence and say good-bye to the 1924 school. Oregon's former Governor Bob Straub (class of 1938) was on hand. Many former teachers and administrators also took part. Charles Bubb (class of 1930) trumpeted the "Star Spangled Banner." Chester Awalt, his daughter Doris Ebere (class of 1928), and Roberta Bubb Sweeney (class of 1931) helped to open the old time capsule. Awalt had been at the dedication ceremonies in 1924. Former Principal Irval Carter did not support the district's decision to sell the property. "It's ridiculous selling out and tearing it down. It's stupidity on the part of the school board. They're going to have a hell of a time knocking it down because it is really put together."[293]

The school buildings on Castro Street were razed in 1987. As Carter predicted, demolition was not an easy task. The wrecking crew "had a hard time taking the buildings down," noted City

Interior of Mayfield Mall It was remodeled as a high tech facility for Hewlett-Packard Company.

Historian Barbara Kinchen.[294] The old school had been built, and later retrofitted, to last.

In the meantime, city officials wanted to revamp city hall, the former First Presbyterian Church just down the street from the high school, and hired contractors to carry out the work. But the massive remodeling job was halted suddenly when workers discovered structural defects that could not be remedied by remodeling. One of the city's project engineers quipped, "there was nothing holding it up but imagination."[295] In 1984 the city negotiated to have a new civic center built for an estimated $8.9 million. The next year the former church was torn down. City offices moved into the Mountain Bay Plaza, formerly known as the IED Building, which had been redeveloped by Perini Land & Development Company. After its inauspicious beginning, Perini had to sink another $4 million into it and had to retrofit it for earthquake standards that had been developed since the building was first constructed. The city paid the going rate of $30,000 per month to rent about 15,000 square feet of office space.

After many delays and cost overruns, the new Mountain View City Hall and Center for Performing Arts opened in 1991 at a cost of $44.5 million, about $15.5 million over budget. It was also built by the Perini Corporation. One of the biggest challenges facing the architect for the civic center was not letting the new complex be dwarfed by the looming eleven-story next door neighbor, Mountain Bay Plaza. The city also carried out a $12 million traffic plan for Castro Street. The street became popularly known in the surrounding high-tech communities as the "home of the $5 lunch" because of all its restaurants, sidewalk cafes and ethnic eateries.

Mountain View Civic Center was a crowning achievement for the city, with its seven-story rotunda and four-story atrium. It blends open space, government buildings, and cultural facilities, one flowing from the other. Pioneer Park reaches to the edge of the building, and leads to the Mountain View Public Library.

The city constructed its new library on the same site as the "shoebox," a nickname the old library earned because it could only accommodate one hundred patrons, and had to store 40,000 books off-site. The new library, adjacent to the civic center and Pioneer Park, was twice the size of the former one and offers underground parking. The building is equipped with state-of-the-art technologies and more than forty miles of fiber-optics and cables were woven through the building to connect on-line computer stations, data communication ports, and self-checkout stations. The projected cost of the facility was $14.5 million, but it came in under budget. Since it opened in 1996, the Mountain View Public Library has become a model for other communities.

As attractive as the new civic center is, did Mountain View make a mistake in opting to build it? The city could have created a civic center at the historic old school, capitalized on its two gymnasiums, swimming pool, and theater-outfitted auditorium at a substantial savings over the $44.5 million it spent for the new civic center. One resident observed, "My argument is when the city bought the back portion [Eagle Park], they could have had the rest of the property: buildings, 2 gyms, pool and an auditorium. Since then, the city has put in a pool and two gyms. It could have preserved the buildings and maintained the uses. They built a new city hall and performing arts center when they could have used the old buildings."[296]

The Castro street merchant community had a different perspective and wondered if government buildings belonged in a business district. Martin Spangler, Jr. felt the city "could have chosen a better place for city hall than prime business property fronting Castro Street. It's a shame to take up space on the main street that's not business."[297]

Besides bidding farewell to the high school during the 1980s, citizens also said good-bye to some of the oldest businesses in Mountain View. Pacific Press Publishing, a pillar of the Mountain View community since 1904, closed its plant in

1984 because of rising energy and housing costs and moved to Idaho. Up until it closed, it employed about 250 people and remained a model business. Many of its workers, all of whom were Seventh-Day Adventist Church members, walked or biked to work from the nearby Villa-Mariposa neighborhood. The property was redeveloped by South Bay Construction and Development Company and became a Hewlett-Packard facility and residential housing.

South Bay was also the developer of the former Ferry-Morse Seed Company, for a time the largest seed packager in the world. The company closed its Mountain View facility in 1985 and relocated to Modesto, California. The property was converted for high technology research and development buildings.

The Oku Nursery, a flower farm operated by the Oku family beginning in 1902 at Wright and Bailey avenues, made way for a new condominium complex "The Lakes of Mountain View." Massao Oku objected when the city annexed his property in 1965 and sued, claiming the nursery sat on greenbelted county land. At first the county board of supervisors sided with him, but after a year-long battle, Oku gave up his stand against city annexation.

Some of the new shopping malls built in the 1970s proved unsuccessful and were closed in the 1980s. By 1981, thirty-six of the 71 stores at the Old Mill were empty. It was converted to office space for a time, and in 1984, one of the

Mountain View's Public Library, 2000.

tenants, Fargo's Pizza, tried to turn it into a hotel. A brief stint as a European-style gourmet produce market did not work either. Although the movie theaters remained open for a while longer, the oversized water wheel was dismantled and hauled away in 1988. By the mid-1990s, the Old Mill was demolished to make way for The Crossings, a new development designed with a new San Antonio Station Caltrain stop in mind. Some of the debris left over from the shopping center demolition was recycled into the new project for base rock in sidewalks, curbing, and streets. The property was developed into more than four hundred residential apartments, townhouses, and homes with some peripheral commercial space. Castro Station, which was the original flagstop for the Castro family just east of the new San Antonio Station, was closed because so few people used the stop. The hundred-year-old flagstop agreement between the Castro family and the railroad was over.

In 1983 Mayfield Mall also closed its doors as a shopping center. Hewlett Packard leased the building with an option to purchase it, which it exercised the following year. The Mayfield Mall property had come full circle. Originally the rancho of a Californio family, it became the Italian Vegetable Gardens and then a regional shopping mall. That venture lasted only a generation before it succumbed to the pressures of Silicon Valley and became one of hundreds of buildings occupied by high technology companies.

The Emporium, sitting on the former Dale orchard, closed in 1995, and several years of controversy about what would happen to that property followed. Home Depot, a large warehouse-style hardware retailer, leased the property to open a store there. Neighbors and city officials opposed this plan, and currently the building is empty.

Sweeping changes transformed Mountain View, especially the commercial developments along El Camino Real and a redeveloped Castro Street. Kaiser Permanente opened a clinic with a large parking structure on the site of the former Palm Plaza. Residents in the surrounding neighborhood became nervous about traffic congestion that might result from these changes, and some formed the Old Mountain View Neighborhood Association (OMVNA) in 1989. Eventually the group developed a preservation and improvement plan for the old neighborhood.

At 5:02 p.m. on October 17, 1989, the Loma Prieta Earthquake struck the San Francisco Bay Area. Mountain View's Emergency Operations Center, located in the basement of the police and fire building, jumped into action. Damage to city-owned buildings was estimated to be about $660,000. The public library had damaged ducting and shelving collapsed. Two firehouses were damaged, but remained open. The Adobe Building,

Rengstorff House in 1974, before it was moved and restored. Lower photo is the restored house on its permanent site in Shoreline Park.

already in need of structural work, suffered another $200,000 worth of damage. The bulk-head at the Eagle Park pool partially collapsed. Damage to private buildings was estimated at almost $6 million. There were no major fires, no deaths, and no reported looting, but there were several gas leaks and congested intersections. The next day, Vice President Dan Quayle, who happened to be at Moffett Field, was told about the local impact of the earthquake. Quayle's informants were very complimentary about Mountain View's emergency response. City Manager Ralph Jaeck described Mountain View's reaction to the earthquake as a "class act."[298]

Dena Bonnell was elected to city council in 1988 and served two terms. She was mayor in 1993-94. Previously she had served on the board of the Mountain View School District and on the Environmental Planning Commission. She was a strong advocate for the preservation of trees, and fellow council member Ralph Faravelli dubbed her Mountain View's "original tree hugger." Bonnell died in 2000.

Ralph Faravelli was elected to the council in 1994 and also served as mayor in 1996 and 1998. During his election campaign, he used Ferry-Morse seed packages of "forget me nots" to remind voters to support him. Ironically, Faravelli had to order the seed packets of the former Mountain View company from Kentucky, since they were no longer packaged here. The seeds must have worked because the voters did not forget Faravelli and elected him to the council. Over the years he supported historic preservation of the Adobe Building and was president of the Mountain View Historical Association.[299]

In 1995 the 1930s-era Adobe Building was slated to be razed so the city could sell the property. Councilman Faravelli voiced the concerns of the Mountain View Historical Association and others who wanted to save the building. The council put a hold on demolition plans to see if the historical association could muster community support to save the Adobe. The effort to save the building was successful, at a cost of $1.2 million, and the Adobe was to be renovated to its first use: a community events venue. It was re-dedicated in 2001.

The hallmark of the last decade of the twentieth century in Mountain View was an embracing of new technologies in city services, including voice mail, e-mail, city web site, on-line building permits, and automatic utility bill payment systems. Interestingly enough, there was a simultaneous new consciousness of things historical.

The landmark Rengstorff House, which had been incorporated into Shoreline Park, was finally restored, and the 1930s Adobe Building won approval for restoration. The Mountain View History Center at the new library was created to replace the Pioneer Room, which had been established in 1967 at the old library. The Centennial Planning Committee actively planned for the one-hundredth anniversary of the incorporation of the City of Mountain View.

The 1990s opened with the appointment of a new city manager, Kevin Duggan. Formerly the city manager for Campbell, Duggan was not new to Mountain View. He attended both Awalt and Saint Francis high schools, and his first job in government was as an intern in Mountain View's city manager's office in 1971. Duggan emphasized the need to facilitate rapid resolution of development proposals from high technology companies. "We don't want to throw our planning regulations out the window. But we need to respond quickly,"[300] Duggan explained. Insofar as municipal governments are not a stumbling block for companies, then the two can maintain a good, working relationship.

City Manager Kevin Duggan who has held the position since 1990.

The city sought to create alternative ways to accommodate new development because large parcels of land were no longer available. Mountain View negotiated long-term leases on city properties, creating corporate campuses that generate substantial revenue for the municipality. Microsoft built a campus of over 500,000 square feet of research and development space on city-owned land on L'Avenida. Likewise, Alza Corporation built almost 500,000 square feet on city-owned Charleston Road properties. SGI (at one time called Silicon Graphics) occupies a half million square feet on Crittenden Lane.

Property formerly used by heavy industry has been transformed to accommodate new tenants. Several buildings in the Ellis Street-Middlefield Road area housed assembly workers building printed circuit boards. Netscape Communications transformed the manufacturing haven and created a campus there. The "Rusty Bucket" on Ellis Street, home of amazing engineering and technological feats "during the halcyon days of Fairchild Semiconductor" was demolished in the 1990s, leaving behind a Superfund toxic clean-up site. It was redeveloped into a campus for Veritas Software, and smaller parcels have been made available to other firms.

Just outside the walls of the far-reaching technological inventions at the Fairchild plant on Ellis Street, a neighborhood wallowed in obsolescence and despair. A short stretch of Fairchild Drive, formerly Bayshore Frontage Road, was known as "motel row" because of a number of 1940s and 1950s-vintage motels. A tall, cinder block sound wall had been erected along the freeway, cutting off all view and therefore the customer base to the motels exacerbating their demise.

Although there were almost no large parcels of developable land left in Mountain View, 2.4 million square feet of new buildings and tenant improvements were under construction at the end of 1999, the highest level of construction ever in the city. Mountain View saw a sales tax revenue of $20 million in fiscal year 1999-2000.[301] A six-story office building, consisting of 150,000 square feet, was under construction next to the Mountain Bay Plaza at Castro and California streets. Camino Bowl's two-acre site was redeveloped into a commercial-residential mixed-use project in June 2000.

City Manager Duggan described "new urbanism"—the late twentieth century reversal of suburbanization—and cites the Crossings at the Old Mill and Whisman Station as good examples of mixed-use developments that have attracted middle-class residents. Here new transit-centered communities of apartments, row houses, and retail businesses have grown up around a hub of rail travel.

One of Mountain View's most enduring attributes is the racial and ethnic diversity of its residents and workers. City Manager Duggan emphasized that Mountain View has diversity "in almost every category you can think of."[302] There are older people and young, recent arrivals and longtime residents. The economic spectrum ranges from day laborers to IPO (initial public offering) beneficiaries. In 1980, a little over a quarter of Mountain View's 58,655 residents belonged to many racial-ethnic groups.[303] New waves of Asian immigrants, particularly from southeast Asia, came to California after the fall of Saigon in 1975. By 2000, just over twenty percent of the total population identified themselves as Asian.[304]

The so-called "digital divide," or the Internet's and technology jobs' inaccessibility to minorities, was the topic of a presentation given by the Reverend Jesse Jackson at SGI in Mountain View in 2001. He appealed to technology firms to overcome the divide by outreach programs and funding education programs. In February 2001, the city sponsored "Culture, Community, Technology. . . . Celebrate Art," an exhibit mounted in honor of Black History Month in the art gallery in the City Hall.

Castro Street's array of ethnic restaurants attests to a multi-cultural clientele. However, racial tensions were evident at some public debates over the fate of a day worker job center. While a surging Silicon Valley economy drew thousands of job-seekers to high tech firms, unskilled workers also streamed into the valley. Early mornings found the workers congregating at a few key intersections around the valley, hoping to be hired for the day as a gardener, a ditch-digger or a trash-hauler. One such impromptu hiring hall had emerged over a period of several years at San Antonio Road and El Camino Real in Los Altos on the border of Mountain View. Saint Joseph the Worker Center,

an employment service run by a Catholic organization and co-founded by the El Camino Hospital Foundation, provided English classes and health referrals, along with job placement for the mostly undocumented immigrants from Mexico.

Merchants along El Camino complained to city officials about the traffic, litter, and other problems caused by congregating workers. Los Altos passed an ordinance in 1999 prohibiting drivers from stopping to hire day workers. In June 2000, Mountain View passed its own ordinance against impeding the public right-of-way. The day worker center needed more space, and task forces were formed to locate a larger center. Even though over eighty sites were considered, none was agreed upon. Mountain View City Council took no action on the issue. The day worker center has vigorous supporters who see it as a humane venue to help the poor gain employment. The retractors claim it is a magnet for illegal aliens and offers no benefits to the community.

An editorial in the *Voice* drew parallels between the contemporary day worker controversy and nineteenth-century Chinese railroad workers who "were denied the most basic elements of a dignified life by their host communities." The article went on to chide communities in the region for failing to "acknowledge those who toil invisibly at the hardest, dirtiest, and most dangerous jobs at the heart of our economic success."[305] Some council members found the editorial to be inflammatory and a misrepresentation of the facts. The issue is likely to be a source of great debate for some time to come.

Mountain View residents became increasingly aware of the environmental costs of the city's industrial history. In 1982, toxic contaminants were found in the ground water beneath five companies bordered by Middlefield Road, Ellis Street, and Whisman Avenue. By 1986 it was clear that the contaminants had sunk into the "deepest aquifers supplying" drinking water to the Santa Clara Valley. In addition, there are two federal Superfund sites at Moffett Field. Estimates of the time needed to clean the ground water range from twenty to one hundred years. Ongoing efforts to stem toxic contamination have shown some positive results. The Charleston Slough Restoration project won awards from the South

Bay Chapter of American Public Works Association and from the American Public Works Association.

Moffett Field posed a safety problem because of the huge increase in population in the immediate vicinity. In 1957, a Republic F-84C *Thunderjet* crashed into a house at the corner of Oak and California streets in Mountain View. Sixteen years later a Navy P-3 *Orion* and a NASA *Condor* crashed over the Sunnyvale Golf Course. Surrounding communities pressured Moffett to curtail its heavy air traffic, which included about 130,000 take offs and landings every year. The 1973 crash induced the Navy to transfer much of its practice "touch and go" landings and take offs to another base.

During the Reagan administration, the American military prospered. Moffett Field's population in early 1980s was about 10,000, including the dependents of military personnel.[306] Not foreseeing the dramatic downsizing the next decade would bring, the Navy sought to build 170 housing units on seventeen acres of unincorporated land at Moffett Boulevard and Middlefield Road. The Navy wanted the city to annex the land so that a sewer hookup would be available.

Mountain View city planners supported the Navy's plans to build housing, provided that a public review of the construction plans took place. The Navy refused public review and wanted housing of its own design and construction. As the housing shortage lingered into the 1980s, however, the Navy had to agree to the city's conditions. The new neighborhood was a prominent entryway into Mountain View, and city officials wanted it to present a good appearance.

In the wake of the fall of the Berlin Wall and the opening of the Soviet bloc countries, the United States reevaluated the real and perceived threats to national security around the world. As a result, hundreds of American military bases were closed or reduced in size. The Navy was ordered to depart from Moffett Field. An official "disestablishment day" was held at Moffett Field in 1994, sixty-one years after the base was commissioned.

The Navy's departure from Moffett had a huge impact on Mountain View economically, socially and politically. Many Navy housing units stood abandoned, a particularly frustrating situation because of a massive housing shortage across the Santa Clara Valley. Stanford University went to great lengths to alleviate its own student housing shortage, by attempting to procure housing both on and off the base, but the school was not successful in its efforts.

In the early 1980s, the question of expanding the use of Moffett Field to non-military air traffic came to the forefront. The idea was proposed by civilian pilots and by San Jose International Airport, which wanted to transfer its general aviation traffic to Moffett. The Navy strongly opposed sharing the base with non-military pilots. An advisory vote was taken in Mountain View in 1983, which indicated the public was decidedly against allowing private use of the base. Similar votes were taken in Sunnyvale with the same result. For once, the two communities agreed.

Mountain View and Sunnyvale both have elected officials who serve on the Community Advisory Committee (CAC) on the future uses of Moffett Federal Airfield. Both cities have expressed interest in annexing portions of the base. They both also support the California Air and Space Center (CASC) in the historic Hangar One. The base's future offers a unique opportunity for cooperation between Mountain View and Sunnyvale. Not since the base was opened in 1930 have the two municipalities so wholeheartedly agreed on anything. Among the possibilities for the future use of the base are: maintaining it as it is; 5 million square feet of research and development space; university housing; light industrial and office space.

Another by-product of the Navy's pullout was a dramatic drop in enrollment in the Whisman School District and the closure of Whisman Elementary School. For twenty years or more, merging the Whisman School District with the Mountain View School District had been debated and a few times voted upon. Voters finally approved the merger in the November 2000 election, and the new district was named the Mountain View-Whisman School District.

NASA-Ames took charge of the former Moffett Field Naval Air Station in 1994. Its space exploration experiments have continued. The 1983 *Pioneer 10* spacecraft, which was manipulated from the Mountain View laboratory, was the first object designed to cross distant planetary orbits and leave the solar system. The space agency wanted to allow air cargo flights from the base, but residents in both Sunnyvale and Mountain View vociferously resisted that proposition. As of the summer of 2000, there were about 65 flights in or out of the base per day.

Space Camp, an intensive summer camp for children, was held at Moffett from 1996 to 2002 when it ran out of funding. It was one of only three sites in the United States (the others in Florida and Alabama) where youngsters learn first-hand about space exploration, aviation, and technological advances in aeronautics. Every year thousands of children went through the Space Camp program. Residents in the City of Mountain View were eligible for scholarships.

Moffett Federal Airfield is being used for a variety of purposes. The Computer Museum History Center at NASA-Ames Research Center holds 3,000 artifacts, 5,000 photographs and 2,000 films in an archive of materials about the history of the computer age. Future plans call for a museum of over 100,000 square feet by the year 2004. The Moffett Field Historical Society, founded in 1993, operated a museum in Hangar One with research material, photographs, memorabilia and artifacts on the history of the base. It also was closed in 2002 because of a shortage of funds but is seeking private funding. The terrorist attack on New York's World Trade Center and the Pentagon in Washington D.C. in 2001, put the precise use of the base in question.

Light rail has led us further on the path of Mountain View's history. Recent years have shown that the milestones are becoming larger than this place. Technological and economic trends have worldwide implications, and impact a population well beyond city limits. As yet it is unclear what the next chapter in this story might be named.

EPILOGUE

I N 1895, BEFORE THE TOWN WAS LIGHTED BY electricity, before airplanes much less airships filled the skies, Mountain View author Mary Julia Gates was startlingly prophetic when she wrote in a published essay:

A city will eventually stretch down to the open water,
and steamers shall come and go from wharves far out
on the reclaimed swamp lands. Here will be electric
lights, street cars, and likely a stray air-ship or more,
and Jacob Shumway would not know the place he
named Mountain View.[307]

Indeed, neither Mr. Shumway nor Mrs. Gates would recognize today's Mountain View. And in another one hundred years at the bicentennial of the city's incorporation, would any of us recognize the Mountain View of 2102?

Marking Mountain View's milestones gives perspective to a wide-ranging history from the anecdotal happenings of a small town to monumental inventions that have tremendous implications the world over. Mountain View's journey places a frustrated farmer blowing up a bank in the same chapter as the establishment of NASA-Ames Research Laboratory. Each is important in its own way, providing a setting and backdrop, one for the other.

The creeks that have always given the city its geography have helped to define Mountain View. Whether flood or drought, open-space or development, in pristine condition or polluted, they have played an important role in the city's history. Like the annual ebb and flow of Stevens Creek, the city has had its own seasons. At times Mountain View has been overflowing with people and businesses, and at other times commerce has slowed to barely a trickle.

Today's interest in revitalizing the natural habitat of the creeks and building trails alongside them also mirrors Mountain View's renewed interest in its own history. Stevens Creek Trail and Permanente Creek Trail have emerged as commuter routes for cyclists and walkers. The creeks connect us with the natural world and remind us to take care of the land and therefore of ourselves.

Crittenden Marsh at lower Stevens Creek is almost thirty acres of a former landfill that has been reclaimed and planted with native plants and grasses. Its hiking and biking trails allow wide, open vistas of Stevens Creek, Moffett Federal Airfield and the South Bay. It has taken years and huge expense to begin to get it to look as it did when Baptist preacher Orrin Crittenden established his dairy farm there in the mid-nineteenth century.

Cities in the county are jockeying for position on the Silicon Valley frontline. Sunnyvale was identified as the "heart of Silicon Valley" in 1980 because it had more high technology firms within its borders than any other municipality. Early in the 1990s, San José proclaimed itself the "capital of Silicon Valley" as part of a marketing and public relations campaign. Late in the 1990s Palo Alto put in its bid to be known as the "birthplace of Silicon Valley" because in a tiny garage there, William Hewlett and David Packard launched what became Hewlett-Packard Corporation. Without understating what Hewlett and Packard accomplished, Mountain View disputes that Silicon Valley began there.

Mountain View can arguably claim the distinction of being the birthplace of Silicon Valley because silicon was first used as a commercial product at Shockley's laboratory on San Antonio Road. The silicon transistors produced there gave rise to the integrated circuit and thus to the computer age. As Mike Cassidy, columnist for the *Mercury*, described the Shockley building, it was a "modest quonset hut, now a furniture store. . . . next to a plumbing supply store, across from a Sears Roebuck."[308] It is certainly as unlikely a birthplace as a garage.

Jacques Beaudouin petitioned the Mountain View City Council to designate the building a historical landmark in 1987, but the city did not respond until thirteen years later. No wonder Palo Alto and others jumped on the bandwagon. Whatever moniker each municipality claims as its own, the phenomenon of Silicon Valley has changed history, has linked this place with people throughout the world, has extended our human reach into space, and will continue to be a major influence in all our lives.

When individuals live long lives, their memories can inform the community about patterns of transformation and change. At an advanced age, Indian Lope Inigo reminded his contemporaries how numerous his tribes people were in an earlier time. He also recalled the prevalence of grizzly bears "all through the woods."[309] Likewise when Mrs. Julia Dale Richardson was interviewed in 1918 she explained how she had witnessed "the trails of the frontier with their ox teams give way to fine highways with the rush of automobiles all day long."[310] Many Mountain View residents today could describe having grown up with acres of orchards surrounding a bustling downtown. And those orchards have been replaced with high tech campuses. What memories are being created today that will be passed on to the next generation?

Plaque marking the site of one time location of Shockley Laboratories. *Photo by Robert Weaver.*

Why We Call it "Mountain View"

Pop Smith, Mountain View's supreme newsman for almost forty years, owns the role of the narrator of the city's history. His tenure began at about the same time that the town was incorporated, and his newspaper reported events, large and small, allowing us a view of that earlier time. Smith also interviewed his seniors, taking readers back another fifty or more years, into the Gold Rush era. Surely Smith deserves our esteem for broadening our vision of the past.

Mountain View's treasure lies in its diversity of people. A wide range of income levels, physical ability, age, education as well as racial and ethnic heritage can make the community an interesting, lively and colorful place to live and work—or it can be a source of painful contention. Each citizen has a choice to make, and that decision will impact the whole.

Transportation provides a thematic framework for the milestones marked in this story. Stage-coaches, trains, cars, dirigibles, airplanes, and light rail cars, have all informed the look of the city: track cut through ranchos, hangars built on dairy farms, freeways slicing through orchards, transit villages springing up along rail corridors. The very landscape is radically altered with each new achievement.

For that reason we must also be careful and deliberate about the alterations we make so that we do not arrive at some distant day and wonder why a building was razed or a whole neighborhood annihilated. Some of Mountain View's most historic buildings, the so-called "granddaddies,"[311] like the Jurian Building, the Mockbee Building, and the former Farmers and Merchants Bank building, attest to longevity, to usefulness, and remind us not to waste. The long-gone railroad depot and high school, coupled with the cost of replacement, leave us wondering about the choices we have made. Can we afford to purchase land and build schools only to raze them when they are in need of maintenance and repair?

At the beginning, stagecoaches passed along El Camino Real. For many years orchards stretched out on either side of the road as far as the eye could see. But gradually the road became less important than the place that grew up around it, and Mountain View became a waystation on the road to the future. The road, as Wendell Berry's verse points out, "is not a way but a place." And this place is Mountain View.

APPENDIX

POPULATION OF MOUNTAIN VIEW BY DECADE

Year	Population
1910	1,161
1920	1,888
1930	3,308
1940	3,946
1950	6,563
1960	30,889
1970	54,132
1980	58,655
1990	67,460
2000	70,708

AREA OF MOUNTAIN VIEW BY DATE

Year	Area (square miles)
1902	1 square mile
1949	1.5 square miles
1958	7.8 square miles
1960	8.3 square miles
2000	12 square miles

CITY MANAGERS

Years	City Manager
1952 - 1954	James Thomas
1954 - 1958	Philip T. Lawlor
1958 - 1973	John O'Halloran
1973 - 1976	Richard B. DeLong
1976 - 1988	Bruce Liedstrand
1989	Ralph Jaeck
1989 - 1990	Nadine Levin (acting)
1990 - current	Kevin Duggan

MAYORS OF MOUNTAIN VIEW

Originally Council members were called Trustees and Mayors were called Presidents. Although we have no official record as to why these titles changed, the minutes begin to use the titles Councilman and Mayor in August 1927.

Chronological Order:

Years	Mayor
1902-04	Daniel Benjamin Frink
1904-06	Benjamin Eastman Burns
1906-08	Julius Weilheimer
1908-09	Julius Weilheimer
1909-10	Benjamin Eastman Burns
1910-12	Nathan H. McCorkel
1912-13	William P. Wright
1913-14	John George Jagels
1914	Charles Coney Minton
1914-16	John George Jagels

Years	Mayor
1916-18	Jacob S. Mockbee
1918-20	James H. Cochran
1920-22	Claude E. Redwine
1922-24	James H. Cochran
1924-26	Earl D. Minton
1926-28	Earl D. Minton
1928-30	Joseph Henry Powell
1930-32	Joseph Henry Powell
1932-34	Abram J. Knight
1934-36	George W. Sohler
1936-37	George W. Sohler
1937-38	Daniel Burke
1938-40	Daniel Burke
1940-42	Daniel Burke
1942-44	Charles N. Lake
1944-46	Charles Newton Higdon
1946-48	Frank Morton
1948-50	Frank Morton
1950-52	Martin J. Spangler, Sr.
1952-52	Martin J. Spangler, Sr.
1952-53	John W. Anderson
1954-56	David L. Tripiano
1956-58	Lawrence Anderson
1958-60	John W. Anderson
1960-62	Charles M. Moore
1962-63	Charles M. Moore
1963-64	Victor Calvo
1964-65	Victor Calvo
1965-66	Charles Gordon
1966-67	Charles Gordon
1967-68	Victor Calvo
1968-70	William R. Jelavich
1970-72	William L. Herfurth
1972-73	W. Ross Wollard
1973-74	Carl E. Anderson
1974-75	Joseph Cusimano
1975-76	Judith Moss
1976-77	Joseph Perez
1977-78	Matthew Allen
1978-79	Richard Wilmuth

Years	Mayor
1979-80	Leslie C. Nichols
1980-81	Matthew Allen
1981-82	Marilyn Perry
1982-83	Patricia Figueroa
1983-84	Ronald D. Packard
1984-85	Maryce Freelen
1985-86	James Zesch
1986-87	Clarence Heppler
1987-88	Robert Schatz
1988-89	Maryce Freelen
1989-90	Norman Shaskey
1990-91	Angelo Frosolone
1991-92	Art Takahara
1992-93	James Cochran
1993-94	Dena Bonnell
1994-95	Robert Schatz
1995-96	Patricia Figueroa
1996-97	Ralph Faravelli
1997-98	Joseph Kleitman
1998-99	Ralph Faravelli
1999-00	Mary Lou Zoglin
2000-01	Rosemary Stasek
2001-02	Mario Ambra
2002-03	Sally Lieber

Council Members of Mountain View*

Year	Name	Mayor in:
November, 1902	Benjamin E. Burns	
	Daniel Benjamin Frink	1902-04
	Dr. Charles O. Gates	
	George A. Pattberg	
	George Swall	
April, 1904	Benjamin E. Burns	1904-06
	Daniel Benjamin Frink	
	Jacob S. Mockbee	
	George Swall	
	Julius Weilheimer	
1906	*Changed to four year terms*	
April, 1904	Benjamin E. Burns	
	Daniel Benjamin Frink	
	Jacob S. Mockbee	
	George Swall	
	Julius Weilheimer	1906-08
April, 1908	William Henry Bates	
	Benjamin E. Burns	1909-10
	Jacob S. Mockbee	
	George Swall	
	Julius Weilheimer	1908-09
August, 1908	Nathan H. McCorkle *(Mockbee resigned July 8, 1908)*	
April 28, 1909	George Parkinson *(Weilheimer resigned April 7, 1909)*	
Feb. 11, 1909	John George Jagels *(Bates resigned December 17, 1909)*	
April, 1910	Benjamin E. Burns	
	John George Jagels *(4 yr. seat)*	
	Nathan H. McCorkle *(2 yr. seat)*	1910-12
	Richard W. McDonald *(4 yr. seat)*	
	George Swall *(4 yr. seat)*	
July 6	Jacob S. Mockbee *(Burns died June 20, 1910)*	
	Called Town Trustees until 1927	
	Called President of the Board until 1927	
Sept. 18, 1911	William P. Wright *(Swall resigned September 12, 1911)*	
1912	Walter A. Clark *(4 yr. seat)*	
	John George Jagels	1913-14
	Nathan H. McCorkle *(2 yr. seat)*	
	Richard W. McDonald	
	William P. Wright *(4 yr. seat)*	1912-13

Year	Name	Mayor in:
Feb 11, 1913	Frederick. L. Peterson (*McCorkle resigned Dec. 4, 1912*)	
1913	*Clark resigned December 3, 1913, post not filled until election*	
Jan 6, 1914	John Luther McPheeters (*Wright resigned Sept. 11, 1913*)	
1914	Herbert G. Childs (*4 yr. seat*)	
	John George Jagels (*4 yr. seat*)	1914-16
	John Luther McPheeters (*4 yr. seat*)	
	Charles Coney Minton (*2 yr. seat*)	1914
	Joseph Henry Powell (*2yr. seat*)	
Sept. 13, 1914	*Minton died, post not filled til 1915*	
1915	James H. Cochran (*Childs resigned March 3, 1915*)	
	Earl D. Minton (*replaced Charles Minton*)	
1916	James H. Cochran	
	John George Jagels	
	John Luther McPheeters	
	Earl D. Minton (*2 yr. seat*)	
	Jacob S. Mockbee	1916-18
1918	James H. Cochran	
	Jacob S. Mockbee	
	Claude E. Redwine	
	P. Milton Smith (*2 yr. seat*)	
	Ray O. Winnegar	
1920	Earl D. Minton (*Winnegar resigned Feb. 4, 1920*)	
1920	James H. Cochran	
	Earl D. Minton (*2 yr. seat*)	
	Jacob S. Mockbee	
	Claude E. Redwine	1920-22
	Leon H. Watson	
1920	*Minton vacated office June 2, 1920 —minutes state that trustee elect failed to qualify as required by law, so office declared vacant.*	
1922	James H. Cochran	1922-24
	Earl D. Minton	
	Jacob S. Mockbee	
	Claude E. Redwine	
	Leon H. Watson	
1923	Oscar W. Whaley (*Mockbee resigned Oct. 3, 1923*)	
1923	*Watson resigned March 7, 1923 and was elected by trustees to be Assistant City Clerk. Resigned this position on March 21, 1923. Reinstated as trustee on March 21, 1923.*	
1924	James H. Cochran	1924-26
	Earl D. Minton	

Year	Name	Mayor in:
1924 (cont.)	Joseph Henry Powell	
	Laurence G. Randall	
	Claude E. Redwine	
1925	*Cochran tendered resignation Jan. 28, 1925, not acted upon.*	
1926	*Cochran tendered resignation Jan. 22, 1926, not acted upon.*	
1926	James H. Cochran	
	Abram J. Knight	1926-28
	Earl D. Minton	
	Joseph Henry Powell	
	Laurence G. Randall	
1928	Abram J. Knight	
	Earl D. Minton	
	Joseph Henry Powell	1928-30
	George W. Sohler	
	Dr. William L. Stansbury, D.D.S.	
1930	Abram J. Knight	
	Earl D. Minton	
	Joseph Henry Powell	1930-32
	George W. Sohler	
	Dr. William L. Stansbury, D.D.S.	
1932	Allan B. Cutter	
	Abram J. Knight	1932-34
	Earl D. Minton	
	Joseph Henry Powell	
	George W. Sohler	
1933	Arthur W. Browne *(Minton resigned April 5, 1933)*	
1934	Arthur W. Browne	
	Daniel Burke	
	Allan B. Cutter	
	Joseph Henry Powell	
	George W. Sohler	1934-36
July 18, 1934	Charles Newton Higdon *(Cutter resigned July 3, 1934)*	
1936	Arthur W. Browne	
	Daniel Burke	1937-38
	Frederick L. Campen	
	Bert E. Knapp	
	Geroge W. Sohler	1936-37
1938	Daniel Burke	1938-40
	Frederick L. Campen	
	Bert E. Knapp	

Year	Name	Mayor in:
1938 (cont.)	Charles N. Lake	
	George W. Sohler	
	Charles Newton Higdon (replaced Sohler)	
1940	Daniel Burke	1940-42
	Frederick L. Campen	
	Charles Newton Higdon	
	Charles N. Lake	
	Ray S. Loucks	
1942	Daniel Burke	
	Frderick L. Campen	
	Charles Newton Higdon	
	Charles N. Lake	1942-44
	Ray S. Loucks	
1942	Malcolm D. Aitken (replaced Loucks)	
1944	Malcolm D. Aitken	
	Daniel Burke	
	Charles Newton Higdon	1944-46
	Charles N. Lake	
	Frank Morton	
1946	Malcolm D. Aitken	
	Charles Newton Higdon	
	Frank Morton	1946-48
	Robert P. Rowe	
	Martin J. Spangler, Sr.	
1948	Paul Fretz	
	Frank Morton	1948-50
	John Parmalee	
	Robert P. Rowe	
	Martin J. Spangler, Sr.	
1950	Paul Fretz	
	Frank Morton	
	John Parmalee	
	Robert P. Rowe	
	Martin J. Spangler, Sr.	1950-52
1952	John W. Anderson	1952-54
	Joseph P. Diaz	
	Hingsberger, Andrew	
	Robert P. Rowe	
	Martin J. Spangler, Sr.	1952
	David L. Tripiano	

Year	Name	Mayor in:
1952 (cont.)	Major General Raymond R. Wright, USMC retired	
1953	Richard O'Brien (replaced Diaz)	
1954	John W. Anderson	
	Lawrence E. Anderson	
	Arthur H. Excell	
	Louis M. Farasyn	
	Richard O'Brien	
	David L. Tripiano	1954-56
	Major General Raymond R. Wright, USMC retired	
1954	Jack Tutman (replaced Excell)	
1956	Lawrence Anderson	1956-58
	John W. Anderson	
	Louis M. Farasyn	
	Vernon Laveroni	
	Charles M. Moore	
	Jack Tutman	
	Major General Raymond R. Wright, USMC retired	
1958	John W. Anderson	
	Carl A. Hansen	1958-60
	Vernon Laveroni	
	Charles M. Moore	
	Jesse J. Nelson	
	Harry W. True	
	Major General Raymond R. Wright, USMC retired	
1960	John W. Anderson	
	Carl A. Hansen	
	Vernon Laveroni	
	Charles M. Moore	1960-62
	Joseph Musso	
	Jesse J. Nelson	
	Harry W. True	
1962	John W. Anderson	
	Victor Calvo	1963-64
	Charles Gordon	
	Vernon Laveroni	
	Charles M. Moore	1963-63
	Joseph Musso	
	Jesse J. Nelson	
1963	William R. Jelavich (replaced Anderson)	
1964	Victor Calvo	1964-65

Year	Name	Mayor in:
1964 (cont.)	Charles Gordon	1965-66
	William R. Jelavich	
	Vernon R. Laveroni	
	Charles M. Moore	
	Joseph Musso	
	Jesse J. Nelson	
1966	Victor Calvo	1967-68
	Charles Gordon	1966-67
	William L. Herfurth	
	William R. Jelavich	
	Vernon R. Laveroni	
	Charles M. Moore	
	Joseph Musso	
1968	Carl E. Anderson	
	Victor Calvo	
	Joseph Cusimano	
	Charles Gordon	
	William L. Herfurth	
	William R. Jelavich	1968-70
	Orville H. Thornall	
1969	Vern Gillmore (replaced Thornall)	
	W. Ross Wollard (replaced Calvo)	
1970	Carl E. Anderson	
	Joseph Cusimano	
	Vern C. Gillmore	
	Charles Gordon	
	William L. Herfurth	1970-72
	William R. Jelavich	
	W. Ross Wollard	
1972	Carl E. Anderson	1973-74
	Joseph Cusimano	
	Charles Gordon	
	William L. Herfurth	
	William R. Jelavich	
	Judith Moss	
	W. Ross Wollard	1972-73
1974	Matthew Allen	
	Carl E. Anderson	
	Joseph Cusimano	1974-75
	Charles Gordon	

Year	Name	Mayor in:
1974 (cont.)	William R. Jelavich	
	Judith Moss	1975-76
	Joseph Perez	
1976	Matthew Allen	1977-78
	Angelo Frosolone	
	Charles Gordon	
	Emily Lyon	
	Judith Moss	
	Joseph Perez	1976-77
	Richard Wilmuth	
1977	Leslie C. Nichols *(replaced Gordon)*	
1978	Matthew Allen	
	Angelo Frosolone	
	Emily Lyon	
	Judith Moss	
	Leslie C. Nichols	1979-80
	Joseph Perez	
	Richard Wilmuth	1978-79
1979	Patricia Figueroa *(replaced Lyon)*	
	Marilyn Perry *(replaced Perez)*	
1980	Matthew Allen	1980-81
	Patricia Figueroa	
	Angelo Frosolone	
	Leslie C. Nichols	
	Ronald D. Packard *(2 yr. term)*	
	Marilyn Perry	1981-82
	Richard Wilmuth	
1982	Patricia Figueroa	1982-83
	Maryce Freelan	
	Angelo Frosolone	
	Leslie C. Nichols	
	Ronald D. Packard	1983-84
	Marilyn S. Perry	
	Richard Wilmuth	
1982	James Zesch *(replaced Wilmuth)*	
1984	Dennis Switick *(replaced Nichols)*	
1984	Patricia Figueroa	
	Maryce Freelan	1984-85
	Clarence Heppler	
	Ronald D. Packard	

Year	Name	Mayor in:
1984 (cont.)	Marilyn Perry	
	Dennis Switick	
	James Zesch	1985-86
1985	Robert Schatz *(replaced Packard)*	
1986	Patricia Figueroa	
	Maryce Freelen	
	Clarence Heppler	1986-87
	Marilyn Perry	
	Robert Schatz	1987-88
	Norman Shaskey	
	James Zesch	
1988	Dena Bonnell	
	James Cochran	
	Maryce Freelen	1988-89
	Angelo Frosolone	
	Robert Schatz	
	Norman Shaskey	1989-90
	Art Takahara	
1990	Dena Bonnell	
	James Cochran	
	Patricia Figueroa	
	Angelo Frosolone	1990-91
	Robert Schatz	
	Norman J. Shaskey	
	Art Takahara	1991-92
1992	Dena Bonnell	1993-94
	James Cochran	1992-93
	Patricia Figueroa	
	Maryce Freelen	
	Robert Schatz	1994
	Norman J. Shaskey	
	Art Takahara	
1994	Municipal elections moved from April to November	
1994	Dena Bonnell	
	James Cochran	
	Ralph Faravelli	1996-97
	Patricia Figueroa	1995-96
	Joseph Kleitman	
	Maryce Freelen	
	Art Takahara	

Year	Name	Mayor in:
Jan, 1996	Stephen Lewis *(replaces Freelen)*	
1996	Mario Ambra	
	Ralph Faravelli	
	Patricia Figueroa	
	Joseph Kleitman	1997-98
	Nancy Noe	
	Rosemary Stasek	
	Mary Lou Zoglin	
1998	Mario Ambra	
	Ralph Faravelli	1998-99
	R. Michael Kasperzak, Jr.	
	Sally Lieber	
	Nancy Noe	
	Rosemary Stasek	2000-01
	Mary Lou Zoglin	1999-00
2000	Mario Ambra	2001-02
	Sally Lieber	2002-03
	Ralph Faravelli	
	R. Michael Kasperzak, Jr.	
	Matt Pear	
	Rosemary Stasek	
	Mary Lou Zoglin	

ENDNOTES

NOTES TO PROLOGUE

[1] Alfred Doten, *The Journals of Alfred Doten*, Vol. 1, Walter Van Tilburg, ed. (Reno: University of Nevada Press, 1973), 394.

[2] Pocket Edition Directory of Mountain View, 1914. No publisher. Copy in the Mountain View Historical Association, Mountain View History Center, Mountain View Public Library.

NOTES TO CHAPTER 1

[3] See for example, Herbert Eugene Bolton, editor, *Historical Memoirs of New California*, by Fray Francisco Palóu, O.F.M., (Berkeley, Ca: University of California Press, 1926); Herbert Eugene Bolton, *Anza's California Expeditions* (Berkeley, Ca: University of California Press, 1930); Juan Crespi, *Fray Juan Crespi, Missionary Explorer on the Pacific Coast*, 1769-1774, by Herbert Eugene Bolton (Berkeley, Ca. University of California Press, 1927).

[4] It was named by Padre Pedro Font in 1776.

[5] Some 19th-century descriptions of birds and geese in the San Francisco Bay and Santa Clara Valley region are in Doten, *Journals*, 315 and 402 and David W. Mayfield, "Ecology of the Pre-Spanish San Francisco Bay Area," Ph.D. diss., San Francisco State University, 1978, 69.

[6] Crespí, *Missionary Explorer*, 285.

[7] George Briggs, "Reminiscences of Mountain View in Olden Times," n.d. clipping in Mockbee Scrapbook, 6, Mountain View History Center, Mountain View Public Library.

[8] Mayfield, "Ecology," 63.

[9] Laurence H. Shoup and Randall T. Milliken, *Inigo of Rancho Posolmi The Life and Times of a Mission Indian* (Novato, CA: Ballena Press, 1999), 8.

[10] Ibid., 4-6.

[11] Crespí, *Missionary Explorer*, 44.

[12] Shoup and Milliken, *Inigo*, 27.

[13] Inigo's name has been spelled a number of different ways, including Yñigo, Indigo, Ynego and others. I have chosen to use the spelling that Shoup and Milliken have used because their book is the most carefully researched biography written on the man. The authors note in the Foreword to their book, "the "I" of old Spanish looks like a "Y."

[14] Shoup and Milliken, *Inigo*, 47.

[15] Mildred Brooke Hoover, Hero Eugene Rensch, Ethel Grace Rensch and William N. Abeloe, *Historic Spots in California*, Fourth Edition, revised by Douglas E. Kyle (Stanford, CA: Stanford University Press, 1990), 401.

[16] United States v. Castro, Docket 257, p. 203 (Circuit Court of Northern California, 1854) National Archives San Francisco Region, Roll 6: Case 369.

[17] Shoup and Milliken, *Inigo*, 102.

[18] Spanish Archives, Expediente 265. National Archives San Francisco Region, Roll 11 p. 625 and 626.

[19] United States v. Castro, Docket 257, p. 57 (Circuit Court of Northern California, 1854) National Archives San Francisco Region, Roll 6: Case 369.

[20] Shoup and Milliken, *Inigo*, 114.

[21] Ibid., 129-130.

[22] Spanish Archives, Expediente 50. National Archives San Francisco Region, Roll 11 p. 401- 408.

[23] Frances Fox, *Luis María Peralta and His Adobe*, illustrated by Ralph Rambo (San Jose: Smith-McKay Printing, 1975), 45 and 66.

[24] Cora Older, "Our Oldest Pioneer, William Dale," Mountain View *Register-Leader*, 15 February 1918, 6.

[25] Ibid.

[26] U.S. v. Castro, Docket 257.

[27] Ibid., p. 86.

[28] Cora Older, *Register-Leader*, 1 March 1918.

[29] Ibid., "Some Early History of Mountain View," *Register-Leader*, 26 July 1918, 2.

30 U.S. v. Castro, Docket 257, p. 383.

31 Ibid., p. 355.

32 Superior Court San Jose, California, Mariano Castro, Probate No. 155, 1871.

33 There has been some argument over the spelling of this name. The original name was Francisca, according to the following sources: H. S. Foote, ed. *Pen Pictures From the Garden of the World or Santa Clara County* (Chicago: The Lewis Publishing Company, 1888), 350 (published while both Francisca and Crisanto were still alive); J. M Guinn, *History of the State of California and Biographical Record of the Coast Counties* (Chicago: The Chapman Publishing Company, 1904), 1344.

34 Fox, *Luis María Peralta*, 20 and 66-67.

35 Clyde Arbuckle and Ralph Rambo, *Santa Clara County Ranchos* (San José, CA: Rosicrucian Press, Ltd., 1973), 28.

36 John Hyde Braly, *Memory Pictures* (Los Angeles: The Neuner Company, 1912), 100.

37 San Jose *Telegraph*, 9 March 1854, 3/2.

Notes to Chapter 2

38 Ralph Herbert Cross, *The Early Inns of California: 1844-1869* (San Francisco: L. Kennedy, 1954), 131-132.

39 Older, "Early History," *Register-Leader*, 26 July 1918, 2.

40 There are two John W. Whismans, each was married for a time to a Hannah; To avoid confusion, this narrative focuses on the one with a significant impact on Mountain View history. He arrived in the valley in 1846 and sold the stage line to Hall & Crandall in fall of 1850.

41 *Alta California* (San Francisco), 12 July 1849, 3/2.

42 Frank Merriman Stanger, "Letters of an Artist in the Gold Rush," *California Historical Society Quarterly*, 22 (1943): 245.

43 Ibid.

44 Frederic Hall, *The History of San Jose and Surroundings: With Biographical Sketches of Early Settlers* (San Francisco: A.L. Bancroft and Co., 1871), 236.

45 San Jose Semi-Weekly *Tribune*, 9 January 1855, 3/3 and 16 February 1855, 3/3.

46 Doten, *Journals of Alfred Doten*, 305.

47 Ibid., 421.

48 Ibid., 305.

49 Mary Julia Gates, *Contributions to Local History, Rancho Pastoria de las Borregas* (San José, CA: Cottle & Murgotten, Printers, 1895), 20.

50 Doten, *Journals*, 422.

51 Older, *Register-Leader*, 1 March 1918.

52 Gates, *Contributions to Local History*.

53 Anna Jagels Leu, "The Schools of Mountain View 1852-1970." Mountain View Historical Association, n.d.

54 Older, "Early History," *Register-Leader*, 26 July 1918, 2.

55 Doten, *Journals*, 441.

56 Susannah Braly diaries, January 22, 1869, California Historical Society, San Francisco.

57 Ibid., September 12, 1870.

58 Santa Clara County Survey Book A, Survey No. 153, p. 161.

59 Linda Sharman Schultz, *Buckeye and Brodeaias The History of a One-Room Schoolhouse* (Cupertino, CA: Cupertino Historical Society, 2000), 63.

60 Ibid., 31.

61 Doten, *Journals*, 310.

62 Ibid., 305.

63 Ibid., 388.

64 Ibid., 377.

65 San Jose *Tribune*, 1 October 1856, 3/2.

66 Doten, *Journals*, 311 and 407.

67 Petition to Santa Clara County Board of Supervisors, January 1, 1868.

68 San Jose *Mercury*, 2 May 1892, 5/5.

69 One source says from the Whismans in 1860 for $10,000: Santa Clara County Deed Book N, p. 170-171, March 19, 1860; another says it was purchased by Sheriff's sale 21 September 1860: California Reports, Supreme Court of the State of California, vol. 30 p. 588.

70 California, Legislature, *The Journal of the Assembly During the Twenty-Third Session of the State of California*, 1880, 215 and 265.

71 San Jose Daily *Morning Times*, 4 March 1890.

72 California, *Journal of the Assembly*, Eleventh Session, 354.

73 Stierlin Road was sometimes misspelled as Sterling Road. It was changed to the correct spelling of the Stierlin family name in the 1930s.

74 Santa Clara County Deed Book 17, p. 154-155.

75 "Plat Map of Town Site of Mountain View," November 18, 1865, Mountain View Historical Association Collection, Mountain View History Center, Mountain View Public Library.

NOTES TO CHAPTER 3

[76] Gilbert Olsen and Richard Floyd, "The San Jose Railroad and Crocker's Pets," in Gloria Hom, ed. *Chinese Argonauts: An Anthology of the Chinese Contributions to the Historical Development of Santa Clara County* (Los Altos Hills, CA: Foothill Community College, California History Center, 1971), 137.

[77] Santa Clara County Deed Book 19, p. 646

[78] Santa Clara County Deed Book O, p. 143-144.

[79] "Pipeline," *Star* (Lockheed newspaper), 10 September 1982.

[80] Munro-Fraser, *History of Santa Clara County, California* (San Francisco, Alley, Bowen and Co., 1881) 264; and Santa Clara County Deed Book T, p. 509-510.

[81] San Jose Weekly *Mercury*, 19 November 1874, quoted in Diane Claerbout, "The Weilheimers: The Jewish Pioneer Family of Mountain View, California," *Western States Jewish History*, Vol. XXX, No. 1, p. 73.

[82] *Mercury*, 18 March 1875, 3.

[83] Leu, "Schools of Mountain View."

[84] *Mercury*, 1 January 1892, 26.

[85] Newspaper interview with William Garliepp, n.d., Mountain View Historical Association, Mountain View History Center, Mountain View Public Library, clipping file.

[86] Older, "Our Oldest Pioneer, William Dale," *Register-Leader*, 15 February 1918, 6.

[87] Report of the County Surveyor A. T. Hermann to the Santa Clara County Board of Supervisors, Road File 3, 6 March 1872.

[88] *Mercury*, 7 March 1878.

[89] Hermann to the Santa Clara County Supervisors, March 6, 1872.

[90] Ibid.

[91] James S. Graham, "Mountain View 90 Years of Fire Department History," 1964, copy in Mountain View History Center, 1.

[92] *Mercury*, 7 March 1885, 2/4.

[93] Ibid., 21 April 1885, 3/3.

[94] Ibid., 10 December 1886, 3/1.

[95] *Register-Leader*, 7 December 1895, 4/6 and Santa Clara County Probate No. 3819.

[96] Angelo F. Semino, "The History of Mayfield Mall," research paper, Mountain View History Center, Mountain View Public Library, 1986, xviii.

[97] Ibid., 71.

[98] Pasquale's son, Angelo, after serving in WWI, returned to Stanford University, earned an engineering degree, and became a successful engineering consultant. He authored a brief history of the vegetable garden land that eventually became the Mayfield Shopping Mall and then a Hewlett-Packard facility.

[99] *Mercury*, 4 January 1885, 5/5.

[100] Ibid., 2 January 1887, 15/3.

[101] Ibid., 15 May 1885, 3/8.

[102] Ibid., 4 February 1885, 3/3 and 23 May 1885.

[103] Ibid., 26 April, 1877, 3.

[104] Ibid., 2 May 1884, 3/3.

[105] United States Census, Santa Clara County, California, 1870.

[106] *Mercury* 31 January 1886, 5/4.

[107] Ibid., 14 February 1886, 4/5; 26 March 1886, 3/1; 21 May 1886, 2/3.

[108] Foote, *Pen Pictures*, 125 and *Mercury*, 29 May 1884, 3/1.

[109] *Mercury*, 9 Oct 1884, 3/4 and 30 October 1884, 3/5.

[110] Ibid., 1 January 1892, 26/1.

[111] "A Day's Drive Among Orchards and Farms," Ibid., 6 Apr 1888, 5/4.

[112] Foote, *Pen Pictures*, 646-647 and Santa Clara County Probate No. 5376.

[113] Roger R. Olmstead, *Scow Schooners of San Francisco Bay*, ed. Nancy Olmstead (Cupertino, CA: California History Center, 1988) 25.

[114] Mountain View *Courier*, 29 August 1885, 2/6.

[115] *Bettys' Santa Clara County Directory* 1889 and *Husted's Directory* 1893.

[116] *Mercury*, 12 August 1887, 3/1.

[117] Ibid., 3 March 1887, 3/7.

[118] Ibid., 14 January 1888, 4/3.

[119] Frank Bacon, *Barnstorming* (San Jose, CA: San Jose Historical Museum Association, 1987) 63.

[120] Ibid., 64.

[121] *Mercury*, 1 January 1892, 26.

[122] Mountain View *Courier*, 29 August 1885, 2/4.

[123] *Mercury*, 8 December 1887, 3.

[124] Ibid., 1 January 1892, 26/1.

125 Ibid., 22 May 1885, 3/8.

126 Graham, "90 Years," 2.

127 *Register*, 13 April 1895, 3/4.

128 *Mercury*, 17 March 1889, 5/4 and 1 January 1892, 26; and Clark promotional flier, 1891, copy at the Mountain View History Center, Mountain View Public Library.

129 *Realty Herald*, circa 1904, copy at the Mountain View History Center, Mountain View Public Library.

130 *Mercury* 1 September 1889, 8/1.

131 Ibid., 12 December 1888, 3/1 and 1 January 1892, 26/1.

132 Ibid., 1 January 1892, 26.

133 *Register*, 2 February 1895, 2/2-3.

134 Ibid., 1 December 1894, 3/3 and 22 June 1906, 2.

135 *Mercury*, 17 June 1891, 3/2.

136 *Register*, 10 March 1894, 3/6

137 Diane Iverson, "Women in Mountain View," research paper 1998, Mountain View History Center, Mountain View Public Library, p. 6.

138 Several entries in *Mercury*, January through March 1900.

139 Schultz, *Buckeye and Brodeaias*; Palo Alto *Times* 19 July 1895, 3/3; and *Register-Leader*, 20 July 1895, 3/2.

140 *Mercury*, 15 April 1897, 2.

NOTES TO CHAPTER 4

141 *Register-Leader*, 2 June 1911, 5/1.

142 This number is in "Petition of Incorporation of the Town of Mountain View" ; the same document in another place says the population was 610; it is 611 in Jeanne Holtzclaw "The First Hundred Years of Mountain View and Its Surroundings" in *Trianon Reflections* (Cupertino, CA: California History Center), Fall 1976.

143 John P. Tomac, "The Mountain View Police 1902-1972," research paper, 1972, Mountain View History Center, Mountain View Public Library.

144 *Register*, 20 February 1904, 3.

145 Handwritten eulogy for Viola Poland delivered by her husband F. Poland 26 October 1904, Woman's Club scrapbook, donated by Diane Keenan, Mountain View History Center, Mountain View Public Library.

146 *Register*, 23 Sept 1904, 3/3.

147 *Register-Leader*, 24 July 1914, 8/6.

148 "The Emersons in Mountain View" by Ethel E. Emerson, presented on 3 November 1974, Mountain View Pioneer and Historical Society.

149 Sanborn Fire Insurance Company Map from 1921.

150 *Register-Leader*, 8 December 1922, 3/7.

151 Becky S. McReynolds, "Chinese Lives in Early Mountain View" (M.A. Thesis, Center for Asian Studies, Stanford University, Winter 1996-97), 51.

152 *Register*, 3 February 1905.

153 *Leader*, 11 August 1905, 4/1; Eugene T. Sawyer, *History of Santa Clara County California with Biographical Sketches* (Los Angeles: Historic Record Company, 1922), 1109-1110; and birth announcement in 1913 of their daughter identified both as "editors."

154 *Register*, 20 April 1906.

155 *Leader*, 27 April 1906, 1/3.

156 *Register*, 4 November 1904, 3/3.

157 Ibid., 9 June 1906, 3; 15 June 1906, 1; and 13 July 1906, 3.

158 "What These Things Mean," *Signs of the Times* Earthquake Special, Pacific Press Publishing, 2 May 1906.

159 Richard B. Lewis, *Streams of Light the Story of Pacific Press* (Mountain View, CA: Pacific Press Publishing Association, 1958), 38.

160 "Watching for the Dawn, A Century of 'Signs'," 9.

161 Graham, "90 Years," 9.

162 Including Herbert G. Childs (1914), James H. Cochran (1915-1928), Dr. William L. Stansbury (1928-1932), Arthur W. Browne (1933-1938), C.N. Lake (1938-1946), Robert Rowe (1946-1954) and Arthur H. Excell (1954-1956).

163 *Leader*, 28 June 1907, 8.

164 Ibid., 1 January 1910.

165 *Register-Leader*, 3 May 1912, 1/6.

166 Ibid., 5 April 1912, 1.

167 For example, *Register* 30 January 1903, 3/4; and Trustee Minutes, 8 June 1904.

168 Mark Thomas, Jr., "Arthur Free," *Association News*, newsletter of the San Jose Historical Museum, May 1987, 7.

169 *Register-Leader*, 14 March 1913, 1.

170 Graham, "90 Years," 12.

171 *Register-Leader*, 23 June 1911, 2/2 and 9 February 1912, 4/2.

172 *Mercury*, 12 July 1950, 8.

[173] *Register-Leader*, 21 June 1912, 1/1.

[174] Ibid., 10 September 1926, 1/4.

[175] *Bittersweet: Memories of Old Mountain View, An Oral History Vol. 1* (Mountain View, CA: Mountain View Public Library), 1980.

[176] *Register-Leader*, 6 June 1919, 8; and 1907-1922 Register of Licenses for the Town of Mountain View, California, in *Bittersweet* Vol. I, 209.

[177] *Bittersweet*, Vol. II, Emilia Lozano Calvo.

[178] Iverson, "Women," 8.

[179] *Register-Leader,* 30 July 1920,1/2.

[180] Ibid., 11 January 1918, 13.

[181] Ibid., 24 May 1918, 1/4.

[182] Ibid., 5 July 1918, 8/1.

[183] Ibid., 5 November 1920, 8; and 8 December 1938.

[184] Ibid., 6 August 1920, 3.

[185] Ibid., 10 October 1924, 1.

[186] June Redwine de Larios as relayed to Wallace Erichsen, 2001.

[187] *Register-Leader,* 15 August 1919, 1/7.

[188] Tomac, "Police."

NOTES TO CHAPTER 5

[189] *Register-Leader*, 7 July 1922, 4/1.

[190] Ibid., 25 May 1923, 1/3 and 27 March 1925, 3.

[191] *Bittersweet*, Vol. I, Tak Hori, 24-33.

[192] *Register-Leader*, 5 June 1925, 1/1; and 29 May 1925, 5/3; and 2 August 1929, 9.

[193] *Bittersweet*, Vol. I, Tak Hori, 24-33.

[194] Wallace Erichsen, interview with the author, 29 January 1999, Los Altos, California.

[195] Mountain View City Council Minutes, 1927, Vol. 1, p. 99.

[196] *Register-Leader,* 2 June 1922, 1.

[197] Erichsen interview.

[198] *Register-Leader*, 31 March 1911, 2.

[199] Martin Spangler, Jr., interview with the author, 16 March 1999, Mountain View, California.

[200] *Bittersweet*, Vol. I, Dorothy Kobayashi Ishimatsu, 45-57.

[201] "Fires of Mountain View 1905-1921," handwritten log of fires, Mountain View History Center, Mountain View Public Library, 2.

[202] *Register-Leader*, 13 January 1928, 1/6.

[203] Erichsen interview.

[204] *Register-Leader*, 14 January 1927, 1/2.

[205] Barbara Lugn, "What's In a (Street) Name?" The *View,* January 1983.

[206] Robert Pack, "House With a Past Shuns Future," Palo Alto *Times*, clipping file Mountain View History Center, Mountain View Public Library, n.d.

[207] *Register-Leader*, 31 July 1931.

[208] Ibid., 12 December 1930, 1/5.

[209] Spencer Gleason, *Naval Air Station Moffett Field*, California: Silver Anniversary 1933-1958 (San Francisco: Globe), 6.

[210] *Register-Leader*, December 1930, Special edition.

[211] DeWitt E. Hogle, "Casting A Giant Shadow: The Macon Makes Memories," in "Scrapbook of Memories: Our City's 85th Birthday," a pamphlet of the Mountain View Historical Association, 15.

[212] San Francisco *Examiner*, 16 October 1933.

[213] *Register-Leader*, 8 January 1932, 3/2.

[214] A.J. Knight, Mayor of Mountain View, memo to the City, 26 November 1932, Mountain View History Center, Mountain View Public Library.

[215] *Register-Leader*, 29 September 1933, 1/1.

[216] Ibid., 14 August 1936, 1/3.

[217] Ibid., 23 May 1938.

[218] Ibid., 27 September 1929.

[219] Pete Silapan as quoted in an oral history interview from "A Project of the Filipino Association of Mountain View, Inc.", n.a.; n.d., Mountain View History Center, Mountain View Public Library.

[220] *Bittersweet* Vol. I, Rin Abey.

[221] Ibid., Ichiro Bill Asada, 7-11.

[222] *Register-Leader*, 22 August 1938, 1.

[223] Ralph Faravelli interview with the author, 18 May 1999, Mountain View, California.

[224] *Register-Leader*, 17 February 1933, 1/2.

[225] "Scrapbook of Memories, Our City's 85th Birthday," 1987, 5.

NOTES TO CHAPTER 6

[226] Barbara Kinchen interview with the author, 13 April, 1999, Mountain View, California.

[227] Tomae, "Police," 11.

[228] "Favorable Beginning for Nielsen," *Valley Journal*, 25 July 1971.

[229] *Weekly Almanac*, 17 September 1986, 3.

[230] *Bittersweet*, Tak Hori, 24-33.

[231] Ibid., Dorothy Kobayashi Ishimatsu, 45-57.

[232] Faravelli interview.

[233] Edna Thompson interview with the author, 13 April, 1999, Mountain View, California.

[234] *Register-Leader*, 14 August 1945, 1.

[235] *Mercury*, 2 February 1962.

[236] *Bittersweet,* Vol. I, Roy Ozawa, 136.

[237] Richard Meyer interview with the author, 23 March, 1999, Mountain View, California.

[238] *Mercury*, 1 August 1954, Magazine Section, 2.

[239] Martin Spangler, Jr. interview with the author, 16 March, 1999, Mountain View, California.

[240] John Turnblad, "Tremendous Growth Recorded in Mt. View," Palo Alto *Times*, 1949, and *Register-Leader*, 17 April 1944, 1/6.

[241] *Bittersweet*, Maria Josepha Miras, 262.

[242] Ibid., Joseph Perez, 254.

[243] Ibid., 261.

[244] Spangler interview.

[245] *Mercury*, 29 November 1963.

[246] *Register-Leader*, 23 May 1930.

[247] Ibid., 1 April 1946 1/3.

[248] City of Mountain View, Economic Industrial Survey, April 1953, 29.

[249] Meyer interview.

[250] *Register-Leader*, 4 April 1954, 1.

[251] Palo Alto *Times*, 4 January 1960.

[252] Tomae, "Police."

[253] "Your Future Lies in Mountain View California." Pamphlet of the Chamber of Commerce, circa 1950s.

[254] Palo Alto *Times*, 12 June 1952.

[255] Ibid., 3 April 1953.

[256] Ibid., 30 June 1952.

[257] *Mercury*, 7 September 1983, Extra 3N.

[258] Palo Alto *Times* 13 May 1954.

[259] A decade later in 1962, Charles Gordon was elected to city council at age 29.

[260] Palo Alto *Times*, August 1954.

[261] Ibid., 16 September 1954.

[262] "Your Future Lies in Mountain View California," Pamphlet of the Chamber of Commerce, circa 1950s.

[263] Thompson interview.

[264] Chuck Carroll, "Auction Closes Mtn. View 'Incubator,'" *Mercury*, June 2000, quote attributed to Rosiland Bivings.

[265] Victor Calvo, telephone conversation with the author, September 6, 2001.

[266] Palo Alto *Times*, 24 October 1962.

[267] Calvo, telephone conversation.

[268] Palo Alto *Times*, 14 October 1959.

[269] Richard Hanner, "Old Rengstorff—A Close Call but Saved by Impassioned Plea," *Valley Journal*, 7 March 1979.

[270] Richard Meyer interview.

[271] Mayfield Mall Brochure, Mountain View History Center, Mountain View Public Library.

[272] *Mercury*, 30 October 1970.

[273] Meyer interview.

[274] "The Face of Mountain View," Pamphlet 1968; 20 square miles was an exaggeration and included unincorporated land. In 2001, Mountain View included twelve square miles.

[275] Meyer interview.

[276] Calvo, telephone conversation.

NOTES TO CHAPTER 7

[277] "Mountain View City Hall gives way to computer age," Palo Alto *Times*, 16 March 1966.

[278] *Mercury*, 8 January 1970.

[279] Ibid.

[280] Ibid. 17 April 1973, 1.

[281] Charles Bricker, "O'Halloran Checks Out of Mountain View," *Mercury*, 12 June 1973, 33.

[282] Ibid., 23 October 1995.

[283] The *View*, December 1980.

[284] Palo Alto *Times Tribune*, May 1980.

[285] *Mercury*, 8 January 1970.

[286] Judith Moss interview with the author, 28 September 2000, Mountain View, California.

[287] Stephen M. Payne, *Santa Clara County Harvest of Change* (Northridge, CA: Windsor Publications, Inc., 1987), 235.

[288] Palo Alto *Times Tribune*, 19 August 1988.

[289] Ibid., 18 August 1988.

[290] *Mercury*, 24 November 1980.

[291] Flo Pallakoff, "City designates historic sites," Mountain View *Sun*, 4 June 1980, 1.

[292] Ed Hering, "Old Mountain View High, City hopes to buy pool, gyms and field, not classrooms." *Mercury*, 7 September 1983.

[293] *Weekly Almanac*, 17 September 1986, 5.

[294] Kinchen interview.

[295] Ruthann Richter, "Mtn. View City Hall starts tumbling down," Palo Alto *Times Tribune*, 26 February 1985, A-3.

[296] Kinchen interview.

[297] Martin Spangler, Jr. interview.

[298] The *View*, November 1989.

[299] Faravelli interview.

[300] Kevin Duggan, interview with the author, 6 June 2000, Mountain View, California.

[301] City of Mountain View, Economic Development Highlights, July 2000, 5.

[302] Duggan interview.

[303] U. S. Commission on Civil Rights, "Background Report on Silicon Valley," by Lenny Siegel, Herb Borock, Linda Kimball and Pam Wyman, (Mountain View, CA: Pacific Studies Center), 24.

[304] United States, U. S. Census Bureau, 2000 Redistricting Data Summary File.

[305] Mountain View *Voice*, 23 June 2000.

[306] The *View*, November 1983.

NOTES TO EPILOGUE

[307] Gates, *Contributions to Local History*, 27.

[308] Mike Cassidy, " It all Started Here," *Mercury*, 11 June 2000.

[309] Doten, *Journals*, 410.

[310] "Moutain View Pioneer Crossed the Plains in Days of Great Gold Rush," n.d. clipping in Dale Collection, Mountain View History Center, Mountain View Public Library.

[311] S.L. Wykes, "Mountain View's granddaddies," *Mercury*, 9 November 1983, B1.

BIBLIOGRAPHY

BOOKS

Arbuckle, Clyde. *Santa Clara County Ranchos*. San José, CA: Rosicrucian Press, Ltd., 1973.

Bacon, Frank. *Barnstorming*. San José, CA: San Jose Historical Museum Association, 1987.

Bolton, Herbert Eugene. *Anza's California Expeditions*. Berkeley: University of California Press, 1930.

Bolton, Herbert Eugene, editor. *Historical Memoirs of New California*, by Fray Francisco Palóu, O.F.M., translated into English from the manuscript in the archives of Mexico. Berkeley: University of California Press, 1926.

Braly, John Hyde. *Memory Pictures*. Los Angeles: The Neuner Company, 1912.

Crespi, Juan. Fray Juan Crespi, *Missionary Explorer on the Pacific Coast, 1769-1774*, by Herbert Eugene Bolton. Berkeley: University of California Press, 1927.

Cross, Ralph Herbert. *The Early Inns of California: 1844-1869*. San Francisco: L. Kennedy, 1954.

Doten, Alfred. *The Journals of Alfred Doten, Vol. 1*, Walter Van Tilburg, ed. Reno: University of Nevada Press, 1973.

Foote, H. S., ed. *Pen Pictures From the Garden of the World or Santa Clara County*. Chicago: The Lewis Publishing Company, 1888.

Fox, Frances. *Luis María Peralta and His Adobe*, illustrated by Ralph Rambo. San Jose: Smith-McKay Printing, 1975.

Gates, Mary Julia. *Contributions to Local History, Rancho Pastoria de las Borregas*. San José, CA: Cottle & Murgotten, Printers, 1895.

Gleason, Spencer. *Naval Air Station Moffett Field, California: Silver Anniversary 1933-1958*. San José: Globe Printing, 1958.

Guinn, J. M. *History of the State of California and Biographical Record of the Coast Counties*. Chicago: The Chapman Publishing Company, 1904.

Hall, Frederic. *The History of San Jose and Surroundings: With Biographical Sketches of Early Settlers*. San Francisco: A.L. Bancroft and Co., 1871.

Hoover, Mildred Brooke, Hero Eugene Rensch, Ethel Grace Rensch and William N. Abeloe. *Historic Spots in California*, Fourth Edition, revised by Douglas E. Kyle. Stanford, CA: Stanford University Press, 1990.

Lewis, Richard B. *Streams of Light the Story of Pacific Press, Mountain View, CA*: Pacific Press Publishing Association, 1958.

Munro Fraser, J.P. *History of Santa Clara County, California*. San Francisco : Alley, Bowen, & Co., 1881.

Olmstead, Roger R. *Scow Schooners of San Francisco Bay*, ed. Nancy Olmstead. Cupertino, CA: California History Center, 1988.

Olsen, Gilbert and Richard Floyd. "The San Jose Railroad and Crocker's Pets," in Gloria Hom, ed. *Chinese Argonauts: An Anthology of the Chinese Contributions to the Historical Development of Santa Clara County*. Los Altos Hills, CA: Foothill Community College, California History Center, 1971.

Payne, Stephen M. *Santa Clara County Harvest of Change*. Northridge, CA: Windsor Publications, Inc., 1987.

Sawyer, Eugene T. *History of Santa Clara County California with Biographical Sketches*. Los Angeles: Historic Record Company, 1922.

Schultz, Linda Sharman. *Buckeye and Brodeaias The History of a One-Room Schoolhouse* Cupertino, CA: Cupertino Historical Society, 2000.

Shoup, Laurence H. and Randall T. Milliken. *Inigo of Rancho Posolmi The Life and Times of a Mission Indian*. Novato, CA: Ballena Press, 1999.

ARTICLES

Briggs, George. "Reminiscenses of Mountain View in Olden Times." n.d. clipping in Mockbee Scrapbook, 6, Mountain View History Center, Mountain View Public Library.

Claerbout, Diane. "The Weilheimers: The Jewish Pioneer Family of Mountain View, California." *Western States Jewish History*, Vol. XXX, No. 1.

Holtzclaw, Jeanne. "The First Hundred Years of Mountain View and Its Surroundings" in *Trianon Reflections*. Cupertino, CA: California History Center, Fall 1976.

Olsen, Gilbert and Richard Floyd. "The San Jose Railroad and Crocker's Pets," in Gloria Hom, ed. *Chinese Argonauts: An*

Anthology of the Chinese Contributions to the Historical Development of Santa Clara County. Los Altos Hills, CA: Foothill Community College, California History Center, 1971.

Stanger, Frank Merriman. "Letters of an Artist in the Gold Rush." *California Historical Society Quarterly,* 22 (1943): 245.

Thomas, Mark Jr. "Arthur Free." *Association News,* newsletter of the San Jose Historical Museum, May 1987.

DOCUMENTS

Mountain View

Trustee Minutes, 8 June 1904.

City Council Minutes, 1927, Vol. 1.

A.J. Knight, Mayor of Mountain View, memo to the City, 26 November 1932.

Economic Industrial Survey, April 1953.

Economic Development Highlights, July 2000.

"Fires of Mountain View 1905-1921," handwritten log of fires, Mountain View History Center, Mountain View Public Library.

Santa Clara County

Santa Clara County Deed Books

Report of the County Surveyor A. T. Hermann to the Santa Clara County Board of Supervisors, Road File 3, 6 March 1872.

Superior Court, San Jose, California, Mariano Castro, Probate No. 155, 1871.

Petition to Santa Clara County Board of Supervisors, January 1, 1868.

California

California. Legislature. *The Journal of the Assembly During the Twenty-Third Session of the State of California,* 1880.

California. Legislature. *The Journal of the Assembly During the Eleventh Session of the State of California,* 1861.

United States

United States v. Castro, Docket 257, p. 203 (Circuit Court of Northern California, 1854) National Archives San Francisco Region, Roll 6: Case 369.

United States v. Castro, Docket 257, p. 57 (Circuit Court of Northern California, 1854) National Archives San Francisco Region, Roll 6: Case 369.

United States Census, Santa Clara County, California, 1870.

United States, U. S. Census Bureau, 2000 Redistricting Data Summary File.

United States Commission on Civil Rights. "Background Report on Silicon Valley." Report by Lenny Siegel, Herb Borock, Linda Kimball and Pam Wyman. Mountain View, CA: Pacific Studies Center.

National Archives. San Francisco Region. Spanish Archives, Expediente 265., Roll 11 p. 625.

INTERVIEWS

Victor Calvo, telephone conversation with the author, September 6, 2001.

Joseph De La Fuente, conversation with the author, 13 April 1999, Mountain View, California.

Kevin Duggan, interview with the author, 6 June 2000, Mountain View, California.

Ruth Job Erichsen, conversation with the author, 29 January 1999, Los Altos, California.

Wallace Erichsen, interview with the author, 29 January 1999, Los Altos, California.

Ralph Faravelli, interview with the author, 18 May 1999, Mountain View, California.

Barbara Kinchen, interview with the author, 13 April 1999, Mountain View, California.

Richard Meyer, interview with the author, 23 March 1999, Mountain View, California.

Judith Moss, interview with the author, 28 September 2000, Mountain View, California.

Carol Olson, interview with the author, 23 March 1999, Mountain View, California.

M. James Spangler, interview with the author, 16 March 1999, Mountain View, California.

Martin Spangler, Jr., interview with the author, 16 March 1999, Mountain View, California.

Edna Thompson, interview with the author, 13 April 1999, Mountain View, California.

Mary Lou Zoglin, interview with the author, 23 March 1999, Mountain View, California.

ORAL HISTORY

Bittersweet: Memories of Old Mountain View, An Oral History Vol. 1 (Mountain View, CA : Mountain View Public Library), 1980.

Silapan, Pete. Quoted in an oral history interview from "A Project of the Filipino Association of Mountain View, Inc.", n.a.; n.d., Mountain View History Center, Mountain View Public Library.

NEWSPAPERS

Mountain View

Courier, 29 August 1885.

Leader, 1905-1910.

Realty Herald, circa 1904.

Register, 1902-1910.

Register-Leader, 1912-1960

Sun, 4 June 1980.

Valley Journal, 25 July 1971.

View, January 1983.

Palo Alto

Times (also known as *Times Tribune*), 1949-1988.

San Francisco

Alta California, 12 July 1849.

Examiner, 16 October 1933.

San Jose

Daily Times, 1890.

Mercury (also known as the *Weekly Mercury, Mercury Herald*, or *Mercury News*), 1870-2001.

Telegraph, 9 March 1854.

Semi-Weekly *Tribune*, 1855-1856.

Other

Signs of the Times, Earthquake Special, Pacific Press Publishing, 2 May 1906.

"Pipeline," *Star* (Lockheed newspaper), 10 September 1982.

Weekly Almanac, 17 September 1986, 3.

MAPS

Plat Map of Town Site of Mountain View, November 18, 1865.

Sanborn Fire Insurance Company Map, 1921.

Santa Clara County Survey Book A, (Ryder Collection) survey no. 153, p. 161.

PAMPHLETS

Chamber of Commerce. "Your Future Lies in Mountain View, California." Pamphlet circa 1950s.

Chamber of Commerce. "The Face of Mountain View." Pamphlet, 1968.

Graham, James S. "Mountain View 90 Years of Fire Department History," 1964, Mountain View History Center, Mountain View Public Library.

Hogle, DeWitt E. "Casting A Giant Shadow: The Macon Makes Memories," in "Scrapbook of Memories: Our City's 85th Birthday, " Mountain View Historical Association.

Emerson, Ethel E. "The Emersons in Mountain View" Mountain View: Mountain View Historical Association, 1974.

Kinchen, Barbara McPheeters. "The 1906 Earthquake in Mountain View." Mountain View: Mountain View Historical Association in cooperation with the Mountain View Public Library, 1994.

Winters, Mildred, Barbara McPheeters Kinchen, and Jeanne Jurian Holtzclaw. "Old Mountain View 1850-1880." Mountain View: Mountain View Historical Association, 1976.

Leu, Anna Jagels. "The Schools of Mountain View 1852-1970." Mountain View Historical Association, n.d.

Leu, Anna Jagels. "The Landings of Mountain View, California 1800-1900." Mountain View: Mountain View Historical Association, 1962.

RESEARCH PAPERS OR THESES

Iverson, Diane. "Women in Mountain View." Research paper 1998, Mountain View History Center, Mountain View Public Library.

Mayfield, David W. "Ecology of the Pre-Spanish San Francisco Bay Area." Ph.D. diss., San Francisco State University, 1978.

McReynolds, Becky S. "Chinese Lives in Early Mountain View." Master's thesis, Center for Asian Studies, Stanford University, Winter 1996-97.

Semino, Angelo F. "The History of Mayfield Mall." Research paper, Mountain View History Center, Mountain View Public Library, 1986.

Tomac, John P. "The Mountain View Police 1902-1972." Research paper, Mountain View History Center, Mountain View Public Library, 1972.

OTHER SOURCES

Bettys' Santa Clara County Directory 1889.

Husted's Directory 1893.

Mayfield Mall Brochure, Mountain View History Center, Mountain View Public Library.

Pocket Edition Directory of Mountain View, 1914.

Susannah Braly diaries, California Historical Society, San Francisco.

Woman's Club Scrapbook donated by Diane Keenan to Mountain View Historical Association.

INDEX

Numbers in **boldface** type refer to photographic inserts.

Y

Z

PHOTO GALLERY

Mountain View,
Santa Clara Co.,
California.

Photos taken
December 13,
1913 —

Castro Street — Looking South. (×)
The building above the cross (×) used
to be that of the Bank of Mountain
View. Chas Fuller kept the books
of this bank several weeks in 1903.

Public Schools

Alonzo

Stevens Creek.
near
Delmas Dam.

January 1914.

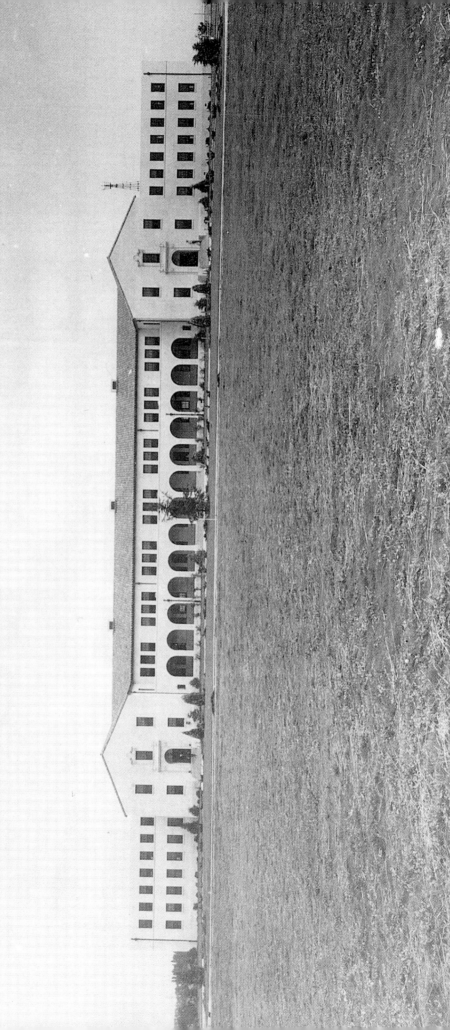

PHOTO GALLERY CAPTIONS

The images in the Photo Gallery are courtesy of the Stocklmeir Library and Archives at the California at the California History Center at De Anza College in Cupertino, California

1. Two pages from the C. R. Fuller scrapbook donated by Steve L Swartz.

2. The Kraljevich family standing amid fruit drying trays on their Mountain View farm.

3. Helping each other with fruit harvesting, members of the Miletich, Givich, Churin, Kalterna, and Milovina families.

4. Three official U.S. Navy photographs of activity at NAS-Sunnyvale and Moffett Field.

5. Original building at Shenandoah Plaza at NAS Sunnyvale.

6. Interior of pilot's compartment of the *Macon*.

7. Retail display of Ferry's seed packets.